The Entangled Eye

THE ENTANGLED EYE

Visual Perception and the
Representation of Nature
in Post-Darwinian Narrative

JAMES KRASNER

New York   Oxford
OXFORD UNIVERSITY PRESS
1992

Oxford University Press

Oxford   New York   Toronto
Delhi   Bombay   Calcutta   Madras   Karachi
Kuala Lumpur   Singapore   Hong Kong   Tokyo
Nairobi   Dar es Salaam   Cape Town
Melbourne   Auckland

and associated companies in
Berlin   Ibadan

Published by Oxford University Press, Inc.,
200 Madison Avenue, New York, New York 10016

Oxford is a registered trademark of Oxford University Press

Library of Congress Cataloging-in-Publication Data
Krasner, James.
   The entangled eye : visual perception and the representation of
nature in post-Darwinian narrative / James Krasner.
p. cm.   Includes bibliographical references and index.
ISBN 0–19–507331–2
1. English fiction—19th century—History and criticism.
2. English fiction—20th century—History and criticism.
3. Literature and science—Great Britain—History.   4. Darwin,
Charles, 1809–1882—Influence.   5. Visual perception in literature.
6. Evolution in literature.   7. Science in literature.   8. Nature in
literature.   9. Narration (Rhetoric)   I. Title.
PR878.S34K7   1992
823'.809356—dc20   91–40095

9 8 7 6 5 4 3 2 1

Printed in the United States of America
on acid-free paper

Acknowledgments

This study was originally composed with the help of a Dean's Fellowship from the University of Pennsylvania and a Mellon Dissertation Fellowship. The process of revision was streamlined by grants from the University of New Hampshire Graduate School and the University of New Hampshire College of Liberal Arts. My thanks to the University of New Hampshire for its firm and respectful support of the various demands of teaching and scholarship. Parts of the first chapter were originally published in *Representations,* 31, Summer 1990; my thanks for the permission to reprint them. Quotations from the works of D. H. Lawrence appear by permission of Laurence Pollinger Ltd. and the Estate of Frieda Lawrence Ravagli. The D. H. Lawrence painting *Fight with an Amazon* is reproduced by permission of Mr. Saki Karavas, whose cordiality and generosity, although widely documented, always merits thanks. Paintings by Bellini, Hobbema, and Botticelli are reproduced by courtesy of the Trustees, the National Gallery London.

The importance of teaching is too often lost in the shuffle of research activity. I would like to thank all the teachers, both formal and informal, who have inspired and endured me over the years, especially William and J. Frances Krasner, William Doyle, David McElroy, Joanna Hubbs, David DeLaura, and Elaine Scarry. The immeasurable concern and attention of Elaine Scarry for this work and for its author should be no surprise to anyone who has known or worked with her, nor should David DeLaura's trenchant and useful engagement with the text. Many thanks also to my colleagues at the University of New Hampshire, particularly Sandhya Shetty for her help with the Conrad chapter and Michael DePorte for his confidence and support. Dennis Taylor's help with the Hardy paintings was more than generous.

Over the months and years Jessamyn Tanner has been a constant reminder of the exuberance and undeniability of physical vision and physical life. Thanks above all to Laura Tanner whose mind has touched this work with the same graceful power and vibrant delicacy with which her life has touched mine.

Contents

The Entangled Eye

Introduction

Literary critics have long held Charles Darwin responsible for two apparently contradictory trends in late-nineteenth and early-twentieth century British fiction. John Alcorn and Roger Ebbatson delineate a group of "nature writers," including Thomas Hardy, Richard Jefferies, H. M. Tomlinson, and D. H. Lawrence, who are inspired by Darwin's writings to celebrate the variety and abundance of exterior nature. Alcorn describes the typical member of what he calls the "naturist tradition" as "a child of Darwin" who "sees man as part of an animal continuum," but is "suspicious of the life of the mind" and "wary of abstractions" (Alcorn x). He adds that "the naturist world is a world of physical organism, where biology replaces theology as the source of psychic health and moral authority" (Alcorn x).

Ebbatson characterizes the nature writers as heirs of both Romanticism and Darwinism who eschew a "dualistic system of mind and inanimate nature" (Ebbatson 5) for "monistic" consciousness. He writes that "the effort of the new school of novelists is to invent a sort of writing which will encompass both the vastness of natural process and the intricate workings of the human spirit" (Ebbatson 26). This attention to exterior nature, Ebbatson argues, places these writers "at the opposite pole to the contemporaneous Flaubertian tradition as perfected by James and his followers" (Ebbatson 4). Alcorn distinguishes the naturist, who perceives a "concrete" natural world, from the modernist, who "if he notices this background of nature . . . tends to see it only as an extension of human thought, a catalyst for desire, an object for manipulation" (Alcorn 121) so that "the natural world . . . remain[s] caught in subjectivity and enigma" (Alcorn 117).

At the same time many critics point to Darwin's theories as the source of the psychological subjectivity that Alcorn considers antinaturist and thus anti-Darwinian. Lionel Stevenson, for example, states that by demonstrating "that mankind must be regarded on the same basis as all other physical phenomena and that therefore human behavior is susceptible to scientific analysis'' Darwinian science ''invaded the territory of fiction'' through the new sciences of psychology and sociology (Stevenson 348). George Levine offers the following summary of Darwin's impact on empirical self-consciousness:

> One of the consequences of the application of Darwinian theory to the obser-
> vation of human behavior is that all observation is ultimately observation of
> the self. . . . The universal is first reduced to the empirical, which cannot
> be universal; the empirical no longer means direct access to the thing in itself
> but mediated access, through one's own perceptual equipment; observa-
> tion, then, is observation of the self perceiving, not of the thing per-
> ceived.   (Levine 218)

Nature, mediated by human perception, becomes a psychological, rather than a physical landscape. This formulation is supported by critics of modernism who describe the modernist landscape in psychological terms. Irving Howe identifies the absence of nature and its transformation ''from an organic setting into a summoned or remembered *idea*'' (Howe 30) as one of the essential characteristics of modernism. Daniel R. Schwarz states that a modernist landscape ''recoils from idealization and control, and orders and expresses the turmoil and anxiety within the author's psyche'' (Schwarz 22). Glen Cavaliero, on the other hand, sees the response to Darwinian science as ''a growing self-consciousness'' resulting in an alienated condition in which humanity is only related to ''the earth'' to the extent that ''the human imagination could make the relation real'' (Cavaliero 2). Darwin is thus held responsible for both the nature writers who turn outward toward the landscape and the modernists who turn inward away from it; his theories bring about both an awareness of the abundance and variety of natural organisms and a self-consciousness about perception that causes nature to disappear into the human mind.

I

In this book I will show the links between these apparently contradictory arguments by suggesting that post-Darwinian nature writers, while profoundly attentive to landscape and biology, choose a mode of representing nature based on visual perception that leads them inevitably toward a more abstract and psychological portrayal of natural landscape. D. H. Lawrence's attention to mental energy, Thomas Hardy's strict adherence to selective principles of perception, and H. M. Tomlinson's and W. H. Hudson's attention to visual ''effects'' and illusions are all indications that the "naturist" way of seeing nature also involves an investigation of perceptual processes. While these nature writers may dislike a "dualistic system of mind and inanimate nature" (Ebbatson 5) their representations of nature are structured around perceptual models that assume such a dualism.

At the same time, by acknowledging the participation of these nature writers in early modernist interiority, I hope to avoid the other branch of the two traditions argument, which portrays exterior nature simply as an expression of the modernist psyche. Alcorn and Ebbatson have done us a critical service in showing that, after Darwin, the literary landscape cannot simply be dismissed as a metaphor for the modernist sensibility. It is already clear that the interiority of modernist narrative can be traced to an empirical tradition shared by Darwin. I will demonstrate that this interiority can be discerned in those very representations that focus on the material presence of exterior nature, and that the tradition of nature writing is thoroughly informed by the empirical self-consciousness of turn-of-the-century British fiction.

The geological theories preceding Darwin greatly expanded the time frame of natural history, and Darwinian theory made the possibilities of natural variation virtually limitless. Critics such as Dwight Culler and George Levine have pointed out that Darwin, in his theoretical writings, needed to emphasize the profound spatial and temporal limitations besetting the human observer without diminishing the grand scheme of evolutionary nature in all its dynamism and multiplicity. I believe that Darwin achieves these conflicting ends by portraying nature as though it is seen through a human, physiologically limited eye. Because evolutionary nature can only be seen through the product of evolution—the human eye—scientists must always be aware of the physical limitations of their own acts of perception; in order to address nature it is therefore necessary to address visual perception.

Consequently, Darwin abandons the omniscient narrative eye common to nineteenth-century scientific and literary discourse and adopts one characterized by misprision, illusion, and limitation. His approach serves the double function of reminding the reader of his or her relative insignificance compared with evolutionary variety and history, and of presenting, through the optical illusions and visual failures to which the physical eye is prone, the formal instability of evolutionary nature. Gillian Beer points out that Darwin's emphasis on the failure of the human mind to fully understand nature "chimes in with his expectation that we should find false approximations, insufficient or imperfect adaptations, if his idea of persisting change and adjustment within organisms and species is correct" (Beer 75). The imperfectly adapted human eye is subject to optical illusion, and

through optical illusion the reader perceives persisting change and adjustment; in Darwin's writing nature appears as a chaotic jumble of animal
parts, continually slipping into and beyond fluid, edgeless animal forms.

The novelists and nature writers who follow Darwin also adopt this
limited, non-omniscient narrative eye. The qualities and limitations of
visual perception are always a narrative concern, but these turn-of-the-
century British writers betray an extraordinary anxiety about their ability to
perceive and to express what they have perceived, particularly when portraying natural landscapes. Nature is the locus of illusions and hallucinations that are rendered to the reader directly, as though he or she were
experiencing them. Moreover, optical illusion and the limitation of vision
is not something that can be willfully chosen and discarded; these authors
portray nature through a narrative eye fixed in position, unable to see past
obstacles, peer through darkness, or accurately interpret the illusions to
which it is prone. Narrative portrayals of nature become narrative portrayals of the perception of nature in which the limitations of visual perception determine the structure of the representation.[1]

The result is a Darwinian nature limited through various processes
of narrative selection. Thomas Hardy's narrative eye moves gradually
from organism to organism, perceiving only one at a time, while the rest of
the landscape remains in shadow or out of focus. Alfred Russel Wallace,
H. M. Tomlinson, and Joseph Conrad portray the tropical jungle either in
terms of familiar European forms or as a psychologically significant but
perceptually deadening darkness. Turn-of-the-century nature writers such
as Richard Jefferies, W. H. Hudson, and D. H. Lawrence reduce natural
forms to patterns of color and motion. In all of these cases, the reader's
ability to imagine natural variety is limited, rather than expanded, by the
optical failure of the narrative eye. Moreover, as it is rendered as the
product rather than the object of perception, the landscape becomes a
reflection of human psychology rather than organic variety. Ironically,
then, Darwin's adoption of the physical eye as a way of portraying the
variation and vitality of evolutionary nature leads to the limitation and
internalization of landscape. Post-Darwinian nature writers, while certainly
followers of Darwin, are very far from the biology-loving, psychology-
hating group that Alcorn describes. Their literary techniques spiral inward;
the deserts of modernist fiction and the lush "naturist" landscapes share a
common psychological ground.

When I speak of the author's "vision" I am not referring to a set of
stylisic idiosyncrasies or thematic tendencies, as many critics do. Rather, I
am referring to the actual imaging process employed by the reader while
reading. What does one "see" (that is, image in one's mind) while one

reads; what is one allowed to image, encouraged to image, granted or denied imagistic access to? Essential to perceptual theory is the principle that our perceptual abilities are neither as accurate nor as complete as they seem. The mind "corrects" vision, so that what we seem to see is significantly more complete, correct, and precise than what we actually perceive in a glance. For the most part, narrative literature offers us such corrected vision; images the reader experiences while reading usually resemble the corrected, completed perceptions rather than the "uneducated" or "primary" lights and colors first perceived. In fact, the narrative eye very often has a fuller, more focused, and more complete visual field than even corrected human vision; the Victorian fictional landscape in particular is seen through a narrative eye that can see for vast distances, can focus intently, can look around corners and trees, into hidden chambers, through fog and darkness, and can almost be in two places at once. In late-nineteenth and early-twentieth century British representations of nature, however, this correcting and completing process is forestalled. The reader is presented with primary images, with incomplete, disoriented, or confusing angles, and with unexplained optical illusions. An author frequently frustrates the reader's expectations in order to create a sense of limited vision or manipulates the succession of images so that the reader's imagination becomes perceptually "uneducated" and perceives uncorrected forms.

It is my contention that these representations cause the reader to image the landscape as though he or she were actually seeing it. The experience of reading these works differs from that of reading other portrayals of nature in that the reader's imagination is limited by constraints very like those imposed on the physical eye. In order to investigate these issues I will describe the reader's imaginative process using terms taken from visual perception theory. An author constructs a narrative in such a way that the reader images certain things in certain sequences, from certain angles and perspectives; in effect, the author creates a perceptual organ with certain powers and characteristics and locates it relative to the fictional landscape. I will refer to this organ as the *narrative eye*. The reader perceives the objects and events that make up the narrative through this narrative eye. In a certain sense it is the eye through which the narrator sees, but because narrators sometimes pretend to see more or less visual information than they actually convey to the reader, I prefer to use a definition based on the reader's imagistic experience. In effect, I will suppose that the reader perceives literary landscapes through an organ of imaginative perception that operates by the same laws and produces the same kinds of images as a physical eye. Psychological experimentation has demonstrated that processes of imagining objects and seeing objects tend to produce very similar mental images that operate in similar ways and can easily be confused with one another. The mind is prone to many of the same optical illusions as is the eye, and imagined and perceived images can even be combined to create perceptual effects.[2] I will, therefore, discuss the images imagined while reading as though they were being seen.

The term *narrative eye* differs from *narrative perspective,* or *point of view,* which describe locations of narrative consciousness, in that it must be described using a perceptual vocabulary. Rather than the question "who sees?" or "who speaks?," we must ask "what is seen and how is it seen?" in order to understand the operation of the narrative eye. Regardless of whether the imagistic information passed to the reader comes through an omniscient or first-person narrator, through external or internal focalization, in defining the properties of the narrative eye we must attend to that visual information itself. Gérard Genette rejects the terms *vision, field,* and *point of view* in order to "avoid the too specifically visual connotations of the terms" (Genette 189). I take the opposite approach; in order to emphasize the visual aspects of the narrative I will refer to the reader *seeing* things in the text, to *narrative vision* and *narrative perception,* to the *visual field,* to the *focus* and *motion* of the narrative eye and to various kinds of optical illusions and perceptual acts using technical terms that I will clarify throughout the argument. I mean these words to suggest the process of imaging that occurs while the reader is reading, but just as Genette needs to prevent his reader from thinking in terms of actual sight, I wish to encourage mine to do so in order to demonstrate that the narrative is organized around a physical model of perception.

Moreover, when I say that I will be discussing *narratives of perception,* I am referring, for the most part, to narrative renditions of single acts of perception—the act of perceiving one object or vista from one location in a single glance. Genette, in his discussion of narrative pause, analyzes a Proustian description as a "perceptual narrative" in which the "impressions, progressive discoveries, shifts in distance and perspective, errors and corrections, enthusiasms or diappointments, etc." (Genette 102) are presented to the reader. In fact, what Genette describes is the narrative presentation of a series of perceptual acts, performed at various times, that might better be called a "narrative of the mind collecting and organizing perceptions." I wish to investigate narratives depicting the mechanisms of single perceptual acts as they take place. By analyzing the operation of the narrative eye I hope to move toward a more optically informed description of the reader's imagistic experience of the literary landscape.

In post-Darwinian British portrayals of nature, as I have suggested, the narrative eye tends to have perceptual powers and characteristics very much like its physical counterpart. In order to demonstrate how the reader is hemmed in by this limited narrative eye, and to make my definition of the term somewhat clearer, I would like briefly to compare certain landscapes described by post-Darwinian authors with those of mid-nineteenth-century novelists, who offer the reader a powerful and agile narrative eye, and Romantic poets, who describe optical failure but still allow the reader a correct and thorough imagistic vision. Although these examples demonstrate the simplest kinds of visual limitation (physical or meteorological obstructions, darkness, distance, and some simple optical illusions), it is clear that in the Romantic and mid-Victorian portrayals the reader sees farther and better through the narrative eye than does the figure in the landscape actually perceiving the scene. Even when the perceiving figure is the narrator, the narrative eye still gives the reader more visual information than the narrator claims to possess. In post-Darwinian portrayals, on the other hand, the reader's eye and the perceiving figure's eye tend to share the same perceptual experience. The reader, therefore, seems to be trapped in the landscape, operating by its rules, and unable to escape the limitations of physical sight.

This contrast between the powerful mid-Victorian narrative eye and the limited post-Darwinian one is apparent in a brief comparison between descriptions of fogbound landscapes by Dickens and Conrad.

> Fog everywhere. Fog up the river, where it flows among green aits and meadows; fog down the river, where it rolls defiled among the tiers of shipping, and the waterside pollutions of a great (and dirty) city. Fog on the Essex marshes, fog on the Kentish heights. Fog creeping into the cabooses of collier-brigs; fog lying out on the yards, and hovering in the rigging of great ships; fog drooping on the gunwales of barges and small boats. Fog in the eyes and throats of ancient Greenwich pensioners, wheezing by the firesides of their wards; fog in the stem and bowl of the afternoon pipe of the wrathful skipper, down in his close cabin; fog cruelly pinching the toes and fingers of his shivering little 'prentice boy on the deck. Chance people on the bridges peeping over the parapets into a nether sky of fog, with fog all round them, as if they were up in a balloon, and hanging in the misty clouds. (*Bleak House* 1)

> When the sun rose there was a white fog, very warm and clammy, and more blinding than the night. It did not shift or drive; it was just there, standing all round you like something solid. At eight or nine, perhaps, it lifted as a shutter lifts. We had a glimpse of the towering multitude of trees, of the immense matted jungle, with the blazing little ball of the sun hanging over it—all perfectly still—and then the white shutter came down again, smoothly, as if sliding in greased grooves. (*Heart of Darkness* 54)

Dickens's narrative eye can pierce the fog so successfully that it sees aits and meadows, distinguishes kinds of ships, moves into eyes and throats and pipe-bowls, and then pulls back to survey the Essex Marches and the Kentish Heights. The fog, while obscuring virtually everything to the figures in the landscape, actually serves as a means by which the reader is given a sense of the breadth and variety of the fictional world. While the narrator continually points to "fog" as the focus of each successive visual field, it is the objects and landscape forms touched or obscured by fog that the reader sees. The initial blankness of the fog always clears to reveal a vividly visible set of objects beneath, behind, or around it; the narrative eye focuses in on marshes, meadows, and ships, or shifts outward to perceive the throats surrounding the fog, then the pensioners surrounding the throats, or a pipe-bowl, then a skipper. It can even adopt the perceptual limitations of the figures in the landscape, as in the last sentence, but we recognize that this limitation, because voluntary and momentary, is yet another manifestation of its perceptual power.

Dickens's narrative eye remains powerful even when the narrative voice is in the first person, as in Esther's description of Chesney Wold.

> I did not dare to linger or to look up, but I passed before the terrace garden with its fragrant odours, and its broad walks, and its well-kept beds and smooth turf; and I saw how beautiful and grave it was, and how the old stone balustrades and parapets, and wide flights of shallow steps, were seamed by time and weather; and how the trained moss and ivy grew about them, and around the old stone pedestal of the sun-dial; and I heard the fountain falling. Then the way went by long lines of dark windows, diversified by turreted towers, and porches, of eccentric shapes, where old stone lions and grotesque monsters bristled outside dens of shadow, and snarled at the evening gloom over the escutcheons they held in their grip. (*Bleak House* 514–15)

Although it is a "gloomy" and "overcast" evening, and although Esther never looks for long and never looks up, the narrative eye perceives the structure and ornamentation of the house in great detail. We notice the facial expressions of the statues, the patterns of wear on the steps, the differences between the foliage in the garden and on the sundial. As Esther moves past them the walls and corners of the building present new and interesting objects to her view, without, it seems, obscuring or impinging upon any portions of her visual field. The gloominess of the evening or the position of Esther's eye are never mentioned as limiting factors to her perceptions, and while this narrative eye does not see through walls or move back to a distance of several miles, the reader still sees significantly more and significantly better than would an actual human eye in the circumstances Esther describes.

Conrad's narrative eye, on the other hand, is placed in the landscape and is subject to the various physical limitations of the figure on the boat. His position is singular and fixed; the perceptual act thus expresses powerlessness and frustration rather than agility and abundance. Here the fog is an actual visual presence we look at rather than through or around; indeed, it surrounds the narrative eye and prevents it from refocusing. When the fog finally does move the narrative eye has the opportunity to perceive objects, but they appear in very limited detail. The jungle is a single vista that the eye cannot willfully change either by the dynamic motion of Dickens's omnisicient narrator or the limited but still effective motion of Esther moving from walks to gardens to porches. The landscape's chief visual characteristics are its size (it fills the narrative eye's visual field almost completely), its "mattedness" (its surface is so dense as to render detailed perception of form impossible), and its stillness (motion perception also fails); Conrad's narrative eye perceives little more than its own failure to perceive any formal variety in this most various of natural landscapes. When not limited by exterior phenomena the narrative eye is limited by fatigue and impatience:

> Sometimes I would pick out a tree a little way ahead to measure our progress toward Kurtz by, but I lost it invariably before we got abreast. To keep the eyes so long on one thing was too much for human patience. (*Heart of Darkness* 53)

Rather than the experienced and knowledgeable overseer of London we see through the fogbound eyes of Charlie Marlow stuck on his steamer and unable to see, or say, hardly anything of nature's variety.

Obviously, finding stylistic contrasts between Dickens and Conrad is easy, but even for such temporally and temperamentally adjacent authors as George Eliot and Thomas Hardy the distinction between the powerful and the failing narrative eye is apparent. Although Eliot pretends to limit her narrative vision, her portrayal of this limitation often points up her ability to transgress those limitations at will. For example, in a landscape description from Chapter 2 of *Adam Bede* Eliot toys with the possiblity of limiting the reader's perceptions to those of the "traveller" surveying the landscape, but ultimately allows the reader to see details the traveller cannot see.

> [F]rom his station near the Green he had before him in one view nearly all the other typical features of this pleasant land. High up against the horizon were the huge conical masses of hill . . . with sombre greenish sides visibly speckled with sheep, whose motion was only revealed by memory, not detected by sight. . . . Then came the valley, where the wood grew thicker . . . that they might take the better care of the tall mansion which

> lifted its parapets and sent its faint blue summer smoke among them. Doubt-
> less there was a large sweep of park and a broad glassy pool in front of that
> mansion, but the swelling slope of meadow wouldn't let our traveller see
> them from the village green.   (*Adam Bede* 26–27)

Eliot pretends to take the perspective of the traveller himself by initially
locating the eye at "his station near the Green." The invocations of memory and imagination seem to be merely parenthetical, but for the reader they
have the same imagistic weight as the parts of the landscape the traveller
actually perceives. Clearly Eliot is not referring to the traveller's memory,
for he is seeing the landscape for the first time. The reader, unlike the
traveller, is able to see the motion of the sheep, and the pool and the lawn
before the mansion; the narrative eye thus sees more than does the traveller's physical eye.

In the second chapter of *Tess,* on the other hand, Thomas Hardy's
narrative eye is aided by neither memory nor imagination. The stranger
perceiving the Blackmoor Vale has a much vaguer sense of landscape than
does Eliot's traveller. The distance at which Hardy's traveller stands makes
the features of the landscape indistinct so that he perceives it primarily as
regions of color.

> The traveller from the coast . . . is surprised and delighted to behold,
> extended like a map beneath him, a country differing absolutely from that
> which he has passed through. Behind him the hills are open, the sun blazes
> down upon fields so large as to give an unenclosed character to the landscape,
> the lanes are white, the hedges low and plashed, the atmosphere colourless.
> Here in the valley, the world seems to be constructed upon a smaller and
> more delicate scale; the fields are mere paddocks, so reduced that from
> this height their hedgerows appear a network of dark green threads over-
> spreading the paler green of the grass. The atmosphere is languorous, and
> is so tinged with azure that what artists call the middle distance par-
> takes also of that hue, while the horizon beyond is of the deepest ultra-
> marine.   (*Tess* 48)

Rather than simply observing the traveller observing, Hardy clearly locates
the narrative eye in the same spot as the traveller's physical eye. We are not
placed "in the valley" but "here, in the valley"; the hedgerows are lines
not from "his height" but from "this height." The viewer perceives the
landscape as a map in the sense that the eye is capable of delineating only
the most obvious visual distinctions such as lanes and hedgerows rather
than in the sense of seeing it precisely. The rest appears only as a group of
adjacent color regions. Eliot's traveller perceives the botanical structure of
distant organic forms.

> He saw instead a foregound which was just as lovely—the level sunlight
> lying like transparent gold among the gently-curving stems of the feathered
> grass and the tall red sorrel, and the white umbels of the hemlocks lining the
> bushy hedgerows.   (*Adam Bede* 27)

Were Hardy's viewer looking at Eliot's landscape he might perceive the
gold swath of sunlight on the grass, but he would not be able to detect, as
does hers, the "gently-curving stems of the feathered grass and the tall red
sorrel" or recognize the tiny white "umbels" of the hemlock. Both authors
mention hedgerows, but Eliot uses the adjective "bushy," which, like
"feathered" and "gently-curving," describes the structure of the plants
that would only be apparent on close observation. Hardy, on the other
hand, uses "plashed," which suggests only their muddy coloration when
seen from afar.

Janice Carlisle has shown how Eliot's narrator alludes to the reader's
reliance upon her; the reader "sees the whole novel within the confines of
the narrator's pool of ink," which brings about "not liberation, but limitation" (Carlisle 195). Eliot, however, sets up the physical eye as a standard,
then demonstrates the ways in which the narrative eye surpasses it. When
there is a choice between the traveller's and the narrative eye, and the
narrative eye sees more than the physical viewer possibly could (such as
hidden objects and the colors of the landscape during different seasons of
the year), then being offered the narrator's view hardly seems a limitation.
While Eliot's eye does not demonstrate the agility of Dickens's, its stated
limitations serve as a foil to its actual power. For example, in her portrayal
of the Hall Farm through physical vision informed by "imagination" she
begins by making a straightforward claim for a physically limited narrative
eye.

> It would be easy enough, by the aid of the nicks in the stone pillars, to climb
> over the brick wall with its smooth coping; but by putting our eyes close to
> the rusty bars of the gate, we can see the house well enough, and all but the
> very corners of the grassy enclosure.   (*Adam Bede* 75)

Within a few paragraphs, however, we discover that the narrative eye is not
as physically constrained as it might seem.

> Yes, the house must be inhabited, and we will see by whom; for imagination
> is a licensed trespasser: it has no fear of dogs, but may climb over walls and
> peep in at windows with impunity. Put your face to one of the glass panes in
> the right-hand window: what do you see? A large open fireplace, with rusty
> dogs in it, and a bare boarded floor . . . And what through the left-hand
> window? Several clothes-horses, a pillion, a spinning-wheel, and an old box
> wide open, and stuffed full of colored rags.   (*Adam Bede* 75)

Despite the elaborate references to a physical body that needs to climb over pillars and press its nose to windows, the figure in the landscape is revealed to be none other than imagination itself. Once again, Eliot mentions what ought to be physical limitations but are not, and, in her references to "trespassing," seems to betray a kind of authorial guilt about the use of the superhuman narrative eye. Carlisle points to this passage as a demonstration of the reader's "perceptual limitations" because "he can only see what the frames of the dining room and kitchen windows reveal" (Carlisle 196). Eliot, however, constructs the passage so that it emphasizes the power of a literary imagination that is not stopped by the physical constraints of gates and walls.

Hardy, on the other hand, in his description of Hintock House from *The Woodlanders,* limits the narrative eye according to the precise physical context of the figure in the landscape. As Grace Melburry looks down on Mrs. Charmond's house she sees what is most apparent to her eye.

> Hintock House appeared immediately beneath her eye. To describe it as standing in a hollow would not express the situation of the manor-house; it stood in a hole. But the hole was full of beauty. From the spot which Grace had reached a stone could easily have been thrown over, or into the bird's-nested chimneys of the mansion. Its walls were surmounted by a battlemented parapet; but the grey lead roofs were quite visible behind it, with their gutters, laps, rolls, and skylights; together with letterings and shoe-patterns cut by idlers thereon. (*Woodlanders* 45)

Hardy's description follows Grace's gaze down the front of the house then up again to the opposite side of the hollow, where "a few sheep lay about which as they ruminated looked quietly into the bedroom windows." This description strikes us as rather odd and comical, starting as it does on the roof, and concentrating more on what seem minor details, such as gutters and shoe patterns, than on major architectural features, such as the front of the house, which is simply "an ordinary manorial presentation." It does highlight those very things that Grace would see looking down from above; shoe-patterns and chimneys and ruminating sheep are closer and appear in greater detail to her than does the housefront, so Hardy makes them appear in greater detail to the reader. Rather than looping around the house or springing forward to peer through the windows, like Eliot's trespassing imagination, Hardy's narrative eye stays with Grace as she descends the zigzag path, and only moves inside the house as she does.

While she may not offer us as many or as varied types of envisionment through her quasi-human narrative eye as does Dickens through his openly omniscient one, Eliot does not relinquish authoritative vision. Her invocation of memory and imagination serve to correct and complete the imperfect physical eye. Dickens's and Eliot's readers receive a great deal of information about a landscape; the narrative eye sees both fully and well. In Hardy and Conrad the narrative eye simply receives perceptual information without correcting or completing it, and the reader must make what he or she will of that information.

The Romantic portrayal of nature often involves claims for optical illusion and visual failure. Like Eliot, but to a much greater degree, Keats and Wordsworth claim a visual confusion, frustration, and disorientation that the reader does not share. In the fifth stanza of Keats's "Ode to a Nightingale," for example, the reader images a great many natural forms through the narrator's supposedly blinded eye.

> I cannot see what flowers are at my feet,
>   Nor what soft incense hangs upon the boughs,
> But, in embalmed darkness, guess each sweet
>   Wherewith the seasonable month endows
> The grass, the thicket, and the fruit-tree wild;
>   White hawthorn, and the pastoral eglantine;
>   Fast fading violets cover'd up in leaves;
>   And mid-May's eldest child,
> The coming musk-rose, full of dewy wine,
>   The murmurous haunt of flies on summer eves.

Keats's "guessing" is like Eliot's imagination; it allows for the perception of objects in the abscence of physical vision. The narrative eye through which the reader sees is unaffected by this visual failure and becomes, if anything, more acutely and broadly perceptive after the apparent blinding of the figure in the landscape. Keats's narrative eye sees grass, thicket, fruit trees, hawthorn, eglantine, violets, leaves, roses, and flies. It also seems to be able to move through time, viewing the "coming musk-rose," as if it were already present, and the flies on summer eves in the dark of night. In Hardy's novels, on the other hand, the narrative eye is often severely impaired by night vision. When Marty South leaves her brightly lit house, "[t]he night in all its fulness met her flatly on the threshold, like the very brink of an absolute void . . . for her eyes were fresh from the blaze. . . ." She is eventually able to make out vague silhouettes because "the pupils of her young eyes soon expanded, and she could see well enough for her purpose" (*Woodlanders* 13). Hardy also emphasizes night vision in the first chapters of *The Return of the Native*.

> It seemed as if the bonfire-makers were standing in some radiant upper story of the world, detached from and independent of the dark stretches below. The

heath down there was now a vast abyss, and no longer a continuation of what
they stood on; for their eyes, adapted to the blaze, could see nothing of the
deeps beyond its influence.   (22)

It "seems" this way both to the bonfire makers and to the reader. While
Keats corrects the narrator's failed vision in a way that makes clear what is,
or could be, actually present although unseen, Hardy's use of words like
void and *abyss,* and his statement that the darkness was "no longer a
continuation of what they stood on" suggests that the natural world exists
for the perceiver only in the way and to the extent that it is perceived. The
reader is offered no "guessed" or "imagined" images to augment his
limited vision, and must, like the figures in the landscape, grope for whatever scant visual impressions are available, so that the description of optical
failure applies to the reader as well.

Wordsworth's various descriptions of optical illusion in *The Prelude*
might be described as examples of optical confusion except that they never
confuse or disorient the reader. As John Alcorn argues, "Wordsworth's
poetic vision presumes a distance between the object (the landscape) and
the subject (the poet)," while the nature writers "are themselves part of the
landscape" (Alcorn 4). In Wordsworth's poetry the reader is insulated from
any personal experience of the narrator's bizarre visual perceptions. In
Book IV, for example, Wordsworth uses the extended metaphor of a boater
perplexed by overlayed reflections in the river to describe his reconstruction
of the past.

> As one who hangs down-bending from the side
> Of a slow-moving boat, upon the breast
> Of a still water, solacing himself
> With such discoveries as his eye can make
> Beneath him in the bottom of the deep,
> Sees many beauteous sights—weeds, fishes, flowers,
> Grots, pebbles, roots of trees, and fancies more,
> Yet often is perplexed and cannot part
> The shadow from the substance, rocks and sky,
> Mountains and clouds, reflected in the depth
> Of the clear flood, from things which there abide
> In their true dwelling,   (IV 256–67)

While the boater may be perplexed by the reflections, the reader is not, for
Wordsworth distinguishes between shadow and substance; there are real
pebbles and roots under the water and real mountains being reflected onto
the surface. The physical circumstances and position of the boater's eye are
so clearly defined that the reader understands precisely how and why the

reflection causing the optical illusion takes place. If Wordsworth represented the illusory blending of mountain and tree root without explanation, then the reader, along with the boater, would experience the optical illusion. Instead, he demonstrates the mechanism of the illusion and thus allows the reader to avoid it. While the eye of the boater is fixed "downbending," the narrative eye roams across the bottom of the stream, among the mountains, and up into the sky to find the objects being reflected—to compose the landscape so that all of the forms overlayed by the perplexed boater's confused vision are placed back in their "true dwelling." We thus remain assured that the poem, like the landscape, is ultimately composed. In Book I, when the narrator hangs above the raven's nest, or is surprised by the uprearing black peak, he is, again, confused, but the narrative eye observes the spatial relationships that define the perceptual experience (imbalance, angle of vision changed by acceleration) so that the reader remains unmoved. The sky seems not a sky of earth to the narrator, and the reader understands why he might feel so, but imaging only an earthly figure clinging to an earthly cliff beneath an earthly sky he or she does not have the same visual experience.

Wordsworth does offer instances in which the narrative eye perceives the illusion along with the narrator, such as the skating episode in Book I, but the reader is again aware of the true placement of the skater relative to the bank, and the true reason for the apparent motion, so the illusion is explicable and predictable rather than confusing and disorienting.

> and oftentimes,
> When we had given our bodies to the wind,
> And all the shadowy banks on either side
> Came sweeping through the darkness, spinning still
> The rapid line of motion, then at once
> Have I, reclining back upon my heels,
> Stopped short; yet still the solitary cliffs
> Wheeled by me—even as if the earth had rolled
> With visible motion her diurnal round!
> Behind me did they stretch in solemn train,
> Feebler and feebler, and I stood and watched
> Till all was tranquil as a dreamless sleep.   (I, 453–63)

This optical illusion is actually a combination of two illusions: the first, known as *induced motion,* is the confusion of fixed for moving objects (here the skater and the landscape) so that the earth seems to be turning. The second, the perception of residual motion after it has stopped, sometimes referred to as the *waterfall effect,* results from the eye becoming fatigued by the continual perception of motion.[3] Both of these illusions are fairly common, both separately and in combination, and Wordsworth's narrator makes clear that he chooses to experience them—in fact, works quite hard to achieve them—on a regular basis. The skater's freedom to manipulate his own perceptions with the confidence that they will return, naturally, to a controlled and predictable state—a world of substance rather than shadow that is "tranquil as a dreamless sleep"—leads the reader to have a similar confidence in this narrative eye. Wordsworth offers us a perceptual experiment that we can ourselves repeat, and that he has re-peated "oftentimes," through a specific manipulation of his body in the landscape. Far from causing fear or uncertainty it offers a particularly intense form of satisfaction, as does the illusion of the boater for whom perceptual "impediments . . . make his task more sweet" (I 270). The narrator expresses his power over the "feebler" illusory state; the portrayal of optical illusion thus expresses control over nature's optical phenomena rather than the opposite.

As many critics have suggested, Wordsworth conceives the poet's role as one of transforming his own responses to visual nature into controlled poetic forms. Wordsworth's mind, states Eugene Stelzig, is

> threatened at all points with disintegration by an astonishing, vertiginous intensity of perception. The formulation of the poet's vision in terms of the landscape always seems to be on the verge of collapsing from the sheer pressure of feeling thought, yet Wordsworth succeeds in controlling and integrating the conjured energies of imagination.   (Stelzig 175)

As Stelzig implies, Wordsworth's narrator does not pass on the threat of disintegration to the reader, but "formulates" his vision, and his verse, so that the reader receives a "controlled" version of vertiginous intensity. Stelzig measures poetic "success" by Wordsworth's ability to contain this threat. None of this suggests that the reader fails to share the narrator's imaginative experience, or that the visually controlled passages are not emotionally transcendent. I am discussing only the visual, not the vision-ary, the imagistic, not the imaginary—the actual images that would be perceived by the narrator's physical eye if he were in a physical landscape. The visionary aspect of the skating passage is that Nature really does move; the visual aspect is that Nature only appears to move because of a certain set of physical conditions that Wordsworth describes in detail.

Wordsworth's critics often foreground the distinction between the visual and the visionary for the purpose of emphasizing the greater impor-tance of the second. Alec King draws a vigorous distinction between physi-cal sight, which he calls a "half-sight" composed of "registering utility images," and true poetic "seeing."

> The force of Wordsworth's "I saw," in so many of his poems, is the sense it suggests of an active and personal act, not of a passive registering of a given image. What his poems ask us to do is to see, not to register a sight photographed as it were on the eyeball. (King 4–5)

Geoffrey Hartman points out that when Wordsworth writes "I behold" he refers "more to the visionary than the visual sense" and negates "the question whether what is seen is willed or received by the mind" (Hartman 22). As Hartman suggests, Wordsworth negates the essential physiological question; he does not pursue or investigate it, and in this negation he manifests a lack of concern for the operations of optical experience. His portrayals of optical illusion offer the reader a mystical experience, not an optical one; the necessity for this distinction is obvious. Were the reader to experience the optical illusion as does the figure in the landscape, then the emotional power of the passage would derive from a false source; the skater's sense of the motion of nature would, in fact, be illusory. Because the skater enters into the illusion with full knowledge of its optical mechanisms, and because the reader is distanced from it as an optical experience, whatever feelings result from it derive from a mystical interaction with Nature, not from disorientation or confusion. Wordsworth thus retains his authority as a purveyor of visionary experience, just as he retained his authority as a poet in the boater simile, through the power of the narrative eye to control optical illusion.

The power to actively control one's visual perception, to move willfully in and out of the illusory state, to contract or expand the powers of the narrative eye, are obviously lacking in D. H. Lawrence's descriptions of nature. His landscapes seethe for visual, rather than visionary, reasons; the reader is placed in the midst of an optical illusion from which he or she cannot withdraw. The description of the mountain landscape from the short story "The Princess" is a good example.

> Then the trail laddered up again, and they emerged on a narrow ridge-track, with the mountain slipping away enormously on either side. The Princess was afraid. For one moment she looked out, and saw the desert, the desert ridges, more desert, more blue ridges, shining pale and very vast, far below, vastly palely tilting to the western horizon. It was ethereal and terrifying in its gleaming, pale, half-burnished immensity, tilted at the west. She could not bear it. (*Collected Stories* v. 2, 496)

The induced motion of the mountain's "slipping away" comes as a surprise to the reader as it does to the Princess; Lawrence has not prepared us for the apparent motion of the landscape as Wordsworth does through references to speed and trajectory in the skating passage. The Princess's sensation of the landscape "tilting" is caused by her inability to determine, at first glance, the actual distance between herself and distant landscape forms. The mind attempts to maintain size constancy so that large distant objects and small near ones, which will make the same size impression on the retina, can be properly placed in a three-dimensional perspective. The Princess's sudden apprehension of the vista creates an initial confusion about which objects are small but near and which are large but far. The illusory "tilting" of the landscape occurs as the focus of the eye moves up the visual field and the mind places the landscape forms farther, then farther away, trying to make them properly conform to their visual context. Had Lawrence wanted the reader to be able to compose the landscape he need only have mentioned the actual location of the distant ridges by saying "more blue ridges shining pale and very vast on the western horizon." He could also have placed the narrative eye at a distance from the Princess so that the reader could perceive her actual physical location relative to the horizon.

Wordsworth does this in the "black peak" passage from Book I of the *Prelude*, which involves the same optical illusion. There the peak seems to "stride" after the narrator, to move with unnatural speed into the sky, because he judges it to be a "huge" distant peak that ought to rise only slowly due to the slight angle at which he views it. While Lawrence's landscape seems to move of its own accord, however, the apparent motion of the black peak results from the rower's own actions, as Wordsworth makes abundantly (and somewhat comically) clear.

> And, as I rose upon the stroke, my boat
> Went heaving through the water like a swan . . .
> I struck and struck again,
> And growing still in stature the grim shape
> Towered up between me and the stars, and still,
> For so it seemed, with purpose of its own
> And measured motion like a living thing,
> Strode after me.   (I 375–85)

The moving peak and the moving boat are both seen from without so that, even if the reader does not recognize the perceptual mechanism at work, the complicity of the rower in his own perceptual confusion becomes apparent. Lawrence's reader, who sees only the mountains moving and the landscape tilting, cannot determine the cause of the illusion, and must suffer through it with the Princess. The frantic motion of the narrative eye, as it moves farther and farther up the visual field attempting to determine the distance of the mountains, suggests no active perceptual power on the Princess's part, and creates only a sense of imbalance and uncertainty for the reader.

The landscape portrayed by these late-nineteenth and early-twentieth century authors is thus one in which character and reader share the same physically unreliable eye. Like an actual person in the landscape the reader is confused by optical illusion and frustrated by optical limitation. Clearly these authors, like all authors, use a range of representational techniques and exceptions can be found, but reading about nature in the works of Hardy, Lawrence, and Conrad, as well as those of their contemporary naturalists and nature writers, involves the reader in a more limited, obscure, confused, and disordered kind of imaging than does reading about a Romantic or mid-Victorian landscape.

II

In the works of Darwin, Hardy, Lawrence, and Conrad, then, reading mimics the physiological process of seeing. The authors' different literary styles must therefore involve different styles of seeing with different scientific and philosophical implications. Gillian Beer discusses the emergence of an "idiosyncratic, often grotesquely individual, yet accessible" (Beer 46) narrative voice that accompanies Victorian novelists' abandonment of teleological narrative ordering. A similarly idiosyncratic narrative eye appears in post-Darwnian literature. Representational strategy indicates an author's aesthetic individualism as well as a specific conception of the perceiving mind. Narrative vision, in its enactment of physiological vision, demonstrates fundamental assumptions about the relationship between the perceiver and the landscape he or she perceives. Consequently, I have chosen to describe each author's narrative vision in terms of the theory of visual perception that it most resembles. Beginning in the first chapter on Darwin, I will establish how the rhetorical styles of his scientific predecessors (William Paley, Charles Lyell, and Thomas Malthus), along with his personal experiences on the *Beagle* voyage, lead to his creation of a mode of scientific narrative representation that, by paralleling empirical modes of envisionment, allows him to portray a varying and evolving natural landscape. Thomas Hardy's Darwinian landscape is also entangled, as Chapter 2 makes clear, but his narrative eye catches the tragedy inherent in such entanglement through the selective perception of distinct forms characteristic of a nativistic perceptual model. The failure of the human eye to perceive the intricacies of Darwinian nature becomes so profound for

British authors describing the jungle that Joseph Conrad, H. M. Tomlinson, and Alfred Russel Wallace can only describe foreign landscapes as composed of familiar forms or no forms at all. Such a familiarization and depopulation of strange lands, Chapter 3 suggests, parallels William James's theory of the memory-based perception of "real" shapes. In the early-twentieth century, nature writers portray a visual world composed of dynamic energy forces rather than of biological organisms. D. H. Lawrence, W. H. Hudson, and Richard Jefferies all perceive natural energy rather than natural form, as Chapter 4 demonstrates, and their landscapes ebb and flow like the visual fields of Gestalt perceptual theory.

I am not arguing for straightforward influence between scientific and literary texts at the turn of the century. Most of the authors I discuss had little specific knowledge of perceptual theory, but their theoretical pronouncements on literary and artistic representation demonstrate that their portrayals of nature do share certain principles of visual organization with specific perceptual theories. Hardy's portrayal of Wessex can be called "nativistic" because his many statements about the way the artist's eye selects forms from the landscape and his stated adoption of certain painterly techniques of focus and perspective are consistent with the Law of Visible Direction that was central to nativistic arguments about binocular vision. D. H. Lawrence openly espouses a field theory of matter and demonstrates, in his paintings as well as in his descriptive prose, principles of segregation and regularization of form consistent with Gestalt perceptual theory. Joseph Conrad's essays on fiction encourage psychological abstraction and the familiarization of perceived images in ways that are consistent with William James's theories of memory-based perception. These parallels between literary style and visual perception theory emerge during this period because both are responding to similar trends in the visualization of nature. Post-Darwinian authors and nativist visual perception theorists were responding to empirical theories that emphasized the fragmentation and disorganization of wholes into parts and the consequent multiplication of formal variety. In both cases their responses involve ways of seeing that regularize perceived form and interiorize the natural landscape.

The conflict between nativistic and empiricist theories of the perception of form spans several centuries and involves philosophers, psychologists, and optical theorists; I can give only a brief summary here.[4] Empiricist philosophers rejected the possibility that certain ideas are innate or native, asserting that all ideas must derive from sensation. In his *Essay Concerning Human Understanding* (1690) Locke applies this to visual perception by arguing that our primary or uneducated visual perceptions of the world, what we see as infants, consists only of sensations such as color, figure, and extension. Locke considers the perception of three-dimensionality to be a complex idea, achievable only through the psychological combination of sensations over time. A baby perceiving a cube or a sphere would see it only as a flat circle or uneven square. In his discussion of what came to be known as the "Molyneaux Question," Locke suggests that a man born blind, who had learned how to distinguish between a cube and a sphere by touch, could not, on first being given sight, distinguish between the sphere and the cube without touching them because his uneducated perception of the sphere would be two-dimensional.

Berkeley takes Locke's empiricist theories a step farther by suggesting that extension in two-dimensional space must also be learned. In his *Essay Towards a New Theory of Vision* (1709), Berkeley maintains that primary vision lacks depth, distance, and limitation of forms, for all of these ideas are derived from the sense of touch. He writes: "That which I see is only variety of light and colors. That which I feel is hard or soft, hot or cold, rough or smooth. What similitude, what connection, have those ideas with these?" (Berkeley sec. 103 p. 69). The connection between that which is seen and that which is touched, or "visible ideas" and "tangible ideas" as Berkeley puts it, is arbitrary and conventional. Consequently, the baby would see neither sphere nor circle, but only lights and colors.

Furthermore, the mind is unextended and only capable of perceiving one point, or "minimum visible," at a time. We perceive forms by combining these minimum visibles; the eye perceives one point at a time, and the mind images each point in succession so that a form is perceived through a kind of mental pointillism. In order to construct the forms of a visual field properly, however, the eye must be trained by touch as to what constitutes a tangibly distinct object—a single formal unit—and what does not.

> According as the mind variously combines its ideas, the unit varies; and as the unit, so the number, which is only a collection of units, also varies. We call a window "one," a chimney "one"; and yet a house, in which there are many windows and many chimneys, has an equal right to be called "one"; and many houses go to the making of one city. In these and the like instances, it is evident the unit constantly relates to the particular drafts the mind makes of its ideas, to which it affixes names. . . . Now, this naming and combining together of ideas is perfectly arbitrary, and done by the mind in such sort as experience shows it to be most convenient—without which our ideas had never been collected into such sundry distinct combinations as they now are. (secs. 109–10 p. 72)

The baby would thus have no way of knowing that the minimum visibles making up the sphere ought to be grouped together until his visual ideas were associated with his tangible ideas through the experience of touching things. Berkeley says that a man born blind and given his sight at a later age, "would not, in the first act of vision, parcel out the ideas of sight into the same distinct collections that others do who have experienced which do regularly coexist and are proper to be bundled up together under one name" (sec. 110 p. 72). The new perceiver could construct a field of color from minimum visibles, but would have no idea of form, distance or magnitude; looking at a man, there would "crowd into his mind the ideas which compose the visible man, in company with all the other ideas of sight perceived at the same time." The landscape would be similarly chaotic and overwhelming; "the sun, the stars, the remotest objects as well as the nearer, would all seem to be in his eye, or rather in his mind" (sec. 41 p. 37). Only after visual experience in concert with tangible experience would he be able to order the visual field properly.

The case most often referred to by empiricist theorists was William Cheselden's 1728 account of a thirteen-year-old boy born blind and given his sight.

> When he first saw, he was so far from making any Judgment about Distances, that he thought all Objects whatever touch'd his Eyes, (as he express'd it) as what he felt, did his Skin; and thought no Objects so agreeable as those which were smooth and regular, tho' he could form no Judgment of their Shape, or guess what it was in any Object that was pleasing to him: . . . but having too many Objects to learn at once, he forgot many of them; and (as he said) at first he learn'd to know, and again forgot a thousand Things in a Day. One Particular only (tho' it may appear trifling) I will relate; Having often forgot which was the Cat, and which the Dog, he was asham'd to ask; but catching the Cat (which he knew by feeling) he was observ'd to look at her stedfastly, and then setting her down, said, So Puss! I shall know you another Time. . . . He said, every new Object was a new Delight, and the Pleasure was so great, that he wanted Ways to express it. . . . A Year after first Seeing, being carried upon Epsom Downs, and observing a large Prospect, he was exceedingly delighted with it, and call'd it a new Kind of Seeing.   (Cheselden 448–50)

Cheselden's patient seems to experience the sort of depthless and formless brilliance, the ravishing intensity of first sight, which Berkeley describes as being characteristic of uneducated vision.

> The objects intromitted by sight would seem to him (as in truth they are) no other than a new set of thoughts or sensations, each whereof is as near to him as the perception of pain or pleasure, or the most inward passions of his soul." (sec. 41 p. 37)

Berkeleyan theories concerning distance and magnitude were largely accepted by the nineteenth century, but a controversy still existed over form. The empiricists maintained Berkeley's belief that the mind is unextended and perceives by minimun visibles. The nativists claimed that the mind has a native ability to perceive whole forms—that the mind is extended. The empiricists explained the perception of form psychologically; forms are constructed by the mind from perceived bits of information. Nativists explained it physiologically; the pattern of light falling on the retina is directly perceived by the mind in whole forms. As Thomas Reid put it, "the object is made up of a trunk, branches and leaves; but the act of mind by which it is perceived, hath neither trunk, branches nor leaves" (206). Hermann von Helmholtz described the distinction between empiricism and nativism as follows:

> Some are disposed to concede to the influence of experience as much scope as possible, and to derive from it especially all notion of space. This view may be called the empirical theory. Others, of course, are obliged to admit the influence of experience in the case of certain classes of perceptions; still with respect to certain elementary apperceptions that occur uniformly in the case of all observers, they believe it is necessary to assume a system of innate apperceptions that are not based on experience, especially with respect to space relations. In contradiction to the former view, this may perhaps be called the intuition theory [nativistic theory] of sense perceptions. (Helmhultz 10)

The dissent of the nativists about the constructed nature of visual form cast doubt upon Berkeley's fundamental teaching—that visual and tangible ideas are unrelated. Empiricists claimed that extension is an idea that can only be derived from the sense of touch, and that the mind therefore cannot be extended. Nativists countered with the charge that the process of perception described by empiricists is physiologically impossible and that in order to perceive form as swiftly as it does the mind must be extended.

For example, Sir William Hamilton argued in his *Lectures on Metaphysics* (posth. 1880) that the theory contradicts our common awareness of how we, as adults, perceive the world.

> [Y]ou cannot imagine a triangle which is not either an equilateral, or an isosceles, or a scalene,—in short, some individual form of a triangle; nay more, you cannot imagine it, except either large or small, on paper or on a board, of wood or of iron, white or black or green; in short, except under all the special determinations which give it, in thought, as in existence, singularity or individuality. (Hamilton Lect. 26, 169)

If the empiricists' theory were true, Hamilton claims, we would not be able to perceive whole forms correctly even as adults, but would always be seeing things in bits and pieces. Everyday experience demonstrates that it is the complete form that we perceive first, only filling in the details later.[5]

> Between two sheep the ordinary spectator can probably apprehend no difference, and if they were twice presented to him he would be unable to discriminate the one from the other. But a shepherd can distinguish every individual sheep; and why? Because he has descended from the vague knowledge which we all have of sheep—from the vague knowledge which makes every sheep, as it were, only a repetition of the same undifferenced unit—to a definite knowledge of the qualities by which each is contrasted from his neighbor.   (Hamilton Lect. 36 pp. 328–29)

To a nativist, perceiving the world is a matter of first perceiving "undifferenced units," and then filling in the specific details. The baby perceives simple two-dimensional forms; the adult, having learned to recognize those forms, can identify them instantly without having to reconstruct them from minimum visibles. A more detailed and particular perceptual process takes place after this initial general perception of form.

> By first having acquired a comprehensive knowledge of it as a whole, we can descend to its several parts, consider these both in themselves, and in relation to each other, and to the whole of which they are constituents, and thus attain to a complete and articulate knowledge of the object. We decompose, and then we recompose.   (Hamilton Lect. 36 pp. 328–29)

A sheep, before it is decomposed and recomposed, is a spatial form having shape and extension, perceived through the eye and vividly outlined in the mind, its visual distinctness corresponding to its tangibile solidity. Actual sheep will differ somewhat from this visual type, but all will be close enough to be recognized as sheep forms. In nativist primary vision, a sheep is a sheep is a sheep.

Nativistic and empirical perception differ in that while the nativistic mind *perceives* forms, the empirical mind *constructs* forms. Hamilton's nativistic shepherd receives the perceptual stimulus of a sheep-shaped form standing before him, and he recognizes it as the "undifferenced unit" named "sheep." He then "descends" to its "several parts," looks more closely at the black muzzle, the short back legs, the scar on the left ear, and recognizes the specific sheep as "Lulu," who is three years old and always delivers strong healthy lambs. The empirical shepherd, on the other hand, receives the stimuli of thousands of tiny visible points: a point of grey from Lulu's slightly dingy back wool, a point of shiny black from the tip of her nose, a point of blue from the branding ink on her haunch, pink from the tender part of the ear, brown from the mud on a hoof, and his mind then assembles the points into a form that it can recognize as "Lulu the sheep." Like Hamilton's model, this involves an element of recognition based on memories of past experience. Before recognition, however, is the mental creation of the image itself, which must occur each time Lulu is perceived. The sheep has no initial distinctness or extension in the shepherd's mind, but it emerges into a form fluidly. Lulu, perceived thus, is not an "undifferenced unit" that is decomposed into specificity. She is a conglomeration of different points of light that come together, not into the typical outline of a sheep, but into the individual outline of a Lulu.

The basic point at issue between empiricists and nativists had strong implications for the regularity and wholeness of perceived forms. Nativists supposed an innate harmony between mind and matter; the stable relationship beween whole perceived forms and whole exterior objects implied a fundamental regularity of organic form. Empiricists, who believed forms are constructed by the mind, embraced a more fragmented and variable conception of form. An empirical narrative eye would thus be well suited to the envisionment of evolutionary nature. Darwin was arguing against biological systematists who believed organic forms occur in typical and immutable species. He suggested that the naming and combining together of unique organisms into species, like the naming and combining of minimum visibles into visual forms, is perfectly arbitrary and done by systematists in the way most convenient for them. In order to portray an evolutionary world, in which species are only loose collections of uniquely varying individuals, Darwin uses a narrative eye that, like the empirical eye, perceives continually recombining parts rather than whole forms. As Robert Richards has convincingly shown, Darwin's populationist conception of species can be traced to his early exposure to sensationalist epistemology. Sensationalists were not—perhaps except for Condillac—strictly empiricist, largely because of their concentration on the mechanisms of brain physiology, however, their belief that "all ideas are imaged sensations" (Richards 21) and their emphasis on learned experience had an empirical cast, particularly in terms of its definition of species form. Sensationalist epistemology "implied that species as abstract entities or individuated essences could not be real: a species could only be a group of like individuals represented by a complex idea (or associated trains of ideas) consisting of particular images" (Richards 39). If species form is correlated to visual form, then the sensationalist and the empiricist conceptions of form are fundamentally similar. Empiricists believed that the eye sees all organisms as composed of unique features, or minimum visibles, and visual similarities are abstractions created by the mind for its own convenience.

Through Darwin's empirical narrative eye the reader images a nature composed of organic minima that can be combined into virtually any form and
that are continually in the process of evolutionary variation. His vision of
nature is thus not unlike Cheselden's patient's delightful chaos.

Those nature writers who follow Darwin tend to portray a more nativistic landscape, one composed of simpler and more regular forms. The
confusion that the multiplicity of external objects implicit in Darwinian
theory causes for post-Darwinian nature writers is often expressed in a
desire to order the landscape into an accurate and intelligible vista, to return
to familiar forms, or to abandon the exterior confusion altogether and live
in the darkened room of the mind. These impulses toward regularizing and
completing forms or turning inward in search of familiarity and regularity
also emerge in turn-of-the-century nativist perceptual theory through the
adoption of cerebral—rather than retinal—models of perception.

The psychophysical postulate (sometimes referred to as the principle
of isomorphism), which asserts that each perception is exactly matched by
one brain event, had long been an element of nativist theory. While some
empiricists had adopted it, it was particularly useful to nativist theory
because it implied the physiological extension of perceived form; if a form
is perceived extended across the retina it must be perceived extended in the
brain. In the nineteenth century most nativist theorists placed emphasis on
the retinal perception of form, suggesting precise linkages between parts of
the retina and parts of the brain.[6] By the end of the century, however, the
brain was more often described as reacting wholistically to stimuli through
chemical and neural processes. William James, in his *Principles of Psychology* (1890), describes cerebral response[7]:

> The only impressions than can be made upon [brain-matter] are through the
> blood, on the one hand, and through the sensory nerve-roots, on the other;
> and it is to the infinitely attenuated currents that pour in through these latter
> channels that the hemispherical cortex shows itself to be so peculiarly sus-
> ceptible. The currents, once in, must find a way out. In getting out they leave
> their traces in the paths which they take. The only thing they *can* do, in short,
> is to deepen old paths or to make new ones; and the whole plasticity of the
> brain sums itself up in two words when we call it an organ in which currents
> pouring in from the sense-organs make with extreme facility paths which do
> not easily disappear.   (James 112)

James goes on to suggest that, because visual perception operates electrochemically, we cannot consider a perception "the sum of distinct psychic
entities" but must instead recognize it to be "one state of mind or nothing"
(James 725–26). This cerebral model combined certain elements of nativism and empiricism by turning the emphasis away from the hard mechanics

of the retina and toward the more fluid and electrochemical dynamics of the brain. Like Hamilton, James suggests formal regularity and wholeness and an essential and reassuring stability between interior and exterior space. Like Berkeley, however, James shows perception to be fluid (if not fragmentary) and dynamic (if not variable), and emphasizes the interiority of the perceptual act. In effect, he places the emphasis on the psyche side of the psychophysical postulate, and thus begins to undermine the material significance of exterior objects even as he asserts their wholeness. For example, James's cerebral model allows for the empiricist suggestion that memories, because electrochemically similar to perceptions, are interchangeable with them. Optical illusions may be based on chemical imbalances that are, in turn, caused by psychological states, and not on misalignments of the retina.

Toward the turn of the century, then, visual perception theory was making the rather contradictory move toward both a more regular and a more interior model of form perception. James's theory and, to an even greater degree, the work of the Gestalt psychologists, attempted to define form in neurological terms; vision was portrayed as being determined by brain chemistry rather than by retinal reproduction. The eye looking at an object became far less important than the operation of the mind perceiving it. These nativistic theories were still physiological rather than psychological, but by focusing on cerebral activity they turned attention away from the interaction of the physical eye with exterior nature.

The revolutionary movement in early-twentieth-century perceptual theory was Gestalt psychology, which combined the physical theories of field dynamics with the psychophysical postulate. It showed that the brain not only perceives through mental chemistry, but that this mental chemistry operates according to the laws of field physics. Rather than supposing discrete neural links between the retina and the brain, Max Wertheimer, Kurt Koffka, and Wolfgang Köhler suggested that the brain operates as an electrochemical field, in which forms are organized according to the laws of physics. Because form is determined by physical laws, the mind will always regularize and organize forms according to principles of regularity, similarity, symmetry, and simplicity.

> Demonstrations of the effectiveness of the internal organizing forces . . . occur at practically every moment of our lives. We are surrounded by rectangular things which look to us rectangular. Even if we disregard the fact of perspective distortion, each one of these cases is a point in hand; for what real rectangle is a mathematically exact rectangle? . . . [T]he fact that we see rectangles everywhere is due to the fact that the true rectangle is a better organized figure than the slightly inaccurate one would be, and that only very

slight dislocation is necessary to change the latter into the former.   (Koffka 140–41)

While Gestalt psychology did not assume innate knowledge of the exterior world, it did suggest that all of nature, including brain matter, operates by the same physical laws so that interior and exterior forms must correspond. The Gestalt "true rectangle" is thus even more regular than Hamilton's "undifferenced units," for the chemistry of the mind actually participates in smoothing out and regularizing perceived nature. There really are typical forms, or ideal electrochemical balances, toward which perception strives. On the other hand, the fundamental nature of the perceptual form has changed. Rather than conceiving of perceived form as a kind of material object that is composed either of wholes or parts, Gestalt theorists describe perceived forms as precarious by-products of dynamic field interactions within the mind.

The progress of visual perception theory through the nineteenth and into the twentieth century is thus marked by a motion toward regular and whole conceptions of perceived form that are linked with interior, cerebral perceptual models. In moving away from the dynamic because fragmentary and variable empirical perception, theorists espouse dynamic because electrochemical and neural nativist perception. Hamilton's reassuringly regular world of whole forms perceived by an innately extended mind had become a profoundly unstable interior world of regular whole forms created by dynamic mental forces.

A similar progress occurs in the perceptual representation of nature by post-Darwinian nature writers. Their narrative limitation of Darwin's entangled nature is manifested in an increasingly interior landscape of whole and regular forms. Darwin, like the empiricists, portrays perceived organic form as fragmented and variable. Those who follow him, while adopting his physiologically limited eye, fail to adopt his empiricist vision. Hardy portrays the tragedy of materiality through a rigidly nativistic narrative eye that perceives tangibly whole and hard-edged forms, but which blurs or overlooks large regions of the landscape. Conrad presents the unfamiliarity of foreign landscape through a Jamesian narrative eye capable of perceiving only a few familiar forms against a black backdrop, and continually blending perceptual and conceptual mental states. Lawrence's psychosexual conception of matter is manifested in a nature composed of homogeneous color regions in a continual state of flux in which forms combine and dissipate by Gestalt principles of regularity. To the first irony, that Darwin's way of portraying an organically unlimited nature leads to a visually limited one, is added the additional irony that post-Darwinian nature writers, in attempting to reassert the wholeness and regularity of exterior nature, generate a psychologically interior and subjective landscape. The interiority of modernism can thus be reconciled with the biological awareness of the nature writers through Darwin's choice of a perceptually limited narrative eye. The perceptual diminishment and simplification of nature accompanying this interiority results from post-Darwinian nature writers, like late-nineteenth and early-twentieth century perception theorists, regularizing formal variety through cerebral modes of narration.

By using an optical vocabulary to discuss narrative operations I hope to describe more precisely the literary envisionment of nature in the post-Darwinian world. I do not, and cannot, hope to investigate the impact of Darwinian theory on Victorian social, scientific, and literary discourse as fully or as eloquently as critics such as Gillian Beer and George Levine. In their enthusiastic and exhaustive intellectual generosity they pursue the manifold entanglements of Darwin's work through the labyrinthine corridors of Victorian society and aesthetics. Other critics, such as Sally Shuttleworth and Roger Ebbatson, demonstrate Darwin's intricate penetrations into the work of specific literary authors with equal zeal. My focus is more specific. I will trace the perceptual limitations placed on Darwinian nature by post-Darwinian portrayals of it. By concentrating on entangled landscapes I have omitted nature writers, most notably George Meredith and E. M. Forster, who tend to describe natural landscapes that are already physically ordered and thus require less perceptual ordering; these authors offer less obvious, although not less important, demonstrations of such limitation. Nor do I wish to join the estimable ranks of literary critics who discuss the visual imagination in relation to painting. The work of critics like Wylie Sypher, George Landow, Mary Ann Caws, and J. B. Bullen is fascinating and essential, particularly for the period I am describing, and there is always a great temptation to describe visual perception in terms of visual art. I have (for the most part) resisted this temptation, except when authors specifically point to paintings as examples of visual perception, because the eye perceiving nature and the eye perceiving a painting are often engaged in different perceptual processes. Similarly, I have tried to avoid comparisons to cinema or photography because the perception of these artforms also involves a distinct set of optical variables.

Investigating the reader's imaginative experience in terms of physical perception will, I hope, allow certain aspects of these authors' literary styles to become more apparent. George Levine describes both his and Gillian Beer's work as relying on the assumption that Victorian writers, like ourselves, could have "absorbed without full consciousness the vision of the world created by . . . science" (vii). I would like to apply this principle more literally than Levine probably intends. The post-Darwinian "vision of the world" . . . that I will investigate is a specific set of representational parameters rather than a general set of imaginative characteristics—acts of vision, not webs of ideas. This does not limit the value of other critical approaches, but serves only as another strategy for understanding the intricate and powerful representations of nature with which post-Darwinian literature abounds.

1

A Chaos of Delight: Perception and Illusion in Darwin's Scientific Writing

It is interesting to contemplate an entangled bank, clothed with many plants of many kinds, with birds singing on the bushes, with various insects flitting about, and with worms crawling through the damp earth, and to reflect that these elaborately constructed forms, so different from each other, and dependent on each other in so complex a manner, have all been produced by laws acting around us.

(ORIGIN 489)

[W]e ought in imagination to take a thick layer of transparent tissue, with spaces filled with fluid, and with a nerve sensitive to light beneath, and then suppose every part of this layer to be continually changing slowly in density, so as to separate into layers of different densities and thicknesses, placed at different distances from each other, and with the surfaces of each layer slowly changing in form.

(ORIGIN 188–89)

Although the entangled bank is Darwin's best-known image, it is not, perhaps, his best imagistic representation of evolutionary nature. The bright insects and wiggling worms certainly demonstrate Darwin's sense of the dynamism and interrelation of natural organisms, but they are too visually distinct to illustrate the formal fluidity of Darwin's organic world. Essential to his portrayal of the natural world is that things are unfocused, fluid, without specific design or fixity, and that they continually slip away from an ever-changing norm. Species blend into one another just as populations, landmasses, and bodily appendages flow and change. There is a softness, an intangibility to Darwinian nature that is not as apparent in the entangled bank as it is in the second passage quoted earlier. This second quotation, from Chapter 6 of the *Origin of Species,* demonstrates the extreme insubstantiality of the Darwinian conception of form; although the structure described can be to some extent understood, it is very difficult to visualize. How can the reader see something that is continually changing from one difference to another, not from one form to another; a structure that mutates without ever developing into anything?

George Levine notes that the formal excess of Darwin's nature leads toward the breaking of boundaries.

> Darwin's observing eye, straining to bring the multiplicity of nature within the rule of law, sees more than law can contain; and his vision of the world is in excess of the theory he can formulate to express it.   (Levine 231)

Dwight Culler also describes Darwin's influence on literary form as a kind of structural lawlessness.

> When all is flux, the reversal cannot be distinguished from any other position, and one thing is quite as meaningless as another . . . but the truth is that this whole Darwinian . . . view is so antithetic to the purposive cast of the human mind that it is very difficult to keep it firmly in focus.   (Culler 244)

Indeed, the organic structure described earlier seems to be always slipping out of focus, moving out of range of the mind's eye, foiling any attempt to cast it purposively into some distinct, imageable form by its excessive variation. The fluxing quality of Darwinian thought and image is also pointed out by Walter F. Cannon, who states that "for Darwin, a 'form' is something unsubstantial, changeable. . . . It is this habit of looking at an apparently rigid structure and imagining it as a plastic one, of 'seeing' it flow into another apparently quite different form" that characterizes "Darwin's vision" (Cannon 160). The described form is so plastic that the mental vision is foiled and the reader is incapable of imaging any form at all. It is all the more startling, then, that the structure being described in this quotation is none other than the human eye itself. What Levine, Culler, and Cannon find in the structure of Darwin's argument and the quality of Darwin's vision can be traced to the very instrument of perception that allows him to look into the natural world. The entangled bank may be intertwined and dynamic, but it does not approach the formless mutability of the entangled eye.

Darwin's portrayal of the eye as a mass of barely differentiated matter was quite unusual for its time. Previously it had generally been portrayed as a mechanism. Darwin's description seems to have been written as a response to William Paley, who, in *Natural Theology,* uses the eye as the set piece of his argument for design.

> I know no better method of introducing so large a subject, than of comparing a single thing with a single thing; an eye, for example, with a telescope. . . . They are made upon the same principles; both being adjusted to the laws by which the transmission and refraction of rays of light are regulated. . . . The lenses of the telescope, and the humours of the eye, bear a complete resemblance to one another, in their figure, their position, and in their power over the rays of light.   (Paley 14–15)

Essential to this argument is that the eye, regardless of its minor limitations, is the most perfect instrument known to humanity, and that its perceptions, like its structure, will be regular and reliable. One of the objects it perceives is another eye, so that the ease with which the reader can visualize descriptions of the eye comes to indicate the power of the eye itself. Opthalmological descriptions of the eye also involve easily imaged metaphors. Benjamin Travers, in his *Synopsis of the Diseases of the Eye and their Treatment* (1821), states that the cornea resembles "in semi-transparency and in color, the ground glass of which ornamental lamps are constructed" (Travers 10). The *processus ciliares* "appear to be radiated folds of the choroid tunic" which are "gathered at their origin like the plaits of a shirt at the wristband." When they are viewed collectively, they "have some resemblance to a radiated flower" (14) while the blood vessels in the ciliary membrane are "arranged in the form of trees with weeping branches" (12). Darwin takes these flowers and tunics, and complicates them into webbed and knotted masses of organic matter. Where Paley's eye sees clearly, and Travers's is clearly seen, Darwin's is both unperceiving and unperceivable. Paley and Travers describe the eye nativistically; all eyes are built on the same ideal model and can be perceived as distinct, regular forms. Darwin's eye, on the other hand, fluxes with the variability of empirically perceived form.

Darwin's revolutionary contribution to nineteenth-century scientific prose is his representation of nature as though seen through an empirically entangled eye. As a scientific writer, Darwin's task was to make nature imagistically comprehensible to his reader. As an evolutionary naturalist, however, he was bound to portray an evolving nature; a set of unstable forms that slip into new forms even as they are being named and represented. Because evolutionary nature lacks regular biological forms, or stable species, Darwin portrays the natural world as lacking distinct visual forms. He does so through the use of representational techniques that disorient the reader's mental vision—imaginative illusions that parallel the perceptual illusions to which physical vision is prone. Dazzled by the dynamism and complexity of Darwin's natural world, the reader struggles unsuccessfully to categorize the multitude of fluxing forms into stable or familiar types. By involving the reader in a perceptual chaos that parallels the organic chaos of the entangled bank, Darwin demonstrates the formlessness of evolutionary nature and the artificiality of a theory of distinct species.

The extraordinary nature of this form of representation can best be understood in the context of the more traditional narrative strategies of other scientific writers, such as William Paley, Thomas Malthus, and Charles Lyell whose works will be discussed in Section I of this chapter. These scientists, who Darwin identifies as his strongest intellectual influences, adopt three distinct narrative strategies, and the intersection of their modes of representation can be seen as the starting point for Darwin's style. The development of Darwin's unique way of seeing and representing nature is traced, in Section II, through his early letters, journals, and scientific articles to its culmination in the rapturous rhetorical illusions of the *Origin of Species*. These illusions, as Section III make clear, allow the reader to see one organic form multiplying, through visual analogy, into hundreds of potential forms, and offer the reader a sense of the formal dynamism of evolutionary nature.

I

Darwin read the works of William Paley at Cambridge and admired them for their logical presentation of complicated natural phenomena. He read Charles Lyell's *Principles of Geology* while on the *Beagle* voyage and credits it with opening his eyes to the uniformitarian operations of nature. Thomas Malthus's *Essay on Population* was read "for amusement" in 1838, and provided, in the geometric pressure of population, the theoretical key to evolutionary theory. All of these authors share a gift for the vivid imagistic presentation of the natural world. Paley's lucid mechanistic metaphors sketch a minute portrait of the body as intricate machine; Malthus's grotesque anecdotes present the reader with a rapaciously expanding organic world; Lyell's undulating mountains and valleys play out the grand narrative of uniformitarian history. For all three authors the natural world is a visual entity that can best be understood by seeing; human vision is extended through literary means to transcend the constraints of time and space. Although Darwin adopts the opposite technique—emphasizing the eye's limitations rather than its strengths—the understanding of scientific investigation as a primarily visual experience ties him to these earlier scientific writers.

Darwin was introduced to Paley's work at Cambridge, where he found that both the *Evidences of Christianity* and the *Natural Theology* "gave me as much delight as did Euclid," and "was the only part of the Academical Course which as I then felt and as I still believe, was of the least use to me in the education of my mind" (*Autobiography* 33). He goes on to admit that he did not "at the time trouble myself about Paley's premises; and taking these on trust I was charmed and convinced by the long line of argumentation." The most charming and convincing quality of Paley's argument for design is his ability, through his methodical use of engaging and highly imageable metaphor, to make the reader see the body as an artifact.

> The chamber of the eye is a camera-obscura, which, when the light is too small, can enlarge its opening; when too strong, can again contract it; and that without any other assistance than that of its own exquisite machinery . . . this hole in the eye, which we call the pupil, under all its different dimensions, retains its exact circular shape. This is a structure extremely artificial. (17)

Paley's long line of argumentation involves the gradual transformation of the bodies of men and animals into machines. The body is broken into parts—parts that are not themselves immediately recognizable as organic—and the reader perceives each as a part of a machine until, bit by bit, the entire body has become mechanical. Paley brings about this transformation by eliding the metaphorical similarity between body function and machine function with a presentation of visual analogy between body part and machine part.

> What contrivance can be more mechanical than the following, viz., a slit in one tendon to let another tendon pass through it? This structure is found in the tendons which move the toes and fingers. The long tendon, as it is called, in the foot, which bends the first joint of the toe, passes through the short tendon which bends the second joint; which course allows to the sinew more liberty, and a more commodious action than it would otherwise have been capable of exerting. There is nothing, I believe, in a silk or cotton mill; in the belts, or straps, or ropes, by which motion is communicated from one part of the machine to another, that is more artificial, or more evidently so, than this perforation. (79)

A cotton mill looks nothing like a leg, but belts and straps do look something like tendons. Similarly, a telescope, no matter how similar its optical principles, looks nothing like an eye, but a telescope's lens does resemble the eye's crystaline lens, and a telescope's diaphragm is not unlike the pupil. By emphasizing these visually analogous forms, Paley makes the mechanical and the organic worlds seem to be ordered both by the same functional principles and by the same visual patterns.

In many cases, Paley's mechanistic reenvisionment is a result of the reader's choosing the course of least imagistic resistance. In the cotton mill passage, the reader is given the choice of imaging either a complicated biological structure that he or she has never actually seen, or a few un-assembled and easily imagable mechanical parts that he or she probably has seen. Some "belts, or straps, or ropes" are much easier to picture than the intersecting and interpenetrating tendons of the toes. Similarly, the many organic structures of the eye are more structurally complicated and less easily imaged by the reader than are a telescope's lenses and diaphragm. By making the body's organs more easily imaged through mechanistic meta-phor Paley influences the reader to think of the body as structurally simple and thus perfect. The power of the narrative eye to perceive the body's parts corresponds to the power of the divine will that designed them. In Paley's nature all body parts, like all machine parts, are perfectly visible because they are perfectly designed.

While Darwin's description of the entangled eye clouds the reader's mind with inchoate fluxing images, Paley's narrative vision is at once so powerful and so precise that the reader can see distant landscapes with one glance, and observe the minute operation of the retina with the next.

> In considering vision as achieved by the means of an image formed at the bottom of the eye, we can never reflect without wonder at the smallness, yet correctness, of the picture, the subtilty of the touch, the fineness of the lines. A landscape of five or six square leagues is brought into a space of half an inch diameter; yet the multitude of objects which it contains are all preserved, are all discriminated in their magnitudes, positions, figures, colors. The prospect from Hampstead-hill is compressed into the compass of a sixpence, yet circumstantially represented. A stage coach, travelling at its ordinary speed for half an hour, passes in the eye only over one-twelfth of an inch, yet is this change of place in the image distinctly perceived throughout its whole progress; for it is only by means of that perception that the motion of the coach itself is made sensible to the eye. (21)

Not only does this passage demonstrate the eye's ability to see precisely at a great distance, it transforms distance into closeness as the narrative eye seems to turn on itself, allowing the reader to both see and feel the minute precision of the optical instrument as the tiny horses pull the miniature stage coach across the retina.

The great success of Paley's mechanistic metaphor rests on its sim-plification of the messiness of organic matter into nativistically regular forms. Machine parts are uniform and can thus be seen with absolute clarity. The Paleyan body opens itself like a watchcase before the eye, one sort of machine being flawlessly perceived by another.

> Examine the contents of the trunk of any large animal. . . . Observe the heart, pumping at the center, at the rate of eight strokes in a minute; one set of pipes carrying the stream away from it, another set bringing, in its course, the fluid back again; the lungs performing their elaborate office, viz. distending and contracting their many thousand vescicles, . . . the stomach exercising its powerful chemistry; the bowels silently propelling the changed aliment; collecting from it, as it proceeds, and transmitting to the blood, an incessant supply of prepared and assimilated nourishment; the blood pursuing its course; the liver, the kidneys, the pancreas, the parotid, with many other known and distinguished glands drawing off from it, all the while, their proper secretions. (104)

In Paley's visual world all is perceivable. He is able to base his entire argument upon the observable because nothing is hidden from his narrative eye and all that is seen conforms to distinct recognizable patterns. In effect, Paley uses visual analogy as the ordering principle of the natural world. In a divinely ordered universe all forms will be built on the same typical pattern so that the investigation of nature primarily consists of a recognition of that essential pattern in all bodies. The playing out of the machine metaphor involves the reader in this process of pattern recognition. For Malthus and Lyell, on the other hand, it is narrative rather than metaphor that best approximates the process of scientific investigation. The scientist's task is to create stories that can explain the past and the present, and perhaps predict the future. Consequently, where Paley celebrates the power of the physical eye, Malthus and Lyell emphasize the importance of a narratively sophisticated and facile imagination. Furthermore, both move away from a simple nativistic conception of the object world to one composed of gradually developing forms.

Darwin writes in his autobiography that in 1838, "I happened to read for amusement 'Malthus on Population,'" and that he was "well prepared to appreciate the struggle for existence which everywhere goes on from long-continued observation of the habits of animals and plants" (*Autobiography* 71). The revelation offered to Darwin by Malthus's *Essay* was that individuals living in the natural world are constantly subjected to intense competitive pressure by the burgeoning growth and reproduction around them. To make this argument convincingly, Malthus must push past the apparent stability and slow gradualness of nature's operations to a vision of nature that is extreme, unlimited, even fantastic in its reproductive hunger.

> Through the animal and vegetable kingdoms, nature has scattered the seeds of life abroad with the most profuse and liberal hand. She has been comparatively sparing in the room and the nourishment necessary to rear them. The germs of existence contained in this spot of earth, with ample food and ample room to expand in, would fill millions of worlds in the course of a few thousand years. (5)

Like the geometrical multiplication of population, Malthus's narratives of growth move from the present and ordinary, to the vast, and finally to the epochal and millennial; the reader's mind must stretch beyond its ordinary limits to accommodate his theory. Malthus sometimes adopts a prophetic tone, as at the end of Chapter 7, when he describes the vices of humanity as "the precursors in the great army of destruction," behind which "sickly seasons, epidemics, pestilence, and plague, advance in terrific array, and sweep off their thousands and ten thousands," and last of all "gigantic inevitable famine stalks in the rear, and with one mighty blow, levels the populations with the food of the world" (49). More often, however, it is the grotesque rather than the prophetic that surfaces in Malthus's vision, as the reader is shown the narratives embedded in the bodies of the populace.

> It cannot fail to be remarked by those who live much in the country that the sons of labourers are very apt to be stunted in their growth, and are a long while arriving at maturity. . . . And the lads who drive plough, which must certainly be a healthy exercise, are very rarely seen with any appearance of calves to their legs; a circumstance, which can only be attributed to a want either of proper or of sufficient nourishment. (25–26)

The rather macabre humor that, as Dwight Culler notes, seems to underly the solemnity of Malthus's pronouncements, is apparent in the image of the calfless ploughboys. Such examples, however, are not purely humorous; Malthus emphasizes the great importance to any scientist or philosopher of being able to expand the imagination past typical forms and patterns into the realm of the outrageous and impossible. He proves his points not so much by showing the most logical possibilities as by showing the logical impossibilities that rest at the basis of Godwin's thought. The image of the sheep with rat-sized heads and the flowers with cabbage-sized heads is a demonstration of organic limitation as well as an exercise of the mind's ability to create the monstrous.

> In the famous Leicester breed of sheep, the object is to procure them with small heads and small legs. Proceeding upon these breeding maxims, it is evident that we might go on till the heads and legs were evanescent quantities, but this is so palpable an absurdity that we may be quite sure that the premises are not just, and that there really is a limit, although we cannot see it

> or say exactly where it is. . . . Though I may not be able . . . to mark the
> limit at which further improvement will stop, I can very easily mention a
> point at which it will not arrive. I should not scruple to assert that were the
> breeding to continue forever, the head and legs of these sheep would never be
> so small as the head and legs of a rat. (58)

Such freedom of imaginative vision is necessary to the logical process in
Malthus. To reason properly one must oppose the plasticity of the imagination to the solidity of the tangible world; one must define the true against the
outrageous. The perceptual limitations of human beings makes such imaginative power of particular importance.

> The shades that are here and there blended in the picture give spirit, life, and
> prominence to her exuberant beauties, and those roughnesses and inequal-
> ities, those inferior parts that support the superior, though they sometimes
> offend the fastidious microscopic eye of short sighted man, contribute to the
> symmetry, grace, and fair proportion of the whole. (133)

Although nature has an overall design, humans are incapable of seeing it
because of their "fastidious microscopic eye." We must concentrate on the
individual points of the picture, the shades and highlights, the roughnesses
and inequalities, like someone with an eye pressed against the canvas, or
like the empirical eye taking in one point at a time. "Intellect," he states,
"rises from a speck," and it is the creative combining of specks that
advances the human race. He adds that "the finest minds seem to be
formed . . . by endeavours to form new combinations, and to discover
new truths," rather than by efforts "to acquire pre-existing knowledge"
(134). Creative imagining, the construction of unusual narratives from the
objective facts of nature, like the creation of different and original designs
from the empirical visual field, is what advances humanity. Those who are
incapable of creative reordering of the visual field will never be able to
approach the truth; those who see in typical forms will be led astray because
it is necessary to imagine the impossible in order to understand the possible.

For Malthus, creating narratives of worlds to come is the essential
scientific endeavor; his studies are of the future rather than the past, and he
puts less stock in actually perceiving nature than in testing the real against
the imagined. The "infinite variety of the forms and operations of nature"
(133) is a stimulant to intellectual activity. We are "awakened" by the
dazzlingly uneven landscape around us (a "perfect" landscape could not
inspire us to the same extent) to a vivid imaginary world. Consequently, the
landscape of Malthus's prose is fantastical; his social and historical narratives are melodramatic and grotesque; bodies expand and contract, seeds
multiply to cover the universe, famine stalks the land. The pressure of

population is made apparent in the brief warping and swelling of forms in Malthus's mininarratives of growth; these narratives exert pressure on the reader's imagination to overcome its spatial and temporal limitations, and to see the world anew. In effect, Malthus accepts Paley's conception of the eye as limited to specific, direct observations, but denies the value of such observations to the scientist. Because the eye cannot see historical development, the scientist must resort to the playful, fantastical imagination.

Where Paley's reader looks at nature and sees so many machines, Malthus's sees the grotesque narrative fantasies of overpopulation. Lyell's reader sees familiar biological and geological structures in rapid, uniform motion. Like Malthus, Lyell glorifies the narrative imagination and demonstrates his points narratively. While Malthus proves his position against impossible imaginary narratives, however, Lyell proves his through scientifically plausible ones. In his *Principles of Geology* Lyell states that the scientist must make an effort of both reason and imagination to "picture" the natural world, as he cannot watch the geological processes of the earth.

> [Because] we cannot watch the progress of their [geological] formations and as they are only present to our minds by aid of reflection, it requires an effort both of the reason and of the imagination to appreciate duly their importance . . . [the scientist must] endeavor to picture to himself the new strata which nature is depicting beneath the water. (Vol. I 97)

It is not enough to understand the formulas of nature's equations; one must also picture its depictions. For Lyell, nature is an expert maker of hidden landscapes, underground panoramas, which it is the job of the scientist both to be aware of and to make visually present to everyone.

In his portrayal of the human failure to perceive geological processes Lyell pictures nature's depictions by attaching the narrative eye to various fantasy creatures; the result is a portrayal of the very phenomena the physical eye cannot see.

> If we were inhabitants of another element—if the great ocean were our domain, instead of the narrow limits of the land, our difficulties would be considerably lessened; although the reader may, perhaps, smile at the bare suggestion of such an idea, an amphibious being, who should possess our faculties, would still more easily arrive at sound theoretical opinions in geology since he might behold, on the one hand, the decomposition of rocks in the atmosphere, or the transportation of matter by running water; and, on the other, examine the deposition of sediment in the sea, and the imbedding of animal remains in new strata. He might ascertain, by direct observation, the action of a mountain torrent, as well as of a marine current; might compare the products of volcanos on the land with those poured out beneath

the waters; and might mark, on the one hand, the growth of the forest, and on the other that of the coral reef. . . . But if we may be allowed so far to indulge the imagination, as to suppose a being entirely confined to the nether world—some "dusky melancholy sprite," like Umbriel, who could "flit on sooty pinions to the central earth," but who was never permitted to "sully the fair face of light," and emerge into the regions of water and air; and if this being should busy himself in investigating the structure of the globe, he might frame theories the exact converse of those usually adopted by human philosophers. He might infer that the stratified rocks, containing shells and other organic remains, were the oldest of created things, belonging to some original and nascent state of the planet. (Vol. I 98–99)

Adopting his fantastical characters, out of pure whimsy it seems, and simply to make a rather obvious point, Lyell's narrative eye descends into the depths, and lays bare the hidden workings of nature. The principle that Lyell is supposedly demonstrating (that limited observational abilities lead to erroneous scientific conclusions) does not require the lengthy defense that is offered. Lyell's fantastical narrative cajoles the reader into expanding his or her imagination beyond the visually verifiable without sacrificing any sicentific authority, thus introducing him or her to the mixture of science and fiction that operates as the proof structure of the work. Once we have imagined nature from the gnomish and amphibian perspectives we are able to form more scientifically accurate theories than our limited human vision would otherwise allow. In order to overcome "prejudice" we must image the invisible; Lyell's fantastical narratives make this imaging process easy. The reader feels that he or she has been given the information to judge objectively because Lyell has so effectively pictured nature's depictions.

Time is as much of a challenge for Lyell as space, however, and his style is most remarkable for the ease and grace with which the narrative eye manipulates the speed of geological change.

The sediment of the Rhone, for example, thrown into the Lake of Geneva, is now conveyed to a spot a mile and a half distant from that where it accumulated in the tenth century, and six miles from the point where the delta began originally to form. We may look forward to the period when this lake will be filled up, and then the distribution of transported matter will be suddenly altered, for the mud and sand brought down from the Alps will thenceforth, instead of being deposited near Geneva, be carried nearly 200 miles southwards, where the Rhone enters the Mediterranian. . . . But, secondly, all these causes of fluctuation in the sedimentary areas are entirely subordinate to those great upward or downward movements of land, which will presently be spoken of, as prevailing over large tracts of the globe. By such elevation or subsidence certain spaces are gradually submerged, or made gradually to emerge. (Vol. I 301–2)

An apparently technical description of sedimentation is made visually dynamic by the speeding up and simplifying of geological processes into imageable arcs of motion; the sediment of the Rhone is "thrown" into the lake of Geneva; soon the lake will be "filled," at which point the deposits will be "suddenly altered," and the river will "carry" them farther southward. The "upward and downward movements of land," undulate with the casual grace of a shaken carpet.

Lyell portrays hundreds of thousands of years of geological metamorphosis in a few paragraphs without disturbing the reader's sense of equilibrium. He also uses several time scales in one description, the rapidity of the passage of time changing with each new image. For example, the arrival of polar bears in Greenland and the resulting change in the ecosystem are described at varying narrative speeds.

> Let us consider how great are the devastations committed at certain periods by the Greenland bears, when they are drifted to the shores of Iceland in considerable numbers on the ice. . . . The Danes of old, when they landed in their marauding expeditions upon our coast, hardly excited more alarm, nor did our islanders muster more promptly for the defence of their lives and property. . . . It often happens, says Henderson, that the natives are pursued by the bear when he has long been at sea and when his natural ferocity is heightened by the keenness of hunger. . . .
>
> Let us cast our thoughts back to the period when the first polar bears reached Iceland, before it was colonised by the Norwegians in 874; we may imagine the breaking up of an immense barrier of ice like that which, in 1816 and the following year, disappeared from the east coast of Greenland, which it had surrounded for four centuries. By the aid of such means of transportation a great many of these quadrupeds might effect a landing at the same time, and the havoc they would make among the species previously settled on the island would be terrific. The deer, foxes, seals, and even birds on which these animals sometimes prey, would be soon thinned down. . . . The plants on which the deer fed . . . would soon supply more food to several insects. . . . The increase of these would furnish other insects and birds with food. . . . The diminution of the seals would afford a respite to some fish.   (Vol. I 453)

Lyell moves from one time-scale to another with extraordinary facility. The effect of the bears on the ecosystem, which occurs over several decades, the breaking up of the ice, which takes a few years, and the interaction between the bears and the Icelanders, which occurs in so many minutes, all take similar amounts of narrative time and are imaged as similar visual motions. Add to this the warring of the Britons and Danes, the actual landing of the bears on the coast, and the colonization of the Norwegians in 874, and there are half a dozen time-scales, all of which seem to be operating at the same narrative pace. The smoothness of natural body motion (a bear chases an Icelander) is echoed by the smoothness of a moving landscape (ice floes touch the coast) or varying populations (fish, seals, and plants scatter and reform into new combinations). Gillian Beer notes that "the past can be played at any speed. Lyell chooses to unroll it at a pace which organises it into a knowable and majestic music" (Beer 45). This smoothness is created by Lyell's facile transition between narrative time-scales that makes all earthly motion seem to take place at an easily observable speed. Lyell's narrative eye perceives all worldly activity as the ebb and flow of physical masses. Although these masses are not entirely formless, we see them in the process of flowing from one imageable form to another over time. In effect, Lyellian narrative time is uniformitarian time; like the crust of the earth, the time-line changes so smoothly and imperceptibly that the reader is never jarred by it. The sense of ordered malleability that is central to uniformitarian theory is thus reflected in the very seamlessness of Lyell's representations of natural history.

Lyell is a master storyteller, utilizing the plasticity of the imagination to transform an inaccessible and inconclusive nature into undeniable parables of uniformitarianism. At the end of the passage describing the polar bears' arrival in Iceland Lyell offers an "actual illustration of what we have here proposed hypothetically," but the example is brief and easily forgettable, and Lyell admits that evidence for such a hypothesis is only "in some degree afforded" by it. For Lyell, as for Malthus, narrative theorizing is a more important scientific tool, or at least a more stylistically convincing one, than is first-hand investigation. Darwin, hiking through the mountains of South America, was able to use Lyell's broad and dynamic narrative vision to construct, from bits and pieces, the "structure of the whole" that was not apparent to the eye alone. Darwin speaks of the "wonderful superiority of Lyell's manner of treating geology," which allowed him, while on the *Beagle* voyage, to understand the structure of the South American landscape.

> On first examining a new district nothing can appear more hopeless than the chaos of rocks; but by recording the stratification and nature of the rocks and fossils at many points, always reasoning and predicting what will be found elsewhere, light soon begins to dawn on the district and the structure of the whole becomes more or less intelligible. (*Autobiography* 44).

Darwin's construction of the landscape from "the chaos of rocks" is like the empirical observer's construction of the visual field from a chaos of minimum visibles. The imaginative prediction of the earth's structure al-

lows scientists to see what is not visible on the surface, and they become
familiar with nature's phenomena by imagistically creating them.

Robert Young notes that "Paley and Malthus influenced Darwin in
very different ways. Paley stresses perfect adaptation; Malthus stresses
conflict. These were, at one level, antithetical. Darwin synthesizes them.
Struggle both explains and produces adaptation" (Young 31). Darwin also
synthesizes the literary and imagistic techniques used by these authors; to
Paley's concentration on visual analogy and dedication to actual visual
perception he adds Malthus's and Lyell's multiplication of possible worlds
through imaginative narrative. Throughout his work Darwin remains an
unwavering adherent to first-hand observation and the investigation of actual rather than hypothetical cases, yet he allows his reader to see his
theories enacted through the optical illusions of his narrative eye. Unlike
his predecessors, Darwin does not structure the scientific representation of
nature around the ability of the human imagination to improve upon the
eye's partial vision. Instead he uses the perceptual dysfunctions of the eye
as the model for an imagined evolutionary nature; the abundant complexity
of Darwinian vision is born out of the powerlessness and the limitation of
the evolving human eye beholding nature, rather than Paley's perfect mechanistic vision or Malthus's and Lyell's expansive narrative imagination.
The entangled eye, itself an evolutionary product, demonstrates evolution
by its own structure, as well as by the images it can and cannot produce. If
we are to see Darwin's nature, we must first look through his eyes.

II

Looking to Darwin's first letters and journal entries describing the Brazilian
jungle and the South American landscape, it becomes immediately apparent that, for Darwin, this new landscape demanded, as Cheselden's patient
said of the Epsom Downs, a "new Kind of Seeing" (Cheselden 450). In a
letter to his father dated February 8, 1832, he writes: "It is utterly useless to
say anything about the scenery, it would be as profitable to explain to a
blind man colours as to a person who has not been out of Europe, the total
dissimilarity of a tropical view" (*Life and Letters* 202). As well as the
newness and unfamiliarity of the scene, Darwin invariably expresses the
intensity of emotion associated with these new scenes, and the difficulty of
putting into words either a description of the landscape or of his feelings
while viewing the landscape. In a letter to F. Watkins he writes: "The
brilliancy of the scenery throws one into a delirium of delight, and a beetle
hunter is not likely soon to awaken from it, when whichever way he turns

fresh treasures meet his eye" (*Life and Letters* 213). Again, to his father: "Whilst viewing such scenes, one feels the impossibility that any description should come near the mark, much less be overdrawn" (*Life and Letters* 204).

In these letters Darwin's desire to express his impressions of the landscape is intense, as is his frustration at being unable to do so. "Whenever I enjoy anything," he writes to his father, "I always either look forward to writing it down, either in my log-book (which increases in bulk), or in a letter; so you must excuse raptures, and these raptures badly expressed" (*Life and Letters* 202). Indeed, Darwin's raptures do seem rather redundant at points: "The day has passed delightfully; delight is however a weak term for such transports of pleasure . . . such a day as this brings with it pleasure more acute than he ever may again experience" (*Beagle Diary* 39); "While seated on the trunk of a decaying tree amidst such scenes, one feels an inexpressible delight" (*Beagle Diary* 70); "I can only add raptures to the former raptures" (*Beagle Diary* 40). James Paradis, in his excellent article "Darwin and Landscape," has discussed the influence of Romanticism on Darwin's early portrayals of nature.

> The aesthetic responses of Darwin to the South American landscape are the deeply felt manifestations of a sensuous bond between perceiver and the perceived. Often . . . the sensation of the moment leads to some more profound reality and truth, some sense of natural supernaturalism determined through intuition. (Paradis 96).

Although there is much to what Paradis says, it is worth noticing that many of Darwin's epiphanic experiences seem to rise from a more physiologically distinguishable source. The sense of rapture almost invariably coincides with descriptions of the failure or confusion of physical vision. A "delirium of delight" results when "a beetle hunter" is surrounded by so many new specimens that "whichever way he turns fresh treasures meet his eye" (*Life and Letters* 213). A "pleasure more acute than he ever may again experience," is caused by the multitude of unusual forest forms, among which "it is hard to say what set of objects is the most striking" (*Beagle Diary* 39). In the following passage, the eye is so distracted by the quantity of forms, colors, motions, and perspectives, that the visual field loses all clear definition.

> The delight one experiences at such times bewilders the mind; if the eye attempts to follow the flight of a gaudy butter-fly, it is arrested by some strange tree or fruit; in watching an insect one forgets it in the stranger flower it is crawling over; if turning to admire the splendour of scenery, the individual character of the foreground fixes the attention. The mind is a chaos of

> delight, out of which a world of future and more quiet pleasure will arise.
> (*Beagle Diary* 39)

Darwin's moments of rapture are neither altogether aesthetic nor altogether intuitive; they arise from visual overstimulation, particularly that sort of overstimulation that involves a disordered and fragmented visual field.

Darwin is in the same position as Berkeley's hypothetical man born blind who is suddenly thrust into a new and unfamiliar visual world that his eye has not been trained to understand. In a world where he "knew not the Shape of any Thing, nor any one Thing from another," Cheselden's patient proclaims that "every new Object was a new Delight" (Cheselden 448, 450). In 1826, James Wardrop recorded the case of a woman whose sight was given to her at the age of forty-six, and whose excitement at seeing again resembles Darwin's.

> On that day she drove in a carriage for an hour in the Regent's Park, and on her way there seemed more amused than usual, and asked more questions about the objects surrounding her, such as "What is that?" it is a soldier, she was answered; "and that, see! see!" these were candles of various colours in a tallow chandler's window. . . . On coming home along Piccadilly, the jewellers' shop seemed to surprise her much, and her expressions made everyone around her laugh heartily.   (Wardrop 538–39)

Darwin describes the experience of walking in the Brazilian forest in much the same way. The objects around him appear in a dazzling, unfamiliar array, each grasping his attention.

> I have been wandering by myself in a Brazilian forest: amongst the multitude it is hard to say what set of objects is most striking; the general luxuriance of the vegetation bears the victory, the elegance of the grasses, the novelty of the parasitical plants, the beauty of the flowers, the glossy green of the foliage, all tend to this end.   (*Beagle Dairy* 39)

The rapture experienced by Wardrop's patient, as by Darwin, is not unmixed. The newly sighted lady says that she is "much confused by the visible world thus for the first time opened to her" and tells her brother, "I see a great deal, if I could only tell what I do see; but surely I am very stupid" (Wardrop 536). Similarly, Darwin's inability "to walk a hundred yards without being fairly tied to the spot by some new and wondrous creature," is called a "pleasant nuisance" (*Beagle Diary* 59). There can be too much newness to this brave new world. In the following passage from the *Beagle Diary,* dated May 9, 1832, Darwin expresses a similar sense of bewilderment and desire to return to a world of familiar forms.

> Many of the views were exceedingly beautiful; yet in tropical scenery, the entire newness, & therefore absence of all associations, which in my own case (& I believe in others) are unconsciously much more frequent than I ever thought, requires the mind to be wrought to a high pitch, & then assuredly no delight can be greater; otherwise your reason tells you it is beautiful but the feelings do not correspond. I often ask myself, why can I not calmly enjoy this; I might answer myself by also asking, what is there that can bring the delightful ideas of rural quiet & retirement, what that can call back the recollection of childhood & times past, where all that was unpleasant is forgotten; until ideas, in their effects similar to them, are raised, in vain we look amidst the glories of this new world for quiet contemplation. (*Beagle Diary* 60)

Because the landscape is so unfamiliar joy only comes to the viewer when his emotions are "wrought to a high pitch"; otherwise, this unfamiliarity is registered as uneasiness and homesickness. Thus, despite Darwin's ebullience in his letters home, his moments of rapture are balanced by those of confusion; he wavers from overwrought joy to overwrought bewilderment, and the possibilities for quiet contemplation are nonexistent. On June 16, 1832, Darwin writes: "As a Sultan in a Seraglio I am becoming quite hardened to Beauty. It is wearisome to be in a fresh rapture at every turn of the road. And as I have before said, you must be that or nothing" (*Beagle Diary* 71). The confusion of uneducated empirical vision can account both for Darwin's sense of euphoria and of frustration. As Gillian Beer notes, it is the visual irregularity and tumultuousness of the foreign landscape that both disturbs Darwin and leads him away from a nativistic understanding of landscape forms.

> One of the crucial discoveries that came to Darwin as a result of the voyage was that the green control of English landscape with its man-induced harmonies and sober beauties could not be considered normative. Beyond England lay other natural landscapes full of tumultuous colour and life. The full range of sense experience fills out and disturbs the narrowly descriptive authority of the scientific collector. (Beer 34)

Once the regular nativistic landscape of "childhood & times past" is left behind, the entanglement of a visually chaotic new world becomes both revealing and disturbing. Darwin's letters seem at points to echo the plaintive words of Wardrop's patient.

> I am well, and see better; but don't tease me with too many questions, till I have learned a little better how to make use of my eye. All that I can say is, that I am sure, from what I do see, a great change has taken place; but I cannot describe what I feel. (Wardrop 536)[1]

The impact of Darwin's visual ravishment, of the eye entangled in an unfamiliar and overwhelming landscape, can be detected both in his style and in his method of approaching the study of the natural world. If we look from these early writings to letters written three years later, we discover that Darwin has found a new way of using the sort of overstimulated vision that he first experienced in the forests of Brazil. In a letter to John Stevens Henslow dated April 18, 1835, he describes his explorations in the Cordilleras:

> This latter rock seems to form the nucleus of the shallow mass, and is seen in the deep lateral valleys, injected amongst, upheaving, overturning in the most extraordinary manner, the overlaying strata. On the bare sides of the mountains, the complicated dykes and wedges of variously coloured rocks, are seen traversing in every possible form and shape the same formations, which, by their intersections, prove a succession of violences. The stratification in all the mountains is beautifully distinct, and owing to a variety in their colouring, can be seen at great distances. I cannot imagine any part of the world presenting a more extraordinary scene of the breaking up of the crust of the globe, than these central peaks of the Andes. . . . I cannot tell you how much I enjoyed some of these views; it is worth coming from England, once to feel such intense delight. At an elevation of from ten to twelve thousand feet, there is a transparency in the air, and a confusion of distances, and a sort of stillness, which give the sensation of being in another world; and when to this is joined the picture so plainly drawn of the great epochs of violence, it causes in the mind a most strange assemblage of ideas. (*Collected Papers* 12)

Again we find the sense of rapture, the confusion of vision, the overwhelming variety and intensity of the perceived landscape. Here, however, the oddities of vision in South America are not simply related as gauges of Darwin's feelings; they are invoked to demonstrate the geological development of the landscape. This passage is part of "a very short sketch of the structure of these huge mountains" that Darwin sent to Henslow. What must Henslow's surprise have been to find the granite of the Cordilleras "upheaving, overturning in the most extraordinary manner," while "complicated dykes" are "seen traversing" the mountains. Rather than layers of porphyritic conglomerate, the reader sees "the breaking up of the crust of the globe." Such a moving landscape is reminiscent of Lyell (whose spell Darwin lay under during the entire *Beagle* voyage), but where Lyell's descriptions of the earth in motion take place entirely in imagination, Darwin's rise out of personal experience. Lyell sits before his geological volumes and imagines the lake of Geneva rising and falling; Darwin stands on a peak in the Andes and sees the churning of the rock and the breaking up of the globe. If anything, the description seems to be an odd combination of Lyell's fluidity of form and Paley's visual analogy. Like Lyell, Darwin sees geology as a dynamic and fluid process, but like Paley, Darwin recognizes the visual similarity between several natural forms. Rather than supposing a divine order, however, Darwin supposes a historical one, and accounts for the similarity between the present landscape and similar stratified ones by assuming "a succession of violences." By doing so, Darwin observes in a single visual field the process of geological change that Lyell portrayed as an imagined narrative; the millennia of independently existing landscapes that make up the natural history of the Cordilleras clutter the eye as though they were present forms. The ordering of the landscape through visual analogy thus allows Darwin to envision a multitude of natural forms in a single geological formation without being overcome by the perceptual exhaustion he experienced in the jungle.

Darwin's article, "Observations on the Parallel Roads of Glen Roy" (1839), offers an even more extensive example of the multiplication of natural forms through visual analogy. In "Roads" Darwin attempts to demonstrate that the unusual geological formations found in many Scottish Glens are not the sedimentary deposits from ancient lakes, as had been assumed, but are rather the beaches of an ancient and receding sea. Although this is a formal paper rather than a letter or a journal entry, Darwin's style changes little. His use of the personal pronoun is particularly noticeable. Darwin describes his personal exploration of geological structures, rather than offering straightforward descriptions of them. In arguing for the existence of a particular shelf he states: "Perceiving its importance I examined it with scrupulous care. . . . It was scarcely possible (especially as I purposely looked at it from every point of view,) to make any mistake. . . . I walked along its whole length" (*Collected Papers* 113). Because of the physiological limitations on his perspective, the geologist must stride up and down the rocks, observing angles, elevations, and outlines to ascertain how the present conformations of the rock might line up with ancient conformations. He continually delineates distant vistas, and at one point puts great emphasis on the fact that Sir David Brewster, the eminent visual theorist, "has seen . . . shelves resembling those of Glen Roy at two points, at a distance of several miles down the valley of the Spey." In his investigation of a shelf at Kilfinnin, Darwin's physical location is crucial to his argument.

> This shelf resembles in every respect those in Glen Roy; it seemed, as I walked along it, perfectly level, as it likewise did, when I viewed it from either end, and when I crossed the valley. . . . These [measurements] I

ascertained by the barometer to be on a perfect level with the commencement
of the shelf, or the watershed, a circumstance which was also apparent by the
eye alone. The line further on disappears from the rockiness of the sides of
the valley. On the south and opposite side of the valley, a broad sloping
terrace extends at a corresponding level for about three quarters of a mile, but
is indistinct owing to the gentle slope of the mountain. Further on it seems
modelled into more than one terrace; and these, though obscure, appear to a
person standing on them perfectly horizontal. . . . After having observed
this shelf from so many points of view, I am prepared positively to assert that
it is in every respect as characteristic a shelf as any in Glen Roy.   (*Collected
Papers* 94–95)

Although Darwin perceives the world directly, like Paley, his eye is neither
clear nor powerful. Darwin has to squint, strain, and walk miles to ascertain
the configurations of the shelves. He does not try to disguise his own
limitations, using the peculiar form of humility that was to become his
stylistic trademark; things are "obscure" and "indistinct," but they are as
clear as human effort and human vision can make them.[2]

Moreover, the proofs Darwin offers are invariably based on the visual
similarity he perceives between actual structures in the glens and seaside
structures he has seen elsewhere in the world. Early in the essay, for
example, he states that at Loch Treig "the gneiss is worn into smooth
concave hollows, the peculiar curves of which, though they cannot be
described, may be readily imagined by calling to mind the form of rocks
washed by a water-fall" (*Collected Papers* 91). Whereas in his early letters
the difficulty of describing unusual natural phenomena left Darwin rap-
turously wordless, he uses analogy in "Roads" to convey a visual impression of the landscape to his readers. Moreover, this is not simply an illustrative comparison, for a few sentences later Darwin asserts that the rock both
appears to have been, and actually was, washed by a waterfall. "Standing
on the precipitous and waterworn rocks," he states, "it required little
imagination to go back to former ages, and to behold the water eddying and
splashing against the steep rocks on one side of the channel, whilst on the
other it was flowing quietly over a shelving spit of sand and gravel." As in
his letter to Henslow, Darwin's vision into the past is excited by a natural
object that he is actually in the process of observing that seems to multiply
before his eyes into the many forms that preceded it, so that both past and
present forms are perceived in the same visual space.

Darwin increases this process of visual multiplication and coalescence
in "Roads" by imaging both past and present analogous forms as well as
analogous forms from other parts of the world. Looking at a present form,
Darwin will compare it to another present form and to a past form in a sort

of imagistic triangulation through history. This process is not simply imaginative playfulness on the naturalist's part, for Darwin puts great faith in these visual triangulations:

> This was the only one spot where I could observe this appearance in an unequivocal manner; but this one point of rock would to my mind carry demonstration with it, even if there were not innumerable other proofs, that the water had remained at the level of the 972 feet shelf for a very long period. (*Collected Papers* 91–92)

Throughout "Roads," Darwin presents this triple coalescence of present form, similar present form, and past form as proof.

> The only other and rather different case of waterworn rock which I noticed, was at the head of Lower Glen Roy. . . . I have frequently observed a similar structure on the rocky shores of protected harbours. Large fragments of rock are scattered on most of the shelves . . . some have fallen recently, whilst others are waterworn, as if they had lain for centuries on a sea coast; and it was in many cases easy to point out, whilst walking along the level shelf, which fragments had been washed by the ancient waves, and which had fallen since. (*Collected Papers* 92)

The reader sees the present form, a similar present form, and the past form, all in the same geological structure. As such, Darwin's atemporal envisioning resembles an empirical optical illusion in which the elements that make up a visual form are ordered, and then are dynamically reordered, so that present and past formations are perceived in the same visual space. Unlike Lyell, Darwin has no desire to offer the reader a panorama of natural history. Rather, he attempts to equip the reader with the wherewithal to see the formal similarity between present and past objects, and the consequent likelihood of their historical relationship, by crowding his or her visual field with a great many similar landscapes. For example, compare the following two presentations of geological history, the first by Lyell and the second by Darwin.

> The history of the eruption of Etna, imperfect and interrupted as it is, affords us, nevertheless, much insight into the manner in which a large part of the mountain has successively attained its present magnitude and internal structure. . . . When hills are thrown up lower down or in the middle zone, and project beyond the general level, they gradually lose their height during subsequent eruptions; for when lava descending from the upper parts of the mountain encounters any of these hills, the stream is divided, and flows round them so as to elevate the gently sloping grounds from which they rise. . . . The lava, therefore, of each new lateral cone tends to detract from the relative heights of lower cones above their bases; so that the flanks

of Etna, sloping with a gentle inclination, envelope in succession a great
multitude of minor volcanos, while new ones spring up from time to time.
(Lyell Vol. II 3)

Whoever walks over these mountains, and believes that each part has been
successively occupied by the subsiding waters of the sea, will understand
trifling appearances, which otherwise, I believe, are unintelligible. Thus in
Upper Glen Roy he will see in the level expanse, an old bay, filled up and
leveled with tidal mud. Again at the Gap of Glen Collarig, with its flat
bottom and cut off sides like a gateway, he will recognise a channel, at last
choked up with matter drifted by the tides, and now left in the state in which
it was when the waters retired from it. . . . I may add, that in South
America I have observed numerous instances of terraces in every respect
similar to these, with sea shells abundantly scattered on their surface; and
therefore where there could exist no obscurity regarding their origin.
(*Collected Papers* 117)

Rather than a sweeping omniscient vision of the rise and fall of landscape,
Darwin's narrative eye is that of the present viewer perceiving multiple past
geological forms in the same visual space as the present one. Although
physically limited by time and space, the Darwinian eye engages in the
continual reordering of the visual field—the perceptual playfulness that
allows for the perception of several similar forms in one—rather than the
steady observation of forms unfolding sequentially in a vast historical
narrative.

The relationship between Darwin's representation of nature and that of
his predecessors can, in general, be considered a matter of the rhetorical
limitation of narrative vision. Paley, Malthus, and Lyell attempt to educate
their readers by offering a narrative vision that is manifestly more powerful
than physical vision. Darwin, on the other hand, creates a representational
style that relies upon limited vision; he asserts the lack of clarity, the lack of
breadth and the temporal limitations of the eye throughout his work. These
constraints make it necessary for the scientist to see several objects in one
perceived form, to condense time and space, as it were, so that past and
present forms are perceivable in a visual flicker like that which characterizes an empirical illusion. The process of induction thus comes to rest on
visual analogies that embody geological history rather than the imagined
narratives that enact it.

Darwin has come a long way from the forests of Brazil. Rather than
being ravished beyond thought by the multiplicity of new forms, he has
developed a strategy of ordering the landscape through visual analogy that
allows him to perceive multiple forms in the same visual field. The visually
confusing landscape that previously denied him the opportunity of quiet

contemplation now leads him into thought by causing in the mind "a most strange assemblage of ideas"—an assemblage consisting of various analogous structures gathered from throughout the world and throughout history. Nor are the landscapes that he describes irrelevant to the development of his way of seeing and representing nature. The *Beagle* first landed on the coasts of Brazil, and Darwin's initial visual ravishment coincides with his sudden exposure to the organic abundance of a tropical jungle. Here he expresses the crowding of visual space and the difficulty of perceiving the many new and interesting forms that people the visual world. Three years later he is hiking through the mountains of Chile, where it is geological history, not organic multiplicity, that is laid out before him. As he climbs from stratum to stratum and peak to peak, it is the number and length of epochs rather than the number of forms that dazzle the eye and the mind. By observing a geologically revelatory landscape in which "the picture is so plainly drawn of the great epochs of violence," Darwin is given a strategy for ordering without simplifying the sort of overcrowded visual field that he found so frustrating in the jungle. Rather than attempting to move the eye back and forth from point to point, to catch every form in the visual field, Darwin keeps the eye stationary, and envisions analogous forms in the same visual space. For Darwin, the scientist's task becomes to imagine the visual analogues associated with a natural form and thus reconstruct the narrative of its history, rather than to imagine the narrative of its history, as does Lyell, and to people that imagined landscape with likely imagined forms. Thus, where Lyell's reader conceives of natural history as a panorama, Darwin's conceives of it as a set of optical illusions—a series of minute variations on visual forms recombined in an inchoate visual field. By combining jungle vision (the eye ravished by multiple forms extended in space), with mountain vision (the eye ravished by multiple forms extended in time), Darwin creates a way of representing nature in which the reader's ravished eye images forms extended in neither time nor space, but condensed into and blossoming analogically out from the single organic form. This new way of seeing can best be called *evolutionary vision*.

III

Darwin's emphasis in the first few chapters of the *Origin of Species* is entirely on first-hand observation. He is quick to condemn those naturalists who have insufficient personal experience. The authorities touted in the first chapter are all livestock breeders, and the common sense of the common farmer is continually invoked, while theoreticians are dismissed. "No breeder doubts how strong is the tendency to inheritance . . . doubts have been thrown on this principle by theoretical writers alone'' (12). Darwin uses the first person plural throughout in order to emphasize the self-evident aspects of his theory: ''When we look to the individuals of the same variety or sub-variety . . . one of the first points which strikes us'' (7); ''Every one must have heard of cases of albinism'' (13); ''When we reflect on the vast diversity'' (7); ''When we attempt to estimate'' (16), and so on. One pictures Darwin leaning over the rails at livestock shows, chatting with men in heavy boots holding pitchforks, while dust-covered, bookish naturalists skulk among their shelves and specimen cabinets.

It is odd, however, that Darwin's first-hand observations are invariably of animal parts rather than whole creatures. As he looks out into the everyday world of breeding and bloodlines, Darwin does not see prize cows and sheep, but udders, bones, ears, and feathers.

> In animals it [the habitat] has a more marked effect; for instance, I find in the domestic duck that the bones of the wing weigh less and the bones of the leg more, in proportion to the whole skeleton, than do the same bones in the wild duck; and I presume that this change may be safely attributed to the domestic duck flying much less, and walking more, than its wild parent. The great and inherited development of the udders in cows and goats in countries where they are habitually milked, in comparison with the state of these organs in other countries, is another instance of the effect of use. Not a single domestic animal can be named which has not in some country drooping ears; and the view suggested by some authors, that the drooping is due to the disuse of the muscles of the ear, from the animals not being much alarmed by danger, seems probable. (11)

Such passages, particularly when offered incidentally in the midst of a discussion of the effects of habit on structure, seem disturbingly Frankensteinian. The reader sees the animal parts both still and in action, but in no case are they elements of a complete body. A duck bone, or an udder, looms for a moment into view, and then is gone. Through this odd and seemingly random presentation of parts, however, Darwin's theoretical purpose is served. One does not take the time—indeed, one is not given the time—to distinctly visualize the bones of the wild duck as compared with those of the domestic duck. Several bones are cast across the surface of the imagination, none apparently belonging to any particular organism; thus, the parts of two distinct species become interchangeable.

This process is even more apparent when more parts from more species are used.

> Hairless dogs have imperfect teeth; long-haired and coarse-haired animals are apt to have, as is asserted, long or many horns; pigeons with feathered

feet have skin between their outer toes; pigeons with short beaks have small feet, and those with long beaks large feet.   (12)

Here, the swiftness of the images, their minute precision, and their strange disassociation, combine to create a welter of whirling animal parts that constricts the possibility of imaging a whole form. Teeth, hair, feathers, wings, and feet from various creatures are jumbled before the reader's vision in a witches' brew of fragmented zoology from which no fully formed creature can emerge. The physiological associations that are set up discursively (hairlessness is linked to bad teeth; long-hair is linked to long horns; short beaks are linked to small feet) are utterly foiled by a visual field so crowded with animal parts that everything seems to be linked to everything. The reader's vision is overwhelmed by a mass of natural fragments that are disassociated from any stable, recognizable forms, just as the young Darwin's eye was dazzled by a landscape so full of new and unusual forms that he could at first only perceive them briefly and in chaotic flashes of perception.

One of the best examples of this fragmentation of bodily form is found in Darwin's description of different breeds of pigeons.

Compare the English carrier and the short-faced tumbler, and see the wonderful differences in their beaks, entailing corresponding differences in their skulls. The carrier, more especially the male bird, is also remarkable from the wonderful development of the carunculated skin about the head, and this is accompanied by greatly elongated eyelids, very large external orifices to the nostrils, and a wide gape of mouth. The short-faced tumbler has a beak in outline almost like that of a finch. . . . The runt is a bird of great size, with long massive beak and large feet; some of the sub-breeds of runts have very long necks, others very long wings and tails, others singularly short tails. The barb is allied to the carrier, but, instead of a very long beak, has a very short and very broad one. The pouter has a much elongated body, wings, and legs; and its enormously developed crop, which it glories in inflating, may well excite astonishment and even laughter.   (21)

What the reader images while reading this passage is, for its very kineses, difficult to describe in words. Because each part is presented so rapidly, while the rest of the bird's body is not mentioned, a detailed imaging of the whole bird is impossible. The part is imaged vividly, floating freely against the hazy background of a pigeon body, followed by another equally vivid part on an equally hazy body and another, and another. The individual parts seem to flicker across the general forms, no part specifically associated with any form, so that the visual form "pigeon" becomes generalized and inexact and the several breeds described become imagistically blended into one fuzzy outline. The forms of nature crowd so vigorously and inevitably into the reader's visual space that they impinge upon one another and flow together, becoming a visual morass rather than an imagistic clutter.

Like the past and present structures of Glen Roy, the analogous pigeon bodies are perceived in the same space, and the reader experiences their motion into and through one another as an empirical illusion. Being fleshly rather than geological, however, Darwin's pigeons have greater plasticity than the parallel roads of Glen Roy. Like Malthus's rat-headed sheep, they partake of the grotesque. Although one has the sense while reading that the individual parts are described vividly, the great majority of the adjectives Darwin uses refer only to size. Eyelids are "greatly elongated"; external orifices are "very large," with "a wide gape of mouth"; one bird has "a long massive beak and large feet"; others have "very long necks, others very long wings and tails," and still others are graced with an "enormously developed crop." The small parts of relatively small animals are repeatedly described as very large, while their bodies are lost from sight. The rapidity of the description thus transforms a nauralists' list of features into a grotesque fantasy, and the reader's mind becomes a carnivalesque space in which the least are made greatest (the "runt is a bird of great size") and the part overwhelms the whole. The body contorts comically, like the pouter's crop that is inflated to cries of astonishment and laughter, some parts ballooning to elephantine proportions, and others sinking from view. The effect, like that of Malthus's outrageous mininarratives, is to create an unfettered, boundlessly active imaginative world through which the real world can be better understood. Unlike Malthus, however, Darwin comes by the effect indirectly, seemingly accidentally, through the reader's imaginative dysfunction rather than through his or her imaginative power. The pigeons' bodies are fragmented and blended, the relationships between wholes and parts are shuffled by the inability of the reader's mental vision to perceive the animal forms distinctly. Like Darwin's eye in the jungle, the reader's mental eye cannot fully focus on any one form before it is presented with another, and the mind becomes a chaos of imagistic delight.

Various studies in visual perception published while the *Origin* was being written describe the sort of fragmentation and coalescence of forms typical of Darwinian vision as the ordinary reaction of the eye to an unusually diverse visual field. For example, Charles Wheatstone's "On some remarkable, and hitherto unobserved, Phenomena of Binocular Vision" (1838) contains many striking parallels to Darwin's vision of nature. By demonstrating that the eye creates a three-dimensional image from two differing pictures, Wheatstone applies the empiricist model to binocular vision; not only is each individual form perceived differently from every other, but the same form is perceived differently by each eye. Before

Weatstone's discovery, the combination of the two ocular images was explained nativistically. Wheatstone quotes Thomas Reid as stating:

> [B]y an original property of human eyes, objects painted upon the centres of the two retinae, or upon points similarly situated with regard to the centres, appear in the same visible place . . . the most plausible attempts to account for this property of the eyes have been unsuccessful; and therefore . . . it must be either a primary law of our constitution, or the consequence of some general law which is not yet discovered.   (Reid in Wheatstone 389)

Wheatstone claimed that the images pictured by each eye do not appear in the same visible space, but are combined into one coalescent image by the mind. (Moving one's finger toward one's nose, or holding up a finger and focusing on a wall beyond it, are ways to foil this coalescence. Moreover, when this is done the slight differences between the two images can usually be observed.) Essential to human vision, then, is that every perceived image is, in fact, two images—each one slightly different from the other, and each containing the potential for visual otherness.

Wheatstone goes on to describe what occurs when two different images are presented, by means of a stereoscope, to the two eyes. If two images differing only in size are placed in the stereoscope, then "it will be seen that, notwithstanding this difference, they coalesce and occasion a single resultant perception." If Wheatstone then places the cards so that both the binocular image and the two monocular images can be seen at the same time, then "the binocular image is apparently intermediate in size between the two monocular ones" (Wheatstone 385). (Something like this effect can be observed by holding an open hand a short distance in front of the face and focusing on something beyond it. The multiple double images blend and the fingers, especially toward the center, seem to be roughly of the same size.) The mind blends images together and in the process of doing so, transforms them into new images.

His description of what occurs when two images differing in form are placed in the stereoscope is even more closely related to Darwin's presentation of the fragmented animal body.

> If we regard a picture with the right eye alone for a considerable length of time it will be constantly perceived; if we look at another and dissimilar picture with the left eye alone its effect will be equally permanent; it might therefore be expected, that if each of these pictures were presented to its corresponding eye at the same time the two would appear permanently superposed on each other. This, however, contrary to expectation, is not the case.
>
> If a and b [Fig. 1] are each presented at the same time to a different eye, the common border [the circle] will remain constant, while the letter within it

[S and A] will change alternately from that which would be perceived by the right eye alone to that which would be perceived by the left eye alone. At the moment of change the letter which has just been seen breaks into fragments, while fragments of the letter which is about to appear mingle with them, and are immediately after replaced by the entire letter. It does not appear to be in the power of the will to determine the appearance of either of the letters. . . . When complex pictures are employed in the stereoscope, various parts of them alternate differently. (Wheatstone 386)

Fig. 1. From Sir Charles Wheatstone, "Contributions to the Physiology of Vision" (1838).

This process of alternating and fragmenting images is much like that which the reader experiences while reading Darwin's description of the pigeons. If, rather than two letters, two pigeons are presented, the common elements of the form will remain constant, while the various body parts will flicker from those distinguishing one breed to those distinguishing the other. Moreover, Wheatstone is adamant that what is seen is a single image in relief, not simply two images superposed. Such a possibility of two forms being perceived not only in one visual space, but as a single object, were both investigated and deemed to be necessary to the process of vision at about the time Darwin was writing the *Origin of Species.*

Another sort of visual blending occurs when, rather than comparing different parts of similar species, Darwin compares the same part from several different species.

What can be more curious than that the hand of man, formed for grasping, that of a mole for digging, the leg of the horse, the paddle of the porpoise, and the wing of the bat, should all be constructed on the same pattern, and should include the same bones, in the same relative positions? (434)

Here, rather than the general forms flowing together, it is the parts that seem to blend into one another, while the bodies of the animals retain their complete, although insubstantial, forms. The reader sees a human hand, a mole's claw, and a horse's hoof, as though superimposed on the same space, while the general outlines of the rest of the body are noticed peripherally, somewhere adjacent to the focus of vision. The rapid presentation of similar hand forms creates the imaging equivalent of the optical phenomenon known as *visual masking;* the "ghost" or residual image of one form does not have time to clear before the next one is presented. In "On the Gradual Production of Luminous Impressions on the Eye" (1849), William Swan argues that residual images are caused by the gradual impression of light on the retina. A ball that is observed falling across the sky will seem to leave a dark streak behind it. This effect is caused, says Swan, by "the portion of the retina over which the image of the ball had passed, not having had time to be fully impressed with the light of the sky at the instant when the passage of the ball again exposed it to the action of that light" (Swan 582). There is, then, a lag between the moment when our eyes are turned to something, and the moment when we perceive it fully; the impression of light upon the eye is gradual. The corollary to this thesis is that the impression of darkness, or of objects, is also gradual.

> It may be supposed that a different explanation of this effect might be afforded by the persistence of the impression of the image of the ball on the eye. That this explanation is identical with that given above, is evident from the image of the ball when seen projected in the sky being sensibly black. For, since blackness is the negation of light, the persistence of a black impression is but a want of light on that portion of the retina where the impression is perceived; and the existence of such an impression, or a want of luminosity after the eye is fully exposed to light, clearly proves that its action on that organ is not instantaneous. (Swan 582)

When another image is introduced into the visual field before the residual image can clear, the first image is overlapped, or "masked" by the second image occupying the same visual space, and the two images (for the brief moment they exist together) are prone to the same sort of blending that Wheatstone noticed by use of his stereoscope. (A simple example of visual masking can be observed by shaking the open hand vigorously back and forth so that the fingers seem to smear together.) Jonathan Crary, in his excellent book *Techniques of the Observer,* has demonstrated that the popularity of stereopticons and kaleidoscopes in the early nineteenth century made visual masking a familiar phenomenon to the nineteenth-century reader.[3] Darwin's rhetorical use of visual masking is thus of a piece with his appeal to common experience of visual playfulness. In Darwin's description of the hands, one form corresponds sufficiently to the next that the residual images assume a general outline, and the whole effect is one of wavering hand/claw/leg/wing/paddle form. The single part from many different species is thus made fluid and interpenetrating, as though the man, the horse, the mole, the porpoise, and the bat were all standing around a circular table and swearing eternal brotherhood.

Darwin thus presents the reader with a vision of the natural world that is both fragmented and fluid. Nature has no clear, monolothic forms, no specially created species, but various biological units that are incessantly flowing, reforming, and rearranging. The reader is being taught to see empirically, and also to see like an evolutionary naturalist. While the causal observer within a hutch of prize pigeons may not be able to tell much difference between the relatively uniform creatures, the trained naturalist will automatically focus in on the specific parts that mark their distinction, and those that indicate their common ancestry.

> Hence I look at individual differences, though of small interest to the system-
> atist, as of the highest importance for us, as being the first step towards such
> slight varieties as are barely thought worth recording in works on natural
> history. And I look at varieties which are in any degree more distinct and
> permanent, as steps leading to more strongly marked and permanent vari-
> eties; and at these latter, as leading to sub-species, and to species.   (51–52)

An evolutionary naturalist sees the natural world as a whirl of bodily fragments and transforming morphological patterns; looking at one creature he sees the hundreds of forms from which it may have arisen and to which it may give rise. Darwin's astute awareness of the naturalist's eye allows him to understand the essential irony of his position. While the task of the Linnaean naturalist, the *systematist* as he calls him here, is to categorize nature according to distinct forms (species), his attention to body parts and organic details leads him unceasingly away from seeing in forms, and toward a fluxing, fragmented visual field.

> Certainly no clear line of demarcation has as yet been drawn between species
> and sub-species—that is, the forms which in the opinion of some naturalists
> come very near to, but do not quite arrive at, the rank of the species: or,
> again, between sub-species and well-marked varieties, or between lesser
> varieties and individual differences. These differences blend into each other
> by an insensible series; and a series impresses the mind with the idea of an
> actual passage.   (51)

Seeing evolution comes to the same thing as being constantly involved in an empirical illusion, for as the mind flashes between the different orderings of the visual field that constitute species and subspecies, as the various differ-ent organic forms crowd, overlap, and mask each other, they seem to blend together like one organic form evolving into another.

Darwinian vision is not entirely Berkeleyan, for bodies are broken into organic parts rather than minimum visibles, but it does make the process of organizing animals in species as capriciously variable as the process of organizing the visual field into forms. Darwin reverses the process of our visual education by pulling apart the visual combinations that make up the appearance of a species into smaller visual (and biological) units. While seeming to define a species of pigeons by stating the name and describing the combination of characteristics associated with that name, he presents a jumble of names and a jumble of images that the reader is incapable of disentangling from one another. Beer states that in his use of language, Darwin is "less interested in singleness than mobility . . . he is more preoccupied with relations and transformation than with limits" (Beer 38). The same can be said of his images, through which he reveals that combining animal parts and giving them a species name, like combining minimum visibles and giving them object names, "is perfectly arbitrary, and done by the mind in such sort as experience shows it to be most convenient" (Berkeley Sec. 109, p. 72). Any evolutionary form has the possibility of becoming any other. Thus the typical task of the naturalist author—the categorization and description of species—is subverted, and the reader is made to see the evolutionary flux of nature by being returned to a state of uneducated biological vision.

IV

Up to this point we have discussed the ways in which Darwin uses visual coalescence and fragmentation to overcome spatial difference, so that several animals are seen in one space. The imagistic coalescence of two contemporaneous forms, however, also allows for a visual triangulation into the past, as in the "Parallel Roads of Glen Roy." The relationship between the pigeon part and the hazy form that the various parts have in common, between the human hand and the wavering hand/paddle/wing, is roughly that of descendant to ancestor. The mental creation of that form in the reader's mind involves him or her in a sudden realization of the process of evolution. As one image masks and blends into the other, we do not see a paddle evolving into a hand, but the transformation of both paddle and hand into a common indistinct form. This form is our vision of the ancestor, and the movement from human hand to hand/paddle/wing/ to porpoise paddle, or from runt pigeon beak, to general pigeon form, to pouter pigeon claw, is a movement backward and forward in time. The reader enacts the mental process of the naturalist puzzling out evolutionary relationships, and thus seems to discover the theory anew. Furthermore, Darwin creates a space in which two species-distinct organisms not only occupy the same place, but where two time-distinct organisms occupy the same moment. As in Glen Roy, the ancestor and its several descendants are all imaged in the same field, in a flicker of organic possibility. This free movement between analogous forms over space and time demonstrates the probability of common ancestry and makes a doctrine of fixed species unimaginable.

Gillian Beer describes Darwin's use of analogy as a narrative process.

> Analogy and morphology are both concerned with discovering structures common to diverse forms. In the case of analogy this communality expresses itself by first ranging two patterns of experience alongside each other, seeking their points of identity, and then using one pattern to extend the other. There is always a sense of story—of sequence—in analogy, in a way that there need not be in other forms of metaphor.   (Beer 80)

Darwin's use of visual coalescence, however, collapses narrative into illusion. The movement of the eye back and forth between two images extends the process of comparison in time and gives it the "speculative, argumentatively extended character of analogy," which "ranges it closer to narrative than to image" (Beer 80). Such a process occurs when one compares the two embryos in the figure from the *Descent of Man* (Fig. 2) (15) by moving the focus of the eye back and forth between them. Were those two images put into a stereopticon, the resulting image would more closely resemble the instantaneous imagistic coalescence of Darwin's visual analogy. While coalescent images illustrate the malleability of Darwin's forms, they are neither "speculative" nor "argumentatively extended"; instead, they strike the reader with the sudden realization of morphological similarity.

Because it is instantaneous, however, the operation of Darwinian narrative illusion frequently bypasses important aspects of evolutionary theory. The most significant of these oversights is that Darwinian empirical vision, by its free movement backward and forward in time, is at odds with the gradual, one-directional motion of biological development. As Beer has pointed out, the evolutionary process (i.e., the growth and development of species) can only be described as a narrative. Forms develop through growth over long periods of time, and the comprehension of such a development depends upon a strict attention to changes in form. Appropriately, Darwin describes Nature as a sharp-eyed monitor of biological life, selecting superior forms with perfectly accurate vision in order to construct a seamless developmental narrative.

> It may be said that natural selection is daily and hourly scrutinising, throughout the world, every variation, even the slightest; rejecting that which is bad, preserving and adding up all that is good; silently and insensibly working, whenever and wherever opportunity offers, at the improvement of each

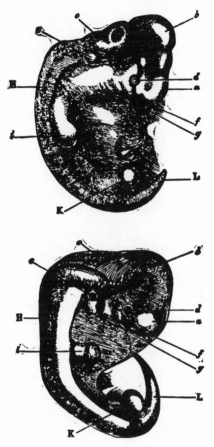

Fig. 2. From Charles Darwin, *The Descent of Man* (G. Appleton & Co., New York, 1895).

organic being in relation to its organic and inorganic conditions of life. (*Origin* 84)

At the same time, however, Darwin goes out of his way to point out how weak-eyed Nature's human children are.

We see nothing of these slow changes in progress, until the hand of time has marked the long lapse of ages, and then so imperfect is our view . . . that

we only see that the forms of life are now different from what they formerly
were.   (*Origin* 84)

Because we cannot observe evolution over time, and because Darwin will
not, like Lyell, allow narrative recreation of history as a method of scientific investigation, we must content ourselves with perceiving the narrative
of evolutionary history in an atemporal fashion, through analogous structures apparent in existing forms. The wisdom of the naturalist is derived not
from a clarity of vision over a long period of time, but through a plastic or
empirical conception of form that allows him to see all times in present
forms. Darwin's narrative eye does not perceive past forms evolving into
present ones because it cannot see into the past. Instead, he chooses two
contemporary organic forms, observed firsthand either by himself or by a
fellow naturalist, and triangulates into the past through their coalescence,
just as he did with geological forms in Glen Roy.

> [I]n the construction of the mouths of insects: what can be more different than
> the immensely long spiral proboscis of a sphinx-moth, the curious folded one
> of a bee or bug, and the great jaws of a beetle?—yet all these organs, serving
> for such different purposes, are formed by infinitely numerous modifications
> of an upper lip, mandibles, and two pairs of maxillae. . . . We have only to
> suppose that their common progenitor has an upper lip, mandibles, and two
> pairs of maxillae, these parts perhaps being very simple in form; and then
> natural selection will account for the infinite diversity in structure and func-
> tion of the mouths of insects.   (*Origin* 434–36)

The various contemporary insects are fragmented and their parts are made
to coalesce, so that the reader perceives a single coalescent insect form
containing all the possibles sizes and styles of lips, mandibles, and maxil-
lae. Darwin sets up visual frames, or holes in time, through which the past
can be seen in natural forms, and the steady, narrative operation of history
is telescoped into a single mercurial image.

   This atemporal presentation of natural history is implicitly condemned
by many critics of Darwin's theory. Adam Sedgwick's proscription of
Darwin's "unflinching materialism" is particularly telling, as it associates
the atemporal comprehension of nature caused by overstimulated vision
with a failure of the moral sense.

> What is it that gives us the sense of right and wrong, of law, of duty, of cause
> and effect? What is it that enables us to construct true theories on good
> inductive evidence? Theories which enable us, whether in the material or the
> moral world, to link together the past and the present. . . . By gazing only
> on material nature, a man may easily have his very senses bewildered (like
> one under the cheatery of an electro-biologist); he may become so frozen up,

by a too long continued and exclusively material study, as to lose his relish
for moral truth, and his vivacity in apprehending it.   (Sedgewick 164–65)

For Sedgewick, the "higher faculties" that allow us to see the world in
terms of cause and effect, to link the past and present narratively, are
essential ingredients of moral consciousness. He accuses Darwin of keeping these high faculties "out of our sight," and thus rendering human
beings "entirely bestial." Beer makes a somewhat similar claim when she
describes "the humanistic core of Lyell's work" as "its insistence on the
power of man's imagination, which allows him to recuperate the stag-
geringly extended time-scale of the physical world" (Beer 44). In both
cases, the "humanistic" is linked to the narrative. A sense of temporal
regularity, of imageable narrative history, is necessary to the maintenance
of human centrality. The dazzled empirical eye does not see causally or
temporally, and so ceases to see humanly.

Furthermore, in the course of the review Sedgewick attempts to make
evolutionary theory appear ridiculous by writing brief and outrageous evolutionary narratives. He asks,

> And how came the Dinosaurs to disappear from the face of Nature? Did they
> tire of the land, and become Whales, casting off their hind-legs? And, after
> they had lasted millions of years as whales, did they tire of the water, and
> leap out again as Pachyderms?   (Sedgewick in Hull 163)

The absurdity that would have resulted had Darwin attempted to portray the
process of evolution as Lyell had portrayed geological uniformitarianism
becomes apparent in such passages. There are a few places in which Darwin approaches a narrative portrayal of one form changing into another,
and it is worth looking closely at one of these to better define the ways in
which Darwinian vision manipulates and collapses narrative envisionment
into coalescence. The most notorious of these passages is that describing
the swimming black bear.

> In North America the black bear was seen by Hearne swimming for hours
> with widely open mouth, thus catching, like a whale, insects in the water.
> Even in so extreme a case as this, if the supply of insects were constant, and
> if better adapted competitors did not already exist in the country, I can see no
> difficulty in a race of bears being rendered, by natural selection, more and
> more aquatic in their structure and habits, with larger and larger mouths, till a
> creature was produced as monstrous as a whale.   (*Origin* 184)

This is indeed an extreme case, so extreme that Darwin edited it from later
editions of the *Origin* to avoid the jocular abuse rained down on him by
critics. Sedgewick credited Darwin with "a wonderful credulity" for be-

lieving that "a white bear, by being confined to the slops floating in a polar basin, might in time be turned into a whale" (Sedgewick in Hull 165). This is, of course, not what Darwin is attempting to demonstrate at all; Darwin never proposes that one contemporary form can evolve into another. As usual Sedgewick has recast Darwin's work in a strictly narrative form. The astonishment of the critics, however, is somewhat forgivable considering the complexity of Darwin's representation. Darwin is here attempting to portray not only past and present forms, but future forms as well. The passage portrays two evolutionary principles at once: bears and whales share a common ancestor, and a bear is capable of evolving into a creature not unlike a whale.

In the first sentence of the passage the reader experiences the sort of Darwinian illusion that has already been discussed. She or he images a bear, and this image is suddenly, with the phrase "like a whale," masked by that of a whale; the combined image is neither whale nor bear, but a general form common to both whale and bear that represents the bear/whale ancestor. It is not enough, however, to make time elastic in one direction; Darwin intends to make the biological future as accessible as the biological past. The extreme vividness, indeed the comic quality, of the second sentence results from the typically Darwinian technique of emphasizing the part over the whole. As the bear evolves its mouth grows larger and larger until it seems almost literally to swallow the body supporting it. When, at the end of the description, Darwin asserts that a "creature was produced as monstrous as a whale," a huge, whalish body is suddenly added to the gigantic mouth. The ease and vividness with which the reader is able to image this transformation relies upon his or her having already imaged the bear/whale coalescence in the first sentence.

Although it is not possible for Darwin to triangulate into the future as he does into the past, the whalish qualities of the bear's body have already been impressed upon the reader's mind in the first image, so that the possibility of a descendant in the bear line being whalish simply involves a further, and slightly expanded, imaging of the whale/bear overlay. The reader never actually sees the bear descendant any more than she or he sees the bear/whale ancestor; both are blurred potential images—inchoate forms that portray a possible rather than an actual organism. The reader cannot, therefore, be said to see a bear turning into a whale, just as he or she was unable to see anything turning into a bear. No imageable narrative of development is portrayed. A bear does not turn into a future organism, it simply slips into the shadows of visual otherness. All the reader is able to see is that forms are changing, that all forms are like those past and future whale/bears, perpetually fragmenting, flowing, and reforming, always flickering empirically between form and form and time and time. Narrative, which documents gradual change over time, is scattered when time is no longer a controlling force. The "story" of evolution can only be told in momentary flashes of optical illusion that demonstrate the visual similarities of organic forms while at the same time denying them both of spatial and temporal integrity.

Darwin is successful in portraying the evolutionary process visually, then, if his reader comes to see all times and all places as present. Such an assertion may seem shocking since Darwin is usually credited with stressing the ineluctability of time and change, and there is no question that steady chronological time is necessary for his theory. In Darwin's work, however, the way in which the reader sees evolution is at odds with the process of evolution itself; the entangled eye offers rather a different message than the entangled bank. Throughout the *Origin* the contrast between the oppressive temporality of Darwin's theory and the playful atemporality of the imagistic operations he uses to portray that theory creates a textual anxiety. Beer draws the distinction between analogy used "simply as an illustrative aid" and analogy as "part of a process of valid argumentation" (Beer 82). The sort of imagistic illusion that has been discussed here is a very provocative illustrative aid; it allows the reader to envision the evolutionary process as well as evolutionary history through the organic imperfections of an empirical eye. Such vision is useful to the naturalist because the fluxing forms of empirical illusion can provide a sense of nature's chaotic bounty and inspiration to investigate the instability of organic forms. It is also useful to the scientific writer who must imaginatively engage the reader with the formal chaos of evolutionary nature. But this empirical eye does not, as Darwin continually emphasizes, allow the naturalist to see natural processes clearly, completely, or accurately. By adopting a representational technique that is at once as compelling and as scientifically imprecise as narrative illusion, Darwin is both helping and hurting his own argument. In discussing Darwin's argumentative techniques George Levine notes that "Darwin must then have it both ways: rhetorically he must appeal to the imagination, while claiming to appeal to the intelligence" (Levine 114). His visual strategies allow the reader to imagine evolution, but, at times, they complicate or nearly contradict the theoretical points that Darwin means to make.[4]

The contrast between Darwinian theory and Darwinian vision becomes problematic when illustration is confused for argument, and time-transcending empirical vision becomes both a strategy for seeing a theory enacted and an example of the theory at work in nature. By portraying an easy flow from one form to another and from one time to another Darwinian vision sidesteps the uglier aspects of Darwin's theory, namely extinction and death. Beer notes the tension created by Darwin's scientific use of the myth of metamorphosis. "Darwin's theory required extinction. . . . Metamorphosis bypasses death. . . . In some ways, evolutionary theory looks like the older concept of metamorphosis prolonged through time, transformation eked out rather than emblazoned" (Beer 111–12). Evolution especially "looks like" metamorphosis through the entangled narrative eye which collapses both time and death into the single coalescent form.

Darwin's emphasis on visual analogy, while always dynamic and chaotic, also seems to admit the possibility of a nativistic ordering of visual nature similar to Paley's. In his chapter on "Mutual Affinities of Organic Beings" Darwin notes that it is necessary to make "the very important distinction between real affinities [body parts demonstrating common ancestry] and analogical or adaptive resemblances [body parts simply reflecting similar use]" (*Origin* 427). According to Beer, the difference between analogies and affinities is one that must be argued through narratively.

> Darwin's aim is to discover analogies which can move beyond the provisional and metaphorical and prove themselves as "true affinities." Analogies may turn out to be homologies. In such a case the parallel narrative patterns reveal actual identity, and the distance between the two patterns vanishes. Total and satisfying congruity is achieved. (Beer 80)

Imagistically, however, "total and satisfying congruity" can be achieved simply through the coalescence of visual patterns regardless of their actual evolutionary relationship. Darwin's visual analogy is not a narrative or an argumentatively extended process; the "argument" takes the form of a sudden and rapturous awareness. The distinction between provisional analogies and true affinities can thus be easily blurred by Darwin's narrative eye because provisionally analogous forms coalesce as readily as do true affinities. For example, Darwin states that the "resemblance, in the shape of the body and in the fin-like anterior limbs, between the dugong, which is a pachydermatous animal, and the whale, and between these mammals and fishes, is analogical" (*Origin* 427). The naturalist who has been trained to make visual comparisons between natural forms will be misled by analogy; "such resemblances will not reveal—will rather tend to conceal their blood-relationship to their proper lines of descent." Reading *Origin of Species* thus accustoms the reader to visualizing nature in a way that, Darwin admits, can obscure as much as it reveals. Had the hand/paddle/wing included a "fin" the reader would as easily have imaged the composite limb, and inadvertently made a scientific error. Darwin's presentation of visually analogous structures in nature gets his reader accustomed to thinking of nature as ordered through visually perceivable patterns, and fails to account for the fact that there is a legitimate biological distinction between visually similar structures.

Moreover, the chaotic fluidity of Darwin's vision can create the desire to freeze his dynamically flickering visual analogues into static, typical patterns, thus transforming an empirical nature into a nativistic one. Gillian Beer describes Darwin's impact on cultural thought in terms of just such a yearning for the formally stable.

> Lying behind the diversity in Darwinian theory, slumbers the form of some remote progenitor, irrecoverable because precedent to history or anterior to consciousness. The idea of "the single form" becomes itself a new and powerful source of nostalgia. . . . The activity of describing development may be history, but it seeks always to reach further back into the past, further and further towards the comforting limits of initiation. . . . So although Darwinian theory brought in its wake heterogeneous enquiry yet a monistic ideal persists. (Beer 127–28)

Thus the legacy of Darwinian vision is twofold; a nativistic, typological and formally stable conception of nature is made at once less accessible and more desirable. Darwin's use of illusion to disorient and confuse the reader creates the same feeling that it created in the young Darwin observing the tropical landscape: the intense yearning for the familiar, the orderly, and the easily perceivable. The reader sees the natural world through uneducated empirical vision that brings, as it did to Darwin in the jungle, a heady, delighted awareness of the multiplicity and mutability of nature. This disorienting expansiveness, however, may also bring uneasiness, consternation, or panic. The reader's impulse may be to push through the masses of feathers, claws, and legs, the entangled bodies and entangled banks, to a landscape of simple nativistic forms that, in Darwin's words, can "call back the recollection of childhood & times past, where all that was unpleasant is forgotten." Darwinian illusion, while offering the reader a visual impression of the empirical flux of nature, also suggests the possibility of and creates the desire for a profoundly stable and nativistic order.

Darwin's illustrative use of empirical vision is ill-matched to his argument for evolution in at least two ways: (1) The shuffling of species allows for a free movement back and forth in time that seems to diminish the rigorous temporality of evolutionary development, and (2) the coalescence of spatially distinct forms into one pattern results in a confusion between visual similarity and developmental difference. The transcendence of time and space, while offering dazzling illustrations of the glorious variability and multiplicity of nature, underplays the essentially narrative and material (temporally and spatially extended), characteristics of evolutionary nature. Darwin's adoption of a limited narrative eye, while making evolutionary nature more visible, also tends to distort it.

The succeeding chapters will demonstrate the ways in which various nature writers choose to reenvision the Darwinian empirical landscape in narrative form. Frequently, the process of locating individual forms in time and space distorts evolutionary nature in the opposite way, regularizing and simplifying the landscape through nativistic modes of envisionment. Where Darwin sacrifices chronological narrative for organic abundance, Hardy, Conrad, and Lawrence sacrifice abundance for perceptual simplicity. Darwin portrays an entangled nature by entangling the eye in its own perceptual processes; however, by doing so he creates the possibility of disentangling perceived nature from physical nature and the desire to reorder nature into simpler and more reassuring forms. The choices made by post-Darwinian nature writers are rarely so distinct as "rapture or nothing"—pure empiricism or pure nativism—but they do demonstrate how, after Darwin, the enraptured empirical eye tends to be replaced by one that perceives nature more nativistically. The variety and abundance of the entangled bank is limited and regularized as nature writers attend to the operation of the entangled eye.

2

The Edges of Sunlight: Visual Selection in the Novels of Thomas Hardy

The temporal location and span of Hardy's career causes his work, like all border territories, to be claimed by divergent groups. For example, the influence of Darwinian theory on Hardy tends to be read in two radically different ways. Critics who consider Hardy a groundbreaker of modernist thought often portray Darwin as a pessimistic philosopher who, along with Nietszche and Schopenhauer, propels Hardy into religious doubt and psychological isolation. Irving Howe alludes very briefly to Darwin as one of a group of thinkers who were "damaging to [Hardy's] faith" (Howe 10). Lionel Stevenson offers the following influence narrative:

> [Hardy] was nineteen when *The Origin of Species* came out, and from the evolutionary theory he drew the inference that the universe is ruled by blind chance rather than any conscious power, either benevolent or malign. He was perpetually aware of the ruthless struggle for survival, as exemplified among plants and animals, so that nature for him was not the kindly foster-mother that Wordsworth loved, but a horrifying spectacle of incessant destruction. . . . Wider reading ultimately made him aware of the pessimistic doctrines of Schopenhauer and von Hartmann; and these reinforced his own vision of mankind as the helpless victim of cosmic forces. (386–87)

In this reading Darwin's theories are significant as general intellectual influences only. The struggle for existence becomes one example of the universal helplessness and victimization of all creatures, and the natural landscape in Hardy's novels, by manifesting this struggle, serves a primarily didactic function. F. B. Pinion says of Hardy's novels that "the human situation and the writer's philosophy of life are reflected so effectively in natural scenes that his thought is communicated wholly in imagery" (Pinion 88). Daniel R. Schwarz describes Hardy's setting as expressing "the turmoil and anxiety within the author's psyche" and as "coterminous with destiny and fate . . . a metaphor for the narrator's and his characters' own moral confusion'' (Schwarz 22). Hardy's Darwinian landscape thus ceases to have material significance and becomes the metaphorical expression of modernist pessimism.

The other approach, favored more often by critics of Victorian literature and of nature writing, involves closer attention to the scientific matter of Darwin's theories and the biological materiality of Hardy's landscape. Critics such as Gillian Beer, Roger Ebbatson, and John Alcorn consider Hardy's awareness of and engagement with the landscape to have been intensified by Darwin's theories. Beer states that Hardy ''shared with Darwin that delight in material life in its widest diversity, the passion for particularity, and for individuality and plenitude'' (Beer 258). Ebbatson describes ''Hardy's unique contribution to fiction'' as his investigation of ''the intimate connexion of man and natural processes'' (Ebbatson 108). Alcorn claims that

> Hardy's better world will emerge from the spontaneity of living things themselves. . . . His concept of nature looks, not to the dead past but to the evolving future. Thus Hardy's popular reputation as an uncompromising pessimist is—as popular reputations often are—false.   (23)

Rather than creating the metaphorically didactic landscape described by Stevenson and Schwarz, these critics suggest that Hardy ''discards metaphor'' (Alcorn 2) to present landscape as a powerful physical presence.

This critical division corresponds to what is usually seen as an essential contradiction in Hardy's portrayal of nature. Hardy's work, it is generally agreed, is at once lyrical and tragic, in Beer's words ''jubilant as well as terrible'' (Beer 257). This ''confusion'' or ''contradiction'' that any reader feels when engaging with Hardy is variously traced to Hardy's conflicting desires for artistry and realism, his conflicting awareness of humanity's relationship to and victimization by nature, or his conflicting emotional needs to draw close to and separate himself from the pleasures of human life. Generally, the tragic or fatalistic elements of Hardy's world are linked to plotting and narrative voice while the lyrical and pastoral aspects are linked to descriptions of nature. In his intricate analysis of voicing in *Tess,* for example, David Lodge suggests that the ''network of imagery and reference'' to plants and animals ''encourages us to think of Tess as essentially 'in touch' with Nature. . . . At such moments we are least conscious of the literary persona of the author, and of his distance from the story.'' When Hardy wishes to emphasize ''that Nature is quite indifferent to her fate,'' however, the narrative voice becomes distanced, ''its moral neutrality emphasized by the sceptical philosopher'' (Lodge 174). Gillian

Beer offers a particularly eloquent reading of this division by demonstrating how both Hardy's narrative determinism and descriptive delight derive from different aspects of Darwin's theories.

> Alongside the emphasis on the apprehension and anxiety, on inevitable over-throw long foreseen, persistingly evaded, there is, however, another prevailing sensation in Hardy's work equally strongly related to his understanding of Darwin. It is that of happiness. Alongside the doomed sense of weighted past and incipient conclusion, goes a plenitude, an "appetite for joy." This finds expression—as it must if at all—in the moment-by-moment fullness of the text. . . . And the drive of his plots is so crushing precisely because of the full sense of life elated in us by the range of sense perception which throng his writing.   (Beer 241, 248)

These readings seem to suggest a fundamental inconsistency in Hardy's style and sensibility—an unbridgeable gap between description and plotting, between happy sensuality and crushing pessimism. While I agree with Alcorn and Beer that nature in Hardy's works is significant as a physical presence and not simply a metaphor for an uncaring universe, I would suggest that Hardy's way of representing this physical nature, and the material qualities implicit in that mode of representation, offer the same sort of tragic ineluctability as does his plotting. I am not simply suggesting, as have many critics including Ebbatson and Beer, that the plants and animals Hardy describes remind the reader of the misery and death of evolutionary struggle; rather, I wish to demonstrate that Hardy's narrative eye, which selects and simplifies the landscape, is at once lyrical and deterministic; its nativistic selection of visual forms limits nature even as it perceives plenitude. At the same time, the very limitations that make his narrative vision tragic allow for a focusing in on, and thus a subjective recentering of, humanity in the natural landscape.

A nativistically perceived nature must be extended in time and space, as Section I of this chapter shows, and Hardy's natural world is seen through an eye capable of perceiving only a limited number of the multitude of natural forms. The sort of optical illusions used by Darwin to multiply natural forms through analogy are thus undercut, as Section II makes clear, and the physical transcendence of formlessness apparent in Darwin's empirical illusions is shown to be impossible. Ultimately, the narrative gaze becomes focused on the interaction between natural and human forms, or upon human forms themselves, as Section III demonstrates. This visual selection of the human figure causes the rest of the landscape to become simplified and humanized. The nativistic Hardyan eye selects humanly significant forms from an entangled Darwinian nature.

I

Hardy combines Darwin's entangled nature with a nativistic perceptual model through an aesthetic of perceptual selection. In his essay "The Science of Fiction" Hardy criticizes naturalist and realist authors for their failure to recognize the essential difference between the artistic representations of nature and nature itself.

> The most devoted apostle of realism, the sheerest naturalist, cannot escape, any more than the withered old gossip over her fire, the exercise of Art in his labour or pleasure of telling a tale. Not until he becomes an automatic reproducer of all impressions whatsoever can he be called purely scientific, or even a manufacturer on scientific principles. If in the exercise of his reason he select or omit, with an eye to being more truthful than the truth (the just aim of art), he transforms himself into a technicist at a move.   (*Life and Art* 86)

It is the task of the artist to "select" those specific forms from the natural world that are significant to telling a tale, rather than to reproduce "all impressions whatsoever." Even if the artist wanted to represent nature so minutely "the impossibility of reproducing in its entirety the phantasmagoria of experience with infinite and atomic truth, without shadow, relevancy, or subordination" would prevent it (*Life and Art* 87). Running throughout Hardy's pronouncements on representation is this principle of selection. In his literary notes he quotes from Schiller ("The artist may be known rather by what he omits") and from Pater ("All art does but consist in the removal of surplusage") (*Literary Notes,* Vol. 2 p. 17, 1722). By basing his aesthetic on selection, Hardy rejects Darwin's rapturous empirical illusions and espouses a representation extended in narrative time. The artist is capable of choosing various forms to portray, but cannot portray them all at once. Like Sedgewick, Hardy associates the narrative with the humanistic; to portray all perceived forms at once, as Darwin does, would cause the artist to become "automatic." The artist's task is to choose those forms out of the entangled mass of nature that express that artist's own idiosyncratic vision, thus offering a limited and humanized landscape.

The following passages from *The Woodlanders* and *Tess,* often quoted as examples of Hardy's "Darwinian" vision of nature, also demonstrate his principle of aesthetic selection. Rather than attempting to reproduce all of the organic forms in these entangled landscapes, Hardy focuses sequentially on each form touched, skirted, or looked past by the figures in the landscape.

> Winterborne followed and kept his eye upon the two figures as they threaded their way through these sylvan masses. . . . They went noiselessly over mats of starry moss, rustled through interspersed tracts of leaves, skirted trunks with spreading roots . . . elbowed old elms and ashes with great forks in which stood pools of water that overflowed on rainy days. (*Woodlanders* 41)

> She went stealthily as a cat through this profusion of growth, gathering cuckoo-spittle on her skirts, cracking snails that were underfoot, staining her hands with thistle-milk and slug-slime, and rubbing off upon her naked arms sticky blights which, though snow-white on the apple-tree trunks, made madder stains on her skin. (*Tess* 179)

Hardy's principle of selection here is human proximity. Giles is able to follow Grace and her father because "some flecks of white in Grace's drapery" are visible through the trees, and it is only the trees past which this white drapery moves that Hardy portrays. Similarly, it is only the forms that Tess brushes against or steps on in her motion through the entangled garden that the reader sees. Consequently, Hardy's entangled landscapes, while still populous, seem controlled and contained when compared with Darwin's. The forest and the garden are overgrown, but the reader can perceive individual forms without having them mutate and multiply in the rapturous clusters of visual analogy. Although Hardy presumes a nature as visually complicated as Darwin's, he does not consider his task to be the scientifically complete representation of such entanglement.

Andrew Enstice offers a practical demonstration of Hardy's "process of selection" (Enstice 11) by comparing his literary landscapes to their actual counterparts. Invariably, the literary versions have fewer details and less complicated visual forms.

> Hardy's art involves the reconstruction of the diverse Dorchester scene, organising and controlling our experience of it. The essential beauty, economy and harmony of the setting are translated, through the author's pen, into something recognisably similar, yet easier to comprehend. (Enstice x)

Hardy's representational strategy is based on limitation rather than on multiplication of forms; therefore, his landscape becomes "organised" and "controlled"—and thus "easier to comprehend"—for the limited narrative eye.

Visual selection is also essential to nineteenth-century nativistic perceptual theory. The nativistic eye has the innate ability to perceive form, and nativistic forms are therefore spatially distinct, having limitations and dimensions. Consequently, nativistic forms cannot coalesce because the eye is incapable of perceiving more than one form in one visual space. To perceive several forms it is necessary for the nativistic eye to move from one to the next—to select forms one at a time from the visual field. Sir David Brewster's article "On the Law of Visible Position in Single and Binocular Vision" (1844), challenges the empiricist claim that the mind can cause differing images to coalesce. Throughout the article Brewster invokes the "Law of Visible Direction," in which it is asserted that "a visible point is seen in the direction of a line perpendicular to the surface of the retina at which the image of the point is formed" (Brewster 351), and that images grow less distinct as they are perceived by parts of the retina farther and farther from its center, or *foramen centrale*. Simply put, the eye must have its center turned toward a form in order to perceive it distinctly, and can consequently fully perceive only one form at a time. In Fig. 3, for example, a nativist would suggest that the eye moves from the cube with *A* as its foremost point to the cube with *X* as its foremost point. According to Brewster, the alternation of the figures is due to the "change in the adjustment of the eye for obtaining distinct vision" (Brewster 367); the fact that both forms seem to occupy the same visible space is immaterial for it is still necessary for the eye to direct itself toward each form separately. Brewster presents this analysis in response to the empiricist claim, enunciated by Sir Charles Wheatstone, that the two figures alternate spontaneously in the perceiver's mind and "while one figure continues it is not in the power of the will to change it immediately" (Wheatstone 382). Brewster claims that the alternation of the two figures is due to a willful and physiologically traceable direction of the eye across the visual field from one form to the other rather than to mental confusion on the part of the perceiver. The forms alternate at whatever rate the eye moves from one point of focus to another across the visual field, not in a spontaneous empirical flicker.

When the visual field is complicated the gradual movement and perceptual limitation of Brewster's nativistic eye become more obvious. Both

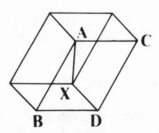

Fig. 3. From Sir David Brewster, "On the Law of Visible Position" (1844).

Brewster and Wheatstone describe the effect caused by looking at a carpet with a complicated pattern in red and green. Where Wheatstone's eye sees the carpet, "as if all the parts of the pattern were in motion" (Wheatstone, Colours 10), Brewster's selects specific patterns from the entangled visual field.

> If we look very steadily and continuously with both eyes at a double pattern—such as one of those on a carpet—composed of two single patterns of different colours, suppose red and green; and if we direct the mind particularly to the contemplation of the red one, the green pattern will sometimes vanish entirely, leaving the red one alone visible; and, by the same process, the red one may be made to disappear.   (Brewster, Colour 10)

While Wheatstone's eye perceives both forms in a coalescent flux, Brewster's concentrates on a single pattern until the others sink into insignificance and the first stands out distinctly as the object of the eye's selective attention.

As is apparent, Wheatstone's portrayal of the psychological combination of forms is significantly closer to Darwin's representations of evolutionary nature, in which forms seem to be in spontaneous motion, flowing together without the reader's control. If two orderings of the visual field are perceived at once, then the spontaneous alternation between one and the other will, like Darwinian vision, deny formal integrity to any one image. On the other hand, if the eye must refocus between orderings, each form is perpetually distinct and has its own formal integrity. Like Darwin's flowing pigeons, the patterns of Wheatstone's carpet are perceived as being in motion into and through one another—a mass of changing and blending patterns perceived in one visual space. Brewster's way of seeing, on the other hand, involves the concentration on one form at a time so that the carpet is perceived as a collection of distinct patterns placed close together.

In his description of artistic perception, Hardy also uses the example of a pattern in a carpet, and his portrayal of the operation of the artistic eye is quite similar to Brewster's description of the nativistic eye at work.

> As, in looking at a carpet, by following one colour a certain pattern is suggested, by following another colour, another; so in life the seer should watch that pattern among general things which his idiosyncrasy moves him to observe, and describe that alone. This is, quite accurately, a going to Nature; yet the result is no mere photograph, but purely the product of the writer's own mind.   (Millgate 158)

In order to create a world that is the expression of a single human consciousness Hardy encourages the artist to "select or omit, with an eye to being more truthful than the truth" (*Life and Art* 86).

Consequently Hardy's narrative eye moves gradually from point to point, describing complete distinct forms, just as Brewster's selects one pattern in the carpet at a time. This selectivity is most obvious when Hardy is describing entangled nature. Rather than perceiving animal parts in confusingly rapid succession, as Darwin's narrative eye does, Hardy's eye moves from organism to organism, perceiving each one distinctly before moving on to the next. Such distinct envisionment is time-consuming, however, and it is impossible for Hardy to represent more than a few organisms in any one passage. Moreover, Hardy's temporally extended perceptual model dictates that his natural world will be represented narratively rather than through visual analogy. Thus, while Darwin's reader is dazzled by an atemporal landscape populated by an infinite number of visually analogous forms, Hardy's perceives a few distinct, vital organisms, each of which is involved in some narratively rendered activity. Clym's furze bank in *The Return of the Native* is one such nativistic landscape.

> His daily life was of a curious microscopic sort, his whole world being limited to a circuit of a few feet from his person. His familiars were creeping and winged things, and they seemed to enroll him in their band. Bees hummed around his ears with an intimate air, and tugged at the heath and furze-flowers at his side in such numbers as to weigh them down to the sod. The strange amber-coloured butterflies which Egdon produced, and which were never seen elsewhere, quivered in the breath of his lips, alighted upon his bowed back, and sported with the glittering point of his hook as he flourished it up and down. Tribes of emerald-green grasshoppers leaped over his feet, falling awkwardly on their backs, heads, or hips, like unskilful acrobats, as chance might rule; or engaged themselves in noisy flirtation under the fern-fronds with silent ones of homely hue. Huge flies, ignorant of larders and wire-netting, and quite in a savage state, buzzed about him without knowing that he was a man. In and out of the fern-dells snakes glided in their most brillant blue and yellow guise, it being the season immediately following the shedding of their old skins, when their colours are brightest. Litters of young rabbits came out from their forms to sun themselves upon hillocks, the hot beams blazing through the delicate tissue of each thin-fleshed ear, and firing it to a blood-red transparency in which the veins could be seen. (*Return* 253)

Although Hardy does engage in a certain amount of comic anthropomorphism here, his major technique is that of focusing on one form, describing it in vivid detail, then moving on to the next. The narrative eye moves patiently, almost languidly, as the reader images bees, butterflies, grasshoppers, snakes, flies, and rabbits as distinct, complete forms. Yet for all its close quarters Clym's clump of furze contains only six species described in six separate sentences, rather a poor showing by Darwinian standards. No animal parts are ever confused with or masked by any others because the reader has a whole sentence to envision the form before another is presented. The animals are not even shown to be interacting with one another; like the patterns in Brewster's carpet, those not focused on become invisible. The only visual constant is Clym, who serves as a point of orientation around which each form is spatially located. Hardy's steady imagistic motion from form to form across the landscape has very little in common with Darwin's sudden envisionment of several forms in one; rather than perceiving a few organic forms as a multitude, Hardy's eye can perceive only six distinct forms, one at a time.

For Hardy, however, the experience of nature cannot be rendered through vision alone; to be in nature is to be touched by it as Elaine Scarry and Gillian Beer have shown. The temporally extended represention of natural forms both reveals the material limitations of Hardy's eye and offers the reader a sense of the tangible distinctness of natural forms. While empiricists claimed that visual and tangible sensations are entirely different and only become associated through convention, nativists believed in an inherent comprehension of form, and thus of the distinct edges of perceived forms. Sir William Hamilton writes,

> [A] perception of the distinction of colours necessarily involves the perception of a discriminating line; for if one colour be laid beside or upon another, we only distinguish them as different by perceiving that they limit each other, which limitation necessarily affords a breadthless line—a line of demarcation. (Hamilton 165)

Darwin's nature, which is seen through uneducated empirical vision, is fluid and edgeless, but Hardy's, which is extended in both time and space, is composed of noncoalescent forms that are tangibly as well as visually distinct. Because the forms are presented gradually, and the reader is not confused into blending one form into the next, the chaotic flux of Darwinian nature is exchanged for a dynamic formal friction. Where Darwin presents masses of animal parts flowing together, Hardy presents a select number of whole animals, all elbowing one another for space in Clym's bank. Such a menagerie is, in this few foot radius, at peace and at play, but there is still a hint of danger in such proximity. Bees circle close to Clym's flesh, butterflies are made to quiver by his breath, flies are "huge" and "savage," and snakes weave through the underbrush. At the center of the description stands Clym, swinging the "glittering point of his hook" up and down through the masses of fluttering, leaping, and sunning creatures.

The tangible hardness and sharpness of this glittering point is opposed to the diaphanous wings of butterflies, legs of grasshoppers, fern fronds, and snake skins, to be ultimately set against the blood pounding through the almost painfully delicate and transparent baby rabbit ears. Beer's reading of touch as an expression of physical pleasure overlooks this tangible danger. The "pleasures of 'forced limitation'" (Beer 256) are called into question on all sides by the possibility of pain. In Darwin the transparency of bodies results from an illusory overlay of one edgeless form upon another, indicating evolutionary relation through visual analogy. In Hardy the transparency of the rabbit ears declares their physical vulnerability rather than their evolutionary dynamism; in a nativistic nature there can be no painless penetration of forms. If forms are distinct and have edges there is always the possibility that these edges may be sharp enough to wound; if patterns of a carpet will not coalesce, neither will bodies.

What is here just a hint of tangible wounding is, as Elaine Scarry has demonstrated at length, explicitly enacted throughout Hardy's work; nature is frequently aggressively and violently tangible. In Chapter 14 of *Tess* sunlight falls "like red-hot pokers upon cupboards, chest of drawers, and other furniture" (136); in Little Hintock forest the "lichen ate the vigour of the stalk, and the ivy slowly strangled to death the promising sapling" while the tree branches are "disfigured with wounds resulting from their mutual rubbings and blows" (*Woodlanders* 41, 234); even raindrops fall like "bullets" (*Collected Stories* 300). Returning to Tess's entangled garden we find that although there are no obviously predatory forms, all the organisms described are in the process of scarring or being scarred by one another.

> The outskirt of the garden in which Tess found herself had been left unculti-
> vated for some years, and was now damp and rank with juicy grass which
> sent up mists of pollen at a touch; and with tall blooming weeds emitting
> offensive smells—weeds whose red and yellow and purple hues formed a
> polychrome as dazzling as that of cultivated flowers. She went stealthily as a
> cat through this profusion of growth, gathering cuckoo-spittle on her skirts,
> cracking snails that were underfoot, staining her hands with thistle-milk and
> slug-slime, and rubbing off upon her naked arms sticky blights which,
> though snow-white on the apple-tree trunks, made madder stains on her
> skin.   (*Tess* 178–79)

Hardy achieves his vision of a gorgeously rapacious nature through the precise description of the sharp and tender surfaces of the undergrowth; there are more words describing the tangible qualities of the garden than its visible aspect. The narrative eye moves through the foliage with the same gradual motion as Tess, noting the specific colors, and distinct, botanically accurate organisms, seeming to catch on one form, then the next, just as Tess's clothing catches on the "sticky blights" of the garden.

Beer's description of Tess as "immersed in this sticky life and death" suggests a rather too-fluid conception of form (Beer 256). Hardy emphasizes the tangible destructiveness of nature by allowing the reader only enough time to image each distinct form fully before it is replaced by the next. The reader has barely imaged the "juicy grass" when "mists of pollen," then "tall blooming weeds," must be envisioned. Nor will Hardy allow for an easy transition from one similar form to another. Rather than offering adjacent images of grass, weeds, and trees, he alternates the analogous with nonanalogous forms, making the reader image grass, then mists, weeds, then colors, cultivated flowers, then Tess, and so forth. The images thus push through the mind without overlapping, and perception is successive rather than compounding. This is particularly noticeable toward the end of the passage, where parts of Tess's body (skirts, feet, hands, arms) alternate with plant parts or excrescences (cuckoo-spittle, cracked snails, thistle-milk, slug-slime, sticky blights). As in Darwin's descriptions, the bodies of both Tess and the plants are fragmented, but here the forms are neither similar enough nor contemporaneous enough to be interchangeable. There is no visual analogy between Tess and the plants, as there is between Darwin's pigeons or the limbs of men and animals; the natural forms, like the patterns in the carpet, touch but never interweave.

One always has the sense while reading a Hardyan description that one has missed something, and there is a strong temptation to go back and reread. This sense of lost complexity, of detail barely missed, is another result of Hardy's nativistic narrative eye, which perceives forms just slowly enough that they can be imaged distinctly, but fast enough that the replacement of one by the next seems somewhat jarring. For example, when the narrator describes "rubbing off upon her naked arms sticky blights which, though snow-white on the apple-tree trunks, made madder stains on her skin," the reader must image Tess's arms, the sticky blights, their whiteness, the tree trunks, and their darker color against Tess's skin all in the space of a few lines, and all for a single visual effect. Although such imaging is possible, it is rather exhausting, and creates the feeling of an impending deadline for the reader. The artful pacing of Hardy's descriptions causes the reader to feel both hurried and delighted by the animals and plants she or he sees. The temptation to move as quickly as possible to the next form, and thus to perceive more of the total landscape, is balanced against the desire to linger over the single form and catch the intensity of its beauty. Darwin's attempt to image all impressions whatever results in an inevitable perceptual coalescence. Hardy's selective vision is sufficiently

slow and detailed that the reader images each form separately, but sufficiently fast and populous as to result in the almost tangible pressing of one
form against another as the narrative eye perceives them in succession. The
perception of a tangible world is thus portrayed as being in itself a tangible
experience; the forms imaged by the reader seem to have dimension and
force enough to create the pressure of population in the reader's mind.

The apparent abundance of Hardy's nature, the sensual "fullness"
that Beer describes results from the limitation and demarcation of the
number of forms portrayed, not from Darwinian overabundance. Hardy's
perception of abundance is necessarily linked to pressure and crowding,
and is thus more Malthusian than Darwin's constantly multiplying forms.
While visual proximity is consummated when two forms coalesce, the
consummation of tangible proximity offers a powerful demonstration of
distinctness; to touch something is at once to become part of it and to feel
one's difference from it. In Hardy's nature it is this double-edged quality of
tangible objects that is the model for natural and perceptual processes; the
proximity of the objects in Hardy's landscapes frequently serves to emphasize their distinctness. In the farewell of Angel and Tess to Talbothays
tangible greeting enacts parting.

> To dissipate the sadness of this recital Tess went and bade all her favourite
> cows good-bye, touching each of them with her hand, and as she and Clare
> stood side by side at leaving, as if united body and soul, there would have
> been something peculiarly sorry in their aspect to one who should have seen
> it truly; two limbs of one life, as they outwardly were, his arm touching hers,
> her skirts touching him, facing one way, as against all the dairy facing the
> other, speaking in their adieux as "we," and yet sundered like the poles.
> (*Tess* 323)

In Tess and Angel's touch is a departure; the coming together of hands and
bodies results in an announcement of their difference, a proclamation of
their perpetual condition of going apart. Because of the paradoxical quality
of tangibility, Hardy is able to emphasize difference simply by reiterating
contact; the more parts of Tess and Angel that touch one another, the more
obvious is their separation.

The tragedy of Hardy's world is frequently enunciated in just these
terms of impenetrability; tangibility both causes scarring and prevents
union. The reader experiences this sense of distinctness of objects through
the almost physically difficult process of envisioning all the pieces of
Hardy's landscapes. The narrative eye hurries from one point to another
and the reader hurries to image each form before the next one pushes it
aside. Hardy's narrative images, like sheep jostling and butting one another

as they rush through a gate, thus exemplify his world of tangibly distinct and frictional objects, while at the same time purveying the delightful "plenitude" mentioned by Beer and Alcorn. If we compare Darwin's and Hardy's entangled banks we find that, ironically enough, Hardy has more effectively represented the Darwinian struggle for the fittest than did Darwin. Where Darwin's forms flux playfully around and through one another, Hardy's tangible forms must compete for space in the landscape, on the page, and in the reader's mind. The Hardyan eye is thus more like Darwin's personified natural selection that is "always intently watching each slight accidental alteration . . . and carefully selecting each" (*Origin* 189) than is Darwin's own narrative eye.

II

While Darwin's vision is phylogenetic, Hardy's is ontogenetic. Hardy limits his vision to individual forms and individual life spans, rejecting the sort of coalescent optical illusions that allow Darwin's forms to transcend time and space by becoming edgeless and multitudinous. In Darwin's nature the individual form blossoms into ancestors and descendants, allowing an easy motion through evolutionary history. Although Hardy's landscape does contain past forms compacted into present ones, the various previous manifestations of those forms are inaccessible to the viewer. Darwin is able to see the breakup of the globe in the Cordilleras, but for Tess the Froom valley is "a level landscape compounded of old landscapes long forgotten" (*Tess* 158); neither Tess nor the reader has access to this history. The impossibility of moving through time, of previous forms replicating themselves in present ones, lies at the root of Tess's tragedy.

Hardy demonstrates the impossibility of overcoming time and place by presenting, then undermining, empirical optical illusions. The characters' desires for access to the past or union with others is portrayed through coalescent illusions that are then explained in noncoalescent, nativistic terms. Alec's practical joke in the cathedral at Kingsbere is all the more cruel because it plays on Tess's yearning for the resuscitation of the grand d'Urberville past.

> She musingly turned to withdraw, passing near an altar-tomb, the oldest of them all, on which was a recumbent figure. In the dusk she had not noticed it before, and would hardly have noticed it now but for an odd fancy that the effigy moved. As soon as she drew close to it she discovered all in a moment that the figure was a living person; and the shock to her sense of not having been alone was so violent that she was quite overcome, and sank down nigh

to fainting, not however till she had recognized Alec d'Urberville in the form. (*Tess* 448–49)

Like Tess, the reader experiences a moment of mystical possibility that is suddenly and intensely reversed by the realization that the apparently moving stone is in fact a feigning human, and the successive realization that the human is the very unmystical Alec D'Urberville. The tangible stone has not become intangible, allowing present and past d'Urberville's to exist together; the possibility for access to an ancestral past is raised and then mockingly withdrawn as time and space are once again asserted in the form of Tess's rapist. Tess cannot overcome her fate any more than spirit can become flesh or ancient forms can coalesce into one present one. The Darwinian leap back and forth along the genealogical line through optical illusion is impossible in Hardy's nativistic world. Where Darwin's rhetorical illusions blur ontogenetic processes into a phylogenetic flux in order to make evolution visible, Hardy foregrounds the tragedy resulting from ontogenetic limitations. While we can imagine the phylogenetic order we must live in the ontogenetic one, and cannot, therefore, escape our inherited fate.

Such narrative explication of empirical illusion occurs throughout Hardy's novel, foiling the union of contemporary as well as temporally distant forms. When Tess first hears Angel's voice coming "as it were out of the belly of a dun cow in the stalls" (*Tess* 164), the narrator is quick to explain that "it had been spoken by a milker behind the animal, whom she had not hitherto perceived." When Angel sees Tess as "a whole sex condensed into one typical form" and calls her "Artemis, Demeter, and other fanciful names" (*Tess* 187) we are dryly informed that the gray background and "the cold gleam of day from the north-east" are responsible for this unification of images, and that "his own face, though he did not think of it, wore the same aspect to her." When Hardy deals with optical illusions that are meant to be experienced by the reader rather than one of his characters he stalls the coalescence before it begins. In the description of Eustacia's profile in *The Return of the Native* the presentation is so meticulously constructed as to undermine the coalescent effect.

A profile was visible against the dull monochrome of cloud around her; and it was as though side shadows from the features of Sappho and Mrs. Siddons had converged upwards from the tomb to form an image like neither but suggesting both. This, however, was mere superficiality. In respect of character a face may make certain admissions by its outline; but it fully confesses only in its changes. (*Return* 61)

The comparison of Eustacia's face with those of Sappho and Mrs. Siddons has the potential to collapse time and space in the same way as do Darwin's descriptions of the geological formations in Glen Roy. Darwin, however, surprises his readers with analogous structures, allowing the conflation of forms to take place accidentally in the reader's mind, while Hardy describes distinct forms presented in spatial relation to one another, causing the operation of illusion to be exposed and transformed into an explanatory narrative. Rather than imaging one form superimposed over another, the reader images the distinct forms of Sappho and Mrs. Siddons moving upward (Hardy even gives us the direction in which to move the spatially extended forms) toward that of Eustacia. As in Brewster's explanation of the Neckar Rhomboid, this apparently atemporal conflation involves the motion of the eye across the visual field from one form to another. The rapturous blending of forms is thus foiled as their conflation is shown to be a temporal process rather than a spontaneous one. Hardy thus demonstrates imagistically what he so often portrays thematically—that the difficulties involved in transcending human nature are essentially the same as the difficulties involved in transcending time and space. Eustacia's tragedy is that she is not Sappho or Mrs. Siddons, and no amount of wishing, or theatrical posing, can transport her from her present condition to theirs. Consequently, the sort of coalescent vision that allows Darwin's forms to transcend time and space is shown to be a distortion of the nature of human experience. The narrative eye brings the reader back to earth by demonstrating that human vision, like human life, cannot transcend its material limitations even through the happy accident of optical illusion.

A similar denial of the possibility of coalescent optical illusion occurs a few chapters later in the description of Eustacia as a divinity.

> In a dim light, and with a slight rearrangement of her hair, her general figure might have stood for that of either of the higher female deities. The new moon behind her head, an old helmet upon it, a diadem of accidental dew-drops round her brow, would have been adjuncts sufficient to strike the note of Artemis, Athena, or Hera respectively, with as close an approximation to the antique as that which passes muster on many respected canvases. (*Return* 73)

J. G. Bullen, in comparing Hardy's portrait of Eustacia to the portrait paintings of Sir Joshua Reynolds, states that in "the manner of the classical composite portrait, he [Hardy] surrounds his central figure with emblems derived from romantic images of women" (Bullen 107). This process of collection, or selection, of visual objects is characteristic of Hardyan nativistic perception. Rather than seeing the coalescence of Eustacia's form with those of Hera and Athena, the reader sees a series of objects collected from the earthly landscape in which Eustacia actually walks—Egdon's new moon, an old helmet, the accidental dewdrops; their presence in the myth-opoeic portrayal causes the divine adornments to degenerate into disguise. Unlike the viewer of Reynolds's *Sarah Siddons as 'The Tragic Muse,'* Rossetti's *Astarte Syriaca* or the *Mona Lisa,* the reader of Hardy's description is not presented with an ideal landscape, but with a hodgepodge of every day objects that never manage to equal more than the sum of their parts. The typological vision of Eustacia as poet, actress, and goddess breaks down as Hardy's narrative eye moves from one object to the next, revealing them to be props rather than symbols.

J. Hillis Miller, in his discussion of the various levels of Hardy's narrative voice, suggests that Hardy allows the reader to see both past and present in the structure of the shearing barn of *Far from the Madding Crowd.*

> The focusing of the point of view, however, is qualified by language which gives the reader a temporal perspective on the barn which no physical vision, cinema, or stage set could provide. The barn as it presently looks is placed in the context of the mind's knowledge of its four centuries of existence. The reader sees the present in the perspective of the past, with that double vision so characteristic of Hardy.   (Miller, *Distance* 60)

Miller's argument rests on Hardy's statement that the procedures of sheep-shearing—the clothing, appearance and language of the men—had not changed in ten generations so that the scene resembles, in Miller's words, "a timeless ritual." Hardy makes it clear, however, that this is an inter-pretation rather than a perception. "Standing before this abraded pile, the eye regarded its present usage, the mind dwelt upon its past history, with a satisfied sense of functional continuity throughout" (195); the viewer does not see the past form in the present one, he only thinks that it must have looked the same. We do not see two temporally distinct images coalescing, only a single "picture of to-day in its frame of four hundred years ago" (196); the past is only a conceptual frame, not another picture. Further-more, Hardy begins the description by placing the barn among other build-ings that now serve new functions.

> One could say about this barn, what could hardly be said of either the church or the castle . . . that the purpose which had dictated its original erection was the same with that to which it was still applied. . . . For once medi-aevalism and modernism had a common standpoint.   (195–96)

This string of disclaimers suggest how unusual Hardy considers this commonality to be. It is not possible to look at the church or the castle and find access to previous times; nor is it possible to look at the D'Urberville mansion or the cathedral at Kingsbere and find oneself present in the past. Hardy certainly portrays present forms adjacent to or surrounded by ancient ones, but this technique allows for the kind of comparison that Beer describes as having the "speculative, argumentatively extended character of analogy" that "ranges it closer to narrative than to image" (Beer 80). Placing Tess above the geological strata of ancient hills, or placing curious Casterbridge children beside the skeletons of Roman soldiers, serves to argumentatively demonstrate the changes in landscape and way of life by allowing the narrative eye to move back and forth between the two forms.

When Hardy portrays an actual disguise, such as Diggory Venn's use of the turves as camouflage, a similar motion of the eye back and forth between body and disguise prevents their overlay. The process of enclosure is portrayed in such painstaking narrative detail that Diggory and the turves are established as entirely distinct entities before their combination can be affected.

> Near him, as in divers places about the heath, were areas strewn with large turves, which lay edgeways and upside down awaiting removal by Timothy Fairway, previous to the winter weather. He took two of these as he lay, and dragged them over him till one covered his head and shoulders, the other his back and legs. The reddleman would now have been quite invisible, even by daylight; the turves, standing upon him with the heather upwards, looked precisely as if they were growing. He crept along again, and the turves upon his back crept with him. Had he approached without any covering the chances are that he would not have been perceived in the dusk; approaching thus, it was as though he burrowed underground.   (*Return* 87–88)

As with Tess in the garden the reader is asked to compare Diggory's body with the entirely nonanalogous forms of the turves, and their formal differences become evident through this comparison. Rather than showing Venn within or behind the turves, Hardy states that they "[stand] upon him with the heather upwards." The reader has no image of a unified form; rather the passage suggests someone with an entangled bank growing on his head. Moreover, the donning of the disguise is a physically arduous and temporally extended task; Venn must "drag" the heavy bundles onto him, and once the two are combined the contrast between the lithe mobility of Venn and the stolid weight of the turves becomes comical. Both the creeping turves and the tunneling man seem singularly silly and uncomfortable. The disguise, which is so effective against Wildeve and Eustacia, has the opposite effect on the reader, making Venn all the more conspicuous. Again, this imagistic obviousness is a result of Hardy's narrative eye moving from one form to another rather than perceiving both at once. In his analysis of the Neckar rhomboid Brewster notes that by "hiding *A* with the finger . . . *X* appears forward, . . . and the same effect is produced by hiding *X, A* becoming then nearest to the eye" (Brewster 367). Hardy's continual shift of focus from man to turves and back has the same effect. A reference to the hiding reddleman is followed by the image of the standing turves; when Diggory moves we first focus on him creeping ("He crept along again"), then on the turves creeping ("and the turves upon his back crept with him"), then again on Diggory burrowing underground. It is almost as though, like Brewster, Hardy had placed a finger over the turves to make Diggory loom forward in the reader's mind, then again over Diggory, so that only one distinct form can be seen at a time. The result is an emphasis on the distinction that is invariably associated with tangible contiguity. The reader sees a man standing on turves, followed by turves standing on man, but the two forms are never united.

A similar avoidance of union through proximity occurs in *The Woodlanders,* when Giles Winterborne meets Grace Melbury in the square at Sherton Abbas. Not only is the disparity between Giles and Grace made apparent at the moment of their touch, but the contiguous distinction between Giles and the tree he carries becomes obvious when man and tree are placed in an urban context.

> It was impossible to avoid re-discovering Winterborne every time she passed that way, for standing, as he always did at this season of the year, with his specimen appletree in the midst, the boughs rose above the heads of the farmers and brought a delightful suggestion of orchards into the heart of the town. When her eye fell upon him for the last time he was standing somewhat apart, holding the tree like an ensign, and looking on the ground. (*Woodlanders* 29)

From the first, the image of Giles beneath the apple tree is perceived by Marty South as an artificial visual effect. The importing of trees into the square, like the placing of one woman's hair on another woman's head, involves a form of transformation that, like Eustacia as goddess or Venn as turves, amounts to little more than a self-announcing disguise. Moreover, as in the case of Venn and the turves, Winterborne is ultimately made to seem somewhat ridiculous (not demeaningly so, as perhaps he is to Grace, but humorously ridiculous) by his attachment to the tree. "Winterborne, being fixed to the spot by his appletree, could not advance to meet her: he held out his spare hand with his hat in it." The contrast between Winterborne's attempt at a polite greeting and the rooted stiffness lent to his body by the tree he holds at once exposes and excuses his humiliation by pointing up the distinction between the two figures. Although the tangible connection of the man and the tree causes an exchange of mechanical functions and motions, as Elaine Scarry argues, this tangible association is never accompanied by a visual union. The effect of the passage turns on the whimsical similarity between the stances of man and tree when the narrative eye moves from one to the other and back again. If Giles were hidden behind the tree, or the two were seen as one, Grace would be confused rather than disdainfully embarrassed as she approaches; however, Giles holds the tree so distinctly beside him—"like an ensign"—that the visual comparison must be narrative. Scarry's description of the "immersion" (97) of man into tree, like Beer's description of Tess "immersed" in the garden, suggests an interpenetration of forms more complete than is possible in Hardy's world. The three figures—tree, man, and woman—form a fragile chain of contiguous distinction; Giles's simultaneous longings to release the tree and to embrace the woman—the hope for union and the desire for separation—are bodied forth equally well by the tangible linkage of the three contiguous yet distinct figures. The impossibility of a mutually desired union is similarly apparent in the contiguity of Tess and Angel's hands in the wash basin.

> The place having been rather hastily prepared for them they washed their hands in one basin. Clare touched hers under the water.
>
> "Which are my fingers and which are yours?" he said, looking up. "They are very much mixed."
>
> "They are all yours," said she, very prettily, and endeavoured to be gayer than she was.   (284)

The reader recognizes that Angel's description of their bodies as "mixed" is wishful thinking, and that Tess's claim to coalescent perception—"They are all yours"—is a vain attempt to disguise her awareness of their separateness.

In Chapter 14 of *Tess,* the narrator goes so far as to make an outright claim for the coalescence of forms that is contradicted by the subsequent description of Tess working. "A field-man is a personality afield; a field-woman is a portion of the field; she has somehow lost her own margin, imbibed the essence of her surrounding, and assimilated herself with it" (*Tess* 137–38). So the narrator claims; yet, in the very next sentence this claim is contradicted by the tangible distinctness and painful edges of the forms surrounding the field-women. "The women . . . wore drawn cotton bonnets with great flapping curtains to keep off the sun, and gloves to prevent their hands being wounded by the stubble." From above and below the women's margins are impinged upon and must be protected from the field into which they have supposedly been assimilated. The claimed coalescent perception of the women as marginless beings is not a Hardyan panorama that is later supplemented by "close-ups." Even from a distance the women's forms stand out brightly and distinctly as the narrative eye perceives them one by one. "There was one wearing a pale pink jacket, another in a cream-coloured tight-sleeved gown, another in a petticoat as red as the arms of the reaping-machine; and others, older, in the brown-rough 'wropper' or over-all." The field-men described in the previous paragraph, with their identical print shirts and leather straps, seem less visually distinct than these women. The narrator describes the eye returning "involuntarily" to Tess, but such unwilled action is belied by the nativistic motion of the narrative eye; Tess does not suddenly appear before the reader's eye, but is selected by the eye as it "returns" in its motion across the visual field. Tess's edgelessness is never actually made visible; we do not see Tess flowing into the field as we see Darwin's pigeons flowing into one another. The use of liquid vocabulary, such as "imbibed," and "assimilated," hints at empirical flow, but bears no perceivable relation to the field being reaped or to the distinct forms of the field-women in it.

What the reader does see of a field-woman afield is far from fluid or edgeless.

> Her binding proceeds with clock-like monotony. From the sheaf last finished she draws a handful of ears, patting their tips with her left palm to bring them even. Then stooping low she moves forward, gathering the corn with both hands against her knees, and pushing her left gloved hand under the bundle to meet the right on the other side, holding the corn in an embrace like that of a lover. She brings the ends of the bond together, and kneels on the sheaf while she ties it, beating back her skirts now and then when lifted by the breeze. A bit of her naked arm is visible between the buff leather of the gauntlet and the sleeve of her gown; and as the day wears on its feminine smoothness becomes scarified by the stubble, and bleeds. (*Tess* 138)

This description is less a picture of Tess than it is a point by point representation of the ways in which the wheat touches and is touched by her. Although very graceful, Tess's laborious fondling of the wheat is never osmotic; her body and the sheaf of wheat never flow into or even disappear behind one another. There seems to be a hint of union in her loverlike embrace, but even as Tess "brings the end of the bond together, and kneels" in an echo of the ritual of marriage the "feminine smoothness" of her skin is made to bleed by the coarse edges of the stubble. The previous reference to Tess as part of the field pales and is forgotten beside the vivid images of proximate distinction, and the myriad references to touch. Tess's movements of leaning, embracing, kneeling, and reaching that cause her body to move forward and down, performing a new action in each position, seem to define her as a narrative entity. Again Tess's motion parallels that of the narrative eye, as it moves onward from point to point across the landscape, and of the images passing through the reader's mind. Where Darwin's forms waver, fragment, and flow into other forms, Hardy's seem to move forward, pressing, and being pressed as they go, like the body through time and space.

Elaine Scarry has pointed out how Hardy's representations of work describe a union between the bodies of workers and the materials of their labor, causing them to be "grafted together so that there ceases to be a clear boundary separating them; the surfaces of the two are continuous with one another" (Scarry 96). J. Hillis Miller offers a similar reading when he points to "the intimate connection of man, implement, and environment" apparent in sheep-shears and hayrakes.

> To see it [the hayrake] as a disconnected "object" is an artificial and deriva-
> tive way of seeing it, for the rake by way of its use reaches out toward all the
> surrounding items in the community and can only by abstraction be detached
> from them.   (Miller, *Distance* 94)

Hayrakes and sheep-shears, however, are also sharp and dangerous, and Tess's body is cut and bleeds in the process of grafting. The loss of boundary experienced by Hardy's workers is not the visual formlessness of Darwin's animals, but a formal contiguity created by the sharing of adjacent surfaces that suggests, and frequently fulfills, the possibility of violence. The temporal immediacy of this violence needs to be borne in mind because it demonstrates a crucial distinction between Darwin's phylogenetic and Hardy's ontogenetic vision. Miller argues that the process of wounding creates a temporal, as well as physical, continuity throughout Hardy's novel.

> Sex, physical violence, and writing all involve a paradoxical act of cutting,
> piercing, or in some way altering some physical object. The paradox lies in
> the fact that the fissure at the same time establishes a continuity. It makes the
> thing marked a repetition and gives it in one way or another the power of
> reproducing itself in the future.   (Miller, *Fiction* 121)

Miller thus demonstrates a temporal continuity implied in the momentary physical interaction of body and object; Tess carries the scar of her labor forward through time. The "grafting" of forms leaves traces on the body, and the tragedy of Hardy's world is marked by such traces because they cannot, as we have seen, be altered once made. By placing the emphasis on temporal continuity rather than on physical contiguity, however, Miller's argument foregrounds repetition, the analogous reproduction of events through time, and deemphasizes the acts of wounding and touching themselves. "Any example of the division which joins is already a repetition, however far back one goes to seek the first one" (Miller, *Fiction* 121). Miller thus suggests that Hardy, like Darwin, offers a time-transcending representation, ordered by analogous patterns.

Hardy's portrayals of sex and violence, however, foreground the temporal and physical limitations of mortal bodies—bodies that cannot be reproduced once destroyed. Tess's rape and Prince's death are tragic because individual lives are not repeatable or changeable; the interaction of tangible bodies in time causes pain and death. Darwin's empirically coalescent bodies are not tragic because they are perceived from an extratemporal perspective. Although the analogical phylogenetic vision in Darwin's work offers a more theoretically powerful version of evolutionary history, Hardy's ontogenetic vision offers a more effective portrayal of the violence and death inherent in Darwin's theory. This sense of ontogenetic limitation is created by Hardy's use of a nativistically limited narrative eye.

III

In his portrayal of entangled nature Hardy describes only a limited number of forms distinctly; when he uncovers empirical illusions he denies the possibility of single visual forms multiplying within the same visual space. Ultimately, Hardy's aesthetic of selection leads away from Darwinian multiplicity and toward a visual landscape in which the human figure is the narrative focus. Gillian Beer ascribes to Hardy "an anthropomorphism which paradoxically denies human centrality and gives the human a fugitive and secondary role in his system of reference but not in his system of value" (Beer 252). She thus echoes many critics who describe humanity as decentered or marginalized in Hardy's landscape so that there is virtually no "place for the human within the natural order"; however, this decentering is counteracted by Hardy's narrative eye. While humanity may be miniature and fugitive on the broad expanse of the Darwinian heath, the single focus of Hardy's physiologically limited eye brings about the imagistic recentering of humanity and the marginalization of entangled nature. Because the artist orders a world idiosyncratically, the objects chosen to perceive will generally be human ones, and the landscape will fall into the periphery of the visual field. An essential principle of the Law of Visible

Direction is that the narrative eye's focus is singular. The eye is directed toward one central figure and thus away from all others, not pulled from point to point so as to be essentially unfocused, as in Darwin's jungle. We have already investigated the way in which Hardy's narrative eye selects forms to be represented, just as Brewster's eye perceives forms distinctly and one at a time. Implicit in such a model of perception is that while the perceiver focuses on the individual form, the rest of the visual field becomes indistinct.

Brewster uses the following experiment in his analysis of the Neckar rhomboid to demonstrate the relative indistinctness of those parts of the visual field that are perceived by the periphery of the retina.

> This experiment may be still more satisfactorily made by holding above the rhomboid a piece of ground glass (the ground side being farthest from the eye), and bringing one edge of it gradually down till it touches the point A, the other edge being kept at a distance from the paper. In this way AX, and all the lines diverging from A, become dimmer as they recede from A, and consequently A becomes the most forward point.   (Brewster 367)

Such singular focusing is an extension of Hardy's consistent practice of representing one form at a time. When he portrays the interaction between humans and nature the narrative eye moves from one form to another, highlighting parts of the landscape one at a time. On the other hand, when he portrays an entire landscape the narrative eye focuses on a single point. In such passages Hardy's aesthetic of selection involves an aesthetic of simplification as well, for as the eye remains focused on one form, the rest of the landscape sinks into formal obscurity, like the area under the curved glass.

An example of Hardyan selection slowing into simplification can be found in Grace Melbury's observation of her husband riding away through the autumnal landscape of the White-Hart Vale. The initial depiction of the organically abundant landscape gradually becomes more and more simplified as Grace concentrates on the visible point of her husband's horse against the darkening sky.

> The conspicuous coat of the active though blanching mare made horse and rider easy objects for the vision. . . . [He rode] surrounded by orchards lustrous with reds of apple-crops, berries, and foliage, the whole intensified by the gilding of the declining sun. The earth this year had been prodigally bountiful, and now was the supreme moment of her bounty. In the poorest spots the hedges were bowed with haws and blackberries; acorns cracked underfoot, and the burst husks of chestnuts lay exposing their auburn contents as if arranged by anxious sellers in a fruit-market. . . . Soon he rose

out of the valley, and skirted a high plateau of the chalk formation on his
right, which rested abruptly upon the fruity district of deep loam, the character and herbage of the two formations being so distinct that the calcareous
upland appeared but as a deposit of a few years' antiquity upon the level vale.
He kept along the edge of this high unenclosed country, and the sky behind
him being deep violet she could still see white Darling in relief upon it—a
mere speck now.   (*Woodlanders* 155)

The initially detailed autumnal fruit and foliage dims to formal indistinctness as Grace follows her husband's path, and the general landscape formations come to assume a homogeneous simplicity. In the early section nature's bounty is apparent: apples, berries, foliage, haws and blackberries,
acorns and chestnuts. As in the description of Tess in the garden, Hardy
arranges the fruits before the reader, crowding the narrative eye with vivid,
distinct forms. As Fitzpiers rides farther away the already selective landscape becomes increasingly featureless; Grace's eye ceases to pick out the
forms that Fitzpiers passes and focuses only on the single form of the horse
Darling. Although it is this point that is receding, the landscape around it
grows dimmer and dimmer. Hardy emphasizes this simplification by portraying the geology of the vale as composed of two formations that are "so
distinct" that the landscape is reduced to three bands: the dark band of the
"fruity district of deep loam," the light band of the "high plateau of the
chalk formation," and the "deep violet" of the sky. The "mere speck" of
Fitzpiers's horse as he rides "along the edge" of the second band com-
pletes the picture. Levine suggests that the very presence of peripheral
forms has the effect of deemphasizing the human: "[I]t is hard to keep the
central character in single focus because so much natural detail incessantly
struggles to displace it" (Levine 231). The reader is being led through this
detail, however, which falls into shadow and insignifance as the eye focuses in on the central human point.

Moreover, Hardy makes clear that this focusing of the vision is a
willful human act that results in an aesthetic form of perception. As Diggory Venn looks up toward the Rainbarrow his specific perception of landscape forms gives way to the intense focus on Eustacia.

The scene before the reddleman's eyes was a gradual series of ascents from
the level of the road backward into the heart of the heath. It embraced
hillocks, pits, ridges, acclivities, one behind the other, till all was finished by
a high hill cutting against the still light of the sky. . . .

As the resting man looked at the barrow he became aware that its
summit, hitherto the highest object in the whole prospect round, was sur-
mounted by something higher. . . . Such a perfect, delicate, and necessary
finish did the figure give to the dark pile of hills that it seemed to be the only

obvious justification of their outline. Without it, there was the dome without the lantern; with it the architectural demands of the mass were satisfied. The scene was strangely homogeneous, in that the vale, the upland, the barrow, and the figure above it amounted only to unity. Looking at this or that member of the group was not observing a complete thing, but a fraction of a thing. (*Return* 20)

The single focus on a human figure creates an aesthetic "unity" and "finish" by rendering the nonhuman part of the landscape "homogeneous"; the sense of homogeneity results from Diggory looking at the specific "member" of Eustacia. Any other focus would fragment the picture into so many hillocks, pits, and ridges, but attention to the human figure offers an aesthetic vision by the elimination of the specific forms of an entangled nature.

Hardy makes explicit reference to focusing on the human figure as an artistic act when he identifies his artistic method as "that of infusing emotion into the baldest external objects either by the presence of a human figure among them, or by mark of some human connection with them" (Millgate 123–24). In these passages we see the perceptual causality implied in this way of seeing; by focusing on "the presence of a human figure among them" through his nativistic narrative eye Hardy allows the forms of nature to fall out of focus and become "the baldest external objects."

In Hardy's writing, the humanized world is always an ordered one; the effect of humanity on nature is to make it, or to attempt to make it, more regular, whether through the naming of constellations, the ploughing of fields, the breeding of domestic animals, the dyeing of cloth, or the cleaning of houses. Perceptually speaking, the humanized landscape is nativistic; it is composed of the same simple, monolithic forms as Sir William Hamilton's primary perceptual landscape. In Hardy's works, however, these forms are the product of concentrated effort on the part of the perceiver, not the product of uneducated vision. Like farming, breeding, or cleaning, perceiving is a form of work for Hardy, and just as the landscape that is most thoroughly worked is the one with the most ploughed fields, the most thoroughly bred animals, and the cleanest and most regular buildings, the landscape that is most intensely perceived is the one in which natural forms are reduced to their simplest, most nativistically primary state. Elaine Scarry describes work in Hardy's fiction as the "reciprocal alterations between man and world," expressed in "a constant set of movements across the passing days and years," that "do not simply happen to occur but are consciously sought" (Scarry 92–94). The nativistic eye, with its steady motion from point to point, its alteration of angle and lens shape that results in an alteration of the perceived landscape, and its conscious direction of its focus can be said to be an organ that is constantly at work ordering the perceived world, just as the tools and hands of Hardy's characters are constantly at work ordering the physical world. Miller notes that in his reciprocal relationship with the land, the Hardyan worker "has yielded to nature in the sense that, for example, his way of cultivating the land is determined by the soil in that region, but at the same time he has made his own mark on nature, a mark which gives it importance and infuses emotion into it" (Miller 93). A similar reciprocal relationship exists between the narrative eye and the landscape. In the short story "The Withered Arm," a woman travelling to the city to find a life-changing cure stops to look across the fields toward her goal.

> She halted before a pool called Rushy-pond, flanked by the ends of two hedges; a railing ran through the center of the pond, dividing it in half. Over the railing she saw the low green country; over the green trees the roofs of the town; over the roofs a white flat facade, denoting the entrance to the county jail. On the roof of this front specks were moving about.   (*Selected Stories* 90)

The focus of Gertrude's glance are the specks on the roof of the jail; the other forms of the landscape represent only the periphery of the visual field. The physical limitations on her vision force Gertrude, and the reader, to see Casterbridge and its surrounding fields through a singular focus. This singularity, however, brings about the emotional transformation of the landscape into a spatial register of her anxiety; the point of her emotional concern is in focus and everything else is peripheral. Similarly, Grace's concentration on Fitzpiers causes the landscape to fall into obscurity, but when her focus shifts to the gleaming blade of Giles Winterborne's shovel as he ascends the hill toward her, the specific peripheral forms of nature come gradually into focus to the extent that they are associated with, or attached to, his face and body (*Woodlanders* 156). Consciousness is unified with landscape through visual perception; because it is the perceived world that is imaged by Hardy's reader, the ordering of perception and the ordering of earth and stone are identical. Hardy's selective vision not only resees, but also remakes the natural landscape into a human artifact. While Darwin returns his reader to a state of primary empirical vision through the playfulness of sensory overstimulation, Hardy returns his to a state of primary nativistic vision through the labor of perceiving a landscape intensely and passionately.

The most extended, and perhaps the most extreme, example of the simplification of nature resulting from a gradual focusing in on a human form can be found in the first chapter of *The Return of the Native*. It is not until the second chapter that a human figure appears, except for the "furze-cutter," who serves as a center of vicarious perception for the narrator rather than as a focal point. As Egdon "embrowns itself" the forms of nature become less and less detailed and more simplified. From the first, the landscape is little more than lightness above and darkness below: "The heaven being spread with this pallid screen and the earth with the darkest vegetation, their meeting-line at the horizon was clearly marked" (11). As the sky grows darker, even this fundamental division is lost.

> The sombre stretch of rounds and hollows seemed to rise and meet the evening gloom in pure sympathy, the heath exhaling darkness as rapidly as the heavens precipitated it. And so the obscurity in the air and the obscurity in the land closed together in a black fraternization towards which each advanced halfway. (*Return* 12)

The setting of the sun over Egdon represents the very gradual focusing of the narrative eye on the highway, and the human figure on it. By the end of the chapter the heath has grown so dark and featureless that the white road and the white hair of Captain Vye stand out as distinctly as if Hardy were creating them out of nothing. Brewster, in his nativistic analysis of the pattern in the carpet, notes that "if we direct the mind particularly to the contemplation of the red [pattern in the carpet] . . . the green pattern will sometimes vanish entirely" (Brewster, Colour 10). As the reader's attention is directed toward the human figure crossing the heath, the heath itself grows darker and darker until it vanishes completely. In its most extended form, then, Hardy's selective vision results in the selecting out of all natural objects; the simplification of landscape leads to its disappearance.

Daniel R. Scwharz suggests that "imagining an experiencing perceiver is itself a movement toward control and order, an effort to exorcise the shadow of darkness that the narrator feels hovers over the heath" (Schwarz 35). In fact, as we have seen, Hardy's vision intensifies and homogenizes the darkness in order to focus upon the human figure; rather than a "quest for form," envisioning the heath involves an escape from the pressure of entangled Darwinian forms. Hardy's eye, is therefore ordering superabundance, not emptiness. Nor is it simply, as Levines states, discovering "the large general patterns . . . without imposing upon the observed world the passion for centrality and dominance to which his own characters so frequently succumb" (Levine 233). Hardy's eye is just as willfully deterministic as is his inexorable plot structure. Through his nativistic portrayals of the natural world Hardy involves the reader in the process of perceptually ordering a landscape. The more intense the focus on what Hardy called the "presence of a human figure among them" or the "mark

of some human connection with them" the "balder" or more featureless
the forms of nature become. Alcorn, by suggesting that post-Darwinian
nature writers are attracted to desolate landscapes because "the microscopic quality of Darwin's vision meant that an arid plain became for the
first time as interesting as a florid life-filled jungle" (Alcorn 5–6) inverts
Hardy's approach. Rather than perceiving entanglement in desolation,
Hardy's eye simplifies entangled nature into desolation in order to foreground humanity.

Hardy's statements about infusing emotion into landscape are part of a
discussion of artists whom he considers to share his approach to representing landscape.

> The method of Boldini, the painter of "The Morning Walk" in the French
> Gallery two or three years ago (a young lady beside an ugly blank wall on an
> ugly highway)—of Hobbema, in his view of a road with formal lopped trees
> and flat tame scenery—is that of infusing emotion into the baldest external
> objects either by the presence of a human figure among them, or by mark of
> some human connection with them.   (Millgate 123–24)

> My art is to intensify the expression of things, as is done by Crivelli, Bellini,
> &c., so that the heart and inner meaning is made vividly visible.   (Millgate
> 183)

Some critics have been at pains to find a stylistic link between Boldini,
Hobbema, Crivelli, and Bellini. Dennis Taylor and J. G. Bullen have been
most successful by linking Hardy's personal attraction to desolate scenery
with his stated aesthetic of "beauty in ugliness," and his penchant for
"dramatic light effects" and vivid visual patterns (Taylor 68) that divide
the landscape into distinct homogeneous regions.[1] Taylor in particular has
shown how Hardy's interest in patterns was influenced by Darwin's evolutionary diagram, which, by spatializing natural history, offered a limited
and obscured, yet still visually comprehensible pattern for evolutionary
variation. If we look at these paintings with an eye to the perceptual model
they seem to demonstrate, it becomes clear that, in keeping with this desire
for visual simplification, Hardy is attracted to those paintings that emphasize the Law of Visible Direction and encourage the reader to focus on a
central human point in a simplified landscape.

In *The Agony in the Garden* (Fig. 4), Bellini renders the landscape in
such smoothly featureless forms that the eye seems to be out of focus
whenever it rests on anything but the human figures. This simplicity of
outline allows no stopping place for the eye unless it rests on Christ. The
painting thus enacts the singular focus and peripheral blurring consistent
with the Law of Visible Direction for the viewer. While Hobbema and

Fig. 4. Bellini, *The Agony in the Garden.* Courtesy of the National Gallery, London.

Boldini do not portray a simplified landscape, the rigorous sightlines of the paintings prevent the viewer from focusing on anything but a human figure. In Hobbema's *The Avenue, Middelharnis* (Fig. 5) the lines of the road, the tree tops, and the horizon all lead the eye toward the human figure, thus locating it directly at the foramen centrale. The viewer consequently focuses on the human figure and allows the rest of the painting to fall out of the direct focus of the eye. Hardy's description of the painting—"[a] view of a road with formal lopped trees and flat tame scenery"—although presumably pointing up its ugliness, calse attention to exactly those features that create this single, central focus: the sightlines created by the road and trees and the "flat" or two-dimensional quality of the rest of the picture due to its being perceived by the periphery of the retina. The same is largely true of Boldini's *The Morning Stroll* (Fig. 6), for although it differs significantly in style from Hobbema's work, it shares the strong geometrical sightlines and the central human figure. Again, Hardy's description of its ugliness calls attention to this geometry by pointing to the wall and the highway as the central features of the painting. In all of these cases there is a willful direction of the reader's or viewer's eye toward a specific point on the landscape, and this direction is emphasized by features of the landscape itself. If the viewer of Hobbema's painting attempts to let his or her eye wander over the canvas it is led inexorably back to the central human point.

Fig. 5. Hobbema, *The Avenue, Middelharnis.* Courtesy of the National Gallery, London.

The operation of these paintings is thus much like the process of reading Hardy describes in his essay "The Profitable Reading of Fiction":

> He [the reader] will see what his author is aiming at, and by affording full scope to his own insight, catch the vision which the writer has in his eye, and is endeavoring to project upon the paper, even while it half eludes him. (*Life and Art* 64)

The viewer of these paintings does not experience the landscape so much as the painter's specific focus upon that landscape, just as Hardy's reader must direct his or her attention toward the same visual phenomena as does Hardy's narrator. J. B. Bullen has shown that Hardy was attracted to Impressionism because it "embodied a highly subjective response to visual stimuli" (Bullen 182). Hardy expresses this subjectivity in terms of clearing the scene through visual selection and omission.

> [The Impressionist's] principle is, as I understand it, that what you carry away with you from a scene is the true feature to grasp; or in other words, what appeals to your own individual eye and heart in particular amid much

that does not so appeal, and which you therefore omit to record.   (Millgate 191).

Once again, it is the selectiveness of the aesthetic technique and the relative featurelessness of the resulting landscape which appeals to Hardy. Bellini and Whistler have quite different styles, and the Impressionist rendering of forms is more consistent with empirical vision than it is with nativistic vision. Hardy's definition of Impressionism by the one element that associates it with nativistic modes of perception demonstrates his eagerness to read all visual phenomena, and judge all art, according to the nativistic model.

J. G. Bullen offers the following passage as an example of Hardy's concentration on "the illuminative medium" of the landscape, rather than its "constituent elements" (Bullen 198), and of the similarity between Hardy's and Turner's landscapes.

> Here, in the valley, the world seems to be constructed upon a smaller and more delicate scale; the fields are mere paddocks, so reduced that from this height their hedgerows appear a network of dark green threads overspreading the paler green of the grass. The atmosphere beneath is languorous, and is so

Fig. 6. Boldini, *The Morning Stroll.* Private collection.

tinged with azure that what artists call the middle distance partakes also of
that hue, while the horizon beyond is of the deepest ultramarine.   (*Tess* 49)

But Hardy represents both the forms and the colors of the landscape in a
simplified fashion. The whole landscape is reduced to a gridwork of two
shades of green topped by two bands of blue; rather than the atmospheric
illumination taking dominance in the description, the color of the light
becomes as homogeneous as the geometrical forms of the fields. To a
certain extent Bullen is falling prey to a Ruskinian dichotomy between
color and outline enunciated, among other places, in *The Elements of
Drawing*. Nativistic theory involved no such dichotomy; the nativistic eye
perceives colored areas, not uncolored forms. Hamilton even offered the
perception of color as evidence for the extension and demarcation of perceived forms, as we have seen, suggesting that the edge of two adjacent
color regions ''affords a breadthless line—a line of demarcation'' (Hamilton 165). Ruskin encourages his students to learn color by abandoning
form altogether.

> Never mind though your houses are all tumbling down,—though your clouds
> are mere blots, and your trees mere knobs, and your sun and moon like
> crooked sixpences,—so only that trees, clouds, houses, and sun or moon are
> of the right colours.   (Ruskin 135)

Hardy's gridwork of light and dark green with the two bands of sky above
seems more in line with Hamilton's conception of form as a limit for color
than with Ruskin's ''shapeless'' colored fields. The color regions do not
blend formally; although Hardy may share Turner's concern with illumination, his landscapes are always composed of materially distinct and present
elements. Moreover, the subsequent focusing in of the narrative eye on the
clubwalkers demonstrates a great attention to formal detail.

> Ideal and real clashed slightly as the sun lit up the figures against the green
> hedges and creeper-laced house-fronts; for, though the whole troop wore
> white garments, no two whites were alike among them. Some approached
> pure blanching; some had a bluish pallor; some worn by the older charac-
> ters . . . inclined to a cadaverous tint, and to a Georgian style.   (*Tess* 49–
> 50)

Like Bellini's landscape, this simplicity of outline allows no resting place
for the eye, so that when the clubwalkers appear in white they immediately
seem to stand forth in brilliant focus. The narrator's description of the
general colors of broad sections of landscape gives way to a distinct tonal
awareness of the different hues of white and styles of dress, and this
awareness of tonal difference is matched by the intricate details of

"creeper-laced housefronts" and "peeled willow wands." Hardy's reader does not seem to see in any detail until the human figures appear on the scene just as Bellini's viewer does not feel comfortable until his or her eye is aligned with the artist's. Hardy "intensif[ies] the expression of things" by directing the reader's vision toward a more intense focus on the most important part of the landscape—the human figure.

While Bullen describes Hardy's mode of envisionment by a comparison with painting many critics describe the nativistic qualities of Hardyan perception through cinematic metaphor. David Lodge compares Hardy's style to film on the grounds that "Hardy uses verbal description as a film director uses the lens of his camera, to select, highlight, distort, and enhance"; Hardy's methods can "be readily analyzed in cinematic terms; long shot, close-up, wide-angle, telephoto, zoom, etc." (Lodge 249). Joan Grundy states that when Hardy "describes Eustacia as 'a creature of light surrounded by an area of darkness' he is describing all living things. . . . But creatures of light surrounded by an area of darkness are exactly what the figures on the cinema screen are, as we watch them from a darkened auditorium" (Grundy 109). In fact, the figures on a cinema screen are creatures of light surrounded by a square or rectangular area of different colored light, surrounded by darkness. The ordering of the visual field into figure and ground patterns, which Grundy describes as a characteristic of cinema, suggests the single focus of the Law of Visible Direction. Similarly Lodge emphasizes the tendency of Hardy's narrative eye to behave according to nativistic principles of selection and singular focus. Hardy's eye has a single focus, is not prone to coalescent images, perceives forms sequentially, and moves willfully across the visual field because it is nativistic, not because it is cinematic. We have come to associate such limitations with the camera because, as perceptual theorists invariably point out, we are unselfconscious about our perceptual states.

Critics often use the cinematic metaphor because terms like "zoom" seem to telp explain the sudden, stunning shifts of perspective Hardy employs. Miller notes that Hardy's "sudden relatively small shifts in perspective" make the reader feel as if the landscape "were suddenly seen through the wrong end of a telescope" (Miller 51). Any reader of Hardy recognizes this sensation, but critics tend to inaccurately describe such shifts as qualities of omniscient vision. Alcorn states that "Hardy's 'bird's-eye view,' . . . was the last of its kind in English literature . . . few novelists would again have the temerity to try to put things together again through the integrating vision of an omniscient narrator" (Alcorn 9). Miller goes so far as to assert that Hardy's narrator "can see everything" (Miller 56). Such shifts in perspective, however, simply result from changing the position of the narrative eye within the landscape, as Penelope Vigar notes (Vigar 34), and involve no violation of physical laws of perspective.

The initial description of Casterbridge comes through Elizabeth-Jane's eye, which focuses on the city from "the summit of a hill within a mile of the place they sought" that "commanded a full view of the town and its environs."

> "It is huddled all together; and it is shut in by a square wall of trees, like a plot of garden ground by a box-edging."
>
> Its squareness was, indeed, the characteristic which most struck the eye in this antiquated borough. . . . It was compact as a box of dominoes. It had no suburbs—in the ordinary sense. Country and town met at a mathematical line.
>
> To the birds of the more soaring kind Casterbridge must have appeared on this fine evening as a mosaic-work of subdued reds, browns, greys, and crystals, held together by a rectangular frame of deep green. To the level eye of humanity it stood as an indistinct mass behind a dense stockade of limes and chestnuts, set in the midst of miles of rotund down and concave field. The mass became gradually dissected by the vision into towers, gables, chimneys, and casements, the highest glazings shining bleared and bloodshot with the coppery fire they caught from the belt of sunlit cloud in the west. (*Mayor* 22–23)

Elizabeth-Jane's view of the city, like Gertrude's view of Casterbridge, is characterized by an intense focusing in on points of interest in the town (towers and gables) that causes the rest of the landscape to become homogeneous (the miles of identical downs and fields and the "belt" of uniform cloud). The "bird's-eye" view occupies only one sentence and is framed by Elizabeth-Jane's human view; it is not maintained throughout the description. Also, the bird's view is just that—what a bird's eye would see from a vertical distance that renders all landscape forms into indistinct color regions—hardly an omniscient perspective. While the sudden shift from "the level eye of humanity" to the bird's view is surprising, it does not suggest unlimited visual power; rather, it points up the limitations, and visual priorities, of both perspectives. Human vision focuses on human architectural forms, thus infusing emotion into the landscape through its perceptual limitations; bird vision elides the color patches of town and field indiscriminately.

Hardy clearly prefers Elizabeth-Jane's idiosyncratically focused vision, which sets the town off from the countryside as effectively as did the builders of its walls, to the undirected color awareness of the bird. Beer's suggestion that Hardy is "a conditional presence capable of seeing things from multiple distances and diverse perspectives almost in the same moment'' (Beer 247), and Miller's similar claim that the ''shifts in perspective involve seeing things simultaneously'' (Miller 52) both overlook the care with which Hardy defines different observers for each different optical location. Hardy's continual invocation of an actual perceiver, even when he needs to invent one to do so, suggests his attention to visual limits. What Beer describes as the ''shifting pace and changing scales'' of Hardy's vision demonstrates neither his ominipotence nor his conception of the narrative eye as a ''zoom lense''; rather, it demonstrates his use of a nativistic optical model specifically located in distinct physical forms.[2]

For Darwin the observer's task is one of comprehending an infinitely varied organic world; for Hardy, it is one of perceiving the material presence of specific tangible forms. This frequently involves a selecting out of natural forms in favor of human ones, and the process of perception becomes an anthropomorphic struggle for aesthetic existence that humans invariably win. The result is not the representation of an entangled landscape so much as ''the product of the writer's own mind''—a landscape selected and simplified by the human will. Where Darwin describes a few general forms squirming through the entangled bank that multiply in the reader's mind into thousands of evolutionary analogues, Hardy portrays the specific plants touched by a woman as she moves through an overgrown garden or a single human form against the blank heath; he thus limits nature to a humanly perceivable scale. As the Hardyan eye moves through nature, brushing up against objects, its tendency is always to direct itself toward the human, thus focusing on and selecting a humanized world out of an entangled natural landscape. The two ways in which Darwin's theories are thought to influence Hardy are both implicit in this way of seeing. Hardy's nativistic vision does suggest the immediacy and sensual abundance of entangled nature by perceiving whole, distinct, tangential forms that seem to have tangible material presence. Yet the same qualities of vision, the same Law of Visible Direction, causes this material nature to fade into a background and become a setting for man's solipsistic centrality. The perceptual simplification of natural vistas surrounding human figures pushes entangled nature toward the homogeneous emptiness of the modernist wasteland. Hardy's vision, by being selective and nativistic, allows us to see nature both as a material presence and as an expression of the human psyche, for Hardy's is an entangled nature reordered, and thus reclaimed, by human vision.

3

The Geometric Jungle: Imperialistic Vision in the Writings of Alfred Russel Wallace, H. M. Tomlinson, and Joseph Conrad

Joseph Conrad is rarely described as a nature writer, or as part of a nature-writing tradition. Critics of *Heart of Darkness* generally consider the landscape irrelevant for one of two opposing reasons. Those who describe the narrative as a "self-examining meditation" (Watt 253), or a "night-journey into the unconscious, and confrontation of an entity within the self" (Guerard 39) accept the landscape's visual absence as demonstrative of psychological interiority. John Alcorn distinguishes between H. M. Tomlinson and Conrad on the grounds that while Tomlinson, the "natur-ist," identifies with "the earth and physical nature," Conrad describes "a descent into the unconscious life of Marlowe [sic] whereby the inner core of his selfhood is revealed as isolated and irrevocably guilty" (Alcorn 55). Chinua Achebe and other critics who focus on the political significance of *Heart of Darkness* tend to be highly critical of the reduction of Africa to "a backdrop," a "metaphysical battlefield" that serves "the role of props for the break up of one petty European mind" (Achebe 788). Rather than emphasizing the reality of Conrad's African landscape, however, these critics generally dismiss it as conventional, the manifestation of a "power-ful collective myth" (Shetty 469) lifted from Victorian imperialist prose. Patrick Brantlinger states that

> Conrad's stress on cannibalism, his identification of African customs with
> violence, lust, and madness, his metaphors of bestiality, death and darkness,
> his suggestion that traveling in Africa is like traveling backward in time to
> primeval, infantile, but also hellish stages of existence—these features of the

story are drawn from the repertoire of Victorian imperialism and racism that
painted an entire continent dark.   (371)

But how, perceptually speaking, is an entire continent painted dark? How is
the visual experience of landscape made conventional? The transformation
of an entire continent, or an entire kind of tropical landscape, into an
imaginative convention reducible not even to forms, but to adjectives suggesting visual absence, is certainly of interest to any study of the perceptual
diminishment of nature. I would like to supplement Brantlinger's study of
"Africanist" literature by reading *Heart of Darkness* in relation to portrayals of the tropical rain forest by Darwin's fellow evolutionary naturalist
Alfred Russel Wallace and the popular travel writer Henry Major Tomlinson.

The tropical jungle is perhaps the most entangled of banks, and the
South American jungles greatly influenced Darwin's conception of natural
and perceptual entanglement, as we have seen. The interaction of white
Europeans with jungles necessarily engages them with Darwinian abundance and variety. In her article "Scratches on the Face of the Country,"
Mary Louise Pratt demonstrates that early nineteenth-century travel writers
perceive foreign landscape through an agile and powerful narrative eye.
Their imperialistic vision first "depopulates" the landscape of indigenous
people, then personifies the "now-empty landscape" as "the metaphorical
'face of the country'—a more tractable face that returns the European's
gaze, echoes his words, and accepts his caresses" (Pratt 146). In the late
nineteenth century this depopulation is pushed even farther, so that the
landscape is depopulated of all foreign forms, inhuman as well as human,
and reinhabited with the architectural forms and artifacts of European civilization. The landscape thus not only returns the European gaze, it also
comes to resemble the European world. While the strength of the narrative
eye in early nineteenth-century travel writing causes portrayals of visual
perception to enact "the physical appropriation" (Pratt 144) of the globe,
the weakness of the narrative eye in late nineteenth- and early twentieth-
century writings—the illusions and hallucinations to which it is prone—
cause perception to enact the colonial transformation of foreign landscapes
into European ones. The Darwinian entanglements of the jungle are cleared
away by a familiarizing narrative eye. Alfred Russel Wallace's portrayal of
an adaptively evolutionary landscape, in which perception mimics manufacture, recreates the jungle as a collection of human artifacts, as Section I
shows. H. M. Tomlinson's hallucinatory refiguring of the jungle as a
fantasy city results, as Section II makes clear, in the assertion of the
imaginary over the actual landscape.

The ultimate disappearance of the landscape in Joseph Conrad's fiction is made inevitable, as Section III demonstrates, by Conrad's redefinition of vision as a conceptual process and exterior nature as an intellectual landscape. As with Hardy's eye, weakness is turned into a solipsistic strength; the limitation of vision results in the elimination of forms unimportant to the individual perceiver; however, because foreign landscapes are being subjected to such familiarization and simplification a political element is added to Conrad's nativism. In all of these works the familiar visual or intellectual forms of European culture are substituted for indigenous forms. This mode of literary vision corresponds to the nativistic perceptual model outlined by William James in his *Principles of Psychology,* which is characterized by the repetitive imaging of familiar forms and the interchangeability of perceptual and conceptual activity. By analyzing this disappearance of the foreign landscape in perceptual terms we can understand how Conrad uses African darkness as a visual, as well as a culturally and morally symbolic, term. Moreover, it will become apparent how the interaction of darkness as cultural symbol and as an indicator of visual and mental absence allows for the easy slippage from colonial to psychological landscape, and the disappearance of Darwin's entangled jungle into formal homogeneity.

I

The failure of the European eye to comprehend an entangled jungle landscape and its tendency to see either no forms at all or only those forms that can be reimagined in familiar terms suggests a parallel between the visual model adopted by these jungle authors and perceptual theories that became dominant in the late nineteenth century, particularly in the writings of William James. James, in his *Principles of Psychology* (1890), departs from the theorists before him by concentrating on cerebral rather than retinal processes, and by adopting a more fluid and wholistic model of brain chemistry. According to James, the brain process that accompanies an optical sensation leaves a "vestige" in the mind; the "forms of habitual and probable things," which are observed more frequently than others, "will plough deep grooves in the nervous system" (James 891). An optical illusion occurs when a visual stimulus—or "optical sign"—excites the memory of a habitually perceived object, and the mind follows the "paths of least resistance and images the habitually perceived object rather than the one actually perceived" with "a quasi-hallucinatory strength" (853). Because the viewer has seen it so many times, the memory of the familiar object asserts its form over the perception of a present but unfamiliar one.

It is not just optical illusion, however, that involves the assertion of the familiar remembered form over the unfamiliar perceived one. All perception involves the correction of forms seen obscurely, obliquely, or from a distance so that they correspond with the "real" form of the object when seen clearly and close up.

> A cross, a ring, waved about in the air, will pass through every conceivable angular and elliptical form. All the while, however, as we look at them, we hold fast to the perception of their "real" shape, by mentally combining the pictures momentarily received with the notion of perculiar positions in space. It is not the cross and ring pure and simple which we perceive, but the cross *so held*, the ring *so held*. From the day of our birth we have sought every hour of our lives to *correct* the apparent form of things, and translate it into the real form by keeping note of the way they are placed or held.　(James 890)

Because the remembered sensation is "so *probable,* so *habitually* conjured up . . . it partakes of the invincible freshness of reality. . . . These optical reproductions of real form are the vividest of all." Remembered familiar objects, what James calls "real" forms, are thus more perceptually dominant, in a sense more visible, than are objects actually being perceived. As we look out across the landscape we do not see the form that is actually there, but the remembered form that most closely corresponds to it.

A Jamesian landscape would consist of a set of objects already familiar to the viewer, or a set of unfamiliar objects that are perceived according to the lineaments of familiar ones. In 1865 James was a member of Louis Agassiz's expedition to the Amazon. In his letters he continually describes the jungle in terms of the New England landscape for which James yearned: "This morning Tom Ward and I took another cruise on shore, which was equally new and strange. The weather is like Newport" (*Letters* 59). James is quick to point out the strangeness of the new landscape, but his representations are always composed of familiar images: "A part of the path hither lay through an orange thicket where the great, hard, sweet, juicy fruit strewed the ground more than ever did apples the good old Concord pike" (*Selected Letters* 21). While this perceptual familiarization expresses James's homesickness, the presentation of the jungle landscape according to familiar visual norms was a common technique of travel writers and naturalists. In *Tropical Nature and Other Essays* (1878), Alfred Russel Wallace begins his "sketch of the characteristics of vegetable life in the equatorial zone" (27), by noting that "Analogous causes" have determined the similarity between the tropical jungle and the "great northern forests of deciduous trees and of Coniferae" (29). He adds that "these

being comparatively well-known to us, will form the standard by a reference to which we shall endeavour to point out and render intelligible the
distinctive characteristics of the equatorial forest vegetation." Wallace's
intent is to make the forms of the jungle visible to the European reader, and
he succeeds in doing so by continually interposing familiar species into the
jungle landscape.

> Turning our gaze upwards from the stems to the foliage, we find two types of
> leaf not common in the temperate zone, although the great mass of the trees
> offer nothing very remarkable in this respect. First, we have many trees with
> large, thick, and glossy leaves, like those of the cherry-laurel or magnolia,
> but even larger, smoother, and more symmetrical. The leaves of the Asiatic
> caoutchouc-tree (*Ficus Elastica*), so often cultivated in houses, is a type of
> this class, which has a very fine effect among the more ordinary-looking
> foliage. Contrasted with this is the fine pinnate foliage of some of the largest
> forest-trees which, seen far aloft against the sky, looks as delicate as that of
> the sensitive mimosa.   (*Tropical Nature* 33–34)

This rather detailed description seems to offer the reader a vivid image of
the jungle's forms, yet the plants the reader actually sees are either native
European species or domesticated trees and houseplants. Although Wallace
claims to be describing plants "not common in the temperate zone," the
reader's upward-turned gaze sees magnolia and mimosa leaves hanging
from the forest roof. A houseplant is offered as the "type" of these un-
named forest leaves, and Wallace goes on to note its "fine effect among the
more ordinary-looking foliage," like an interior decorator commenting on
the appointments of a well-decorated house. Wallace continually succumbs
to the temptation to describe the jungle in more familiar, and often more
domesticated and artificial terms. The Polyalthea is "completely covered
with star-shaped flowers, three inches across and of a rich orange-red
colour, making the trees look as if they had been artificially decorated with
brilliant garlands" (35).[1] This familarizing comparison between tropical
and European forms goes beyond the botanical.

> The observer new to the scene would perhaps be first struck by the varied yet
> symmetrical trunks, which rise with perfect straightness to a great height
> without a branch, and which, being placed at a considerable average distance
> apart, give an impression similar to that produced by the columns of some
> enormous building.   (*Tropical Nature* 30)

The effect of this replacement of tropical botany with European architecture
is to present the reader with an unfamiliar natural landscape that looks like a
familiar, unnatural one. Writing for the English reader who is experiencing
the jungle from an easy chair, surrounded by northern architecture, and not

by northern forests, Wallace pushes his portrayal of the forest toward the most imagistically accessible of familiar forms, allowing the reader's mind to follow its "paths of least resistance," so that the architectural jungle appears with a "quasi-hallucinatory strength." In effect, Wallace's rhetorical strategy is the equivalent of James's homesickness; both cause the viewer to recast present perceptual experience in familiar terms. By using artificial rather than natural analogues, however, Wallace undermines his own rhetorical framework. Analogous climatic causes can be traced between jungle trees and deciduous trees, but not between jungle trees and pillars; Wallace's demonstration of a scientific principle falls second to his representation of the jungle in vividly imageable European terms.

An even more remarkable humanization of the jungle is yet to come. Immediately after drawing the visual parallel between trees and cathedral pillars, Wallace makes the following observation.

> All are tall and upright columns, but they differ from each other more than do the columns of Gothic, Greek, and Egyptian temples. Some are almost cylindrical, rising up out of the ground as if their bases were concealed by accumulations of the soil . . . [others have] thick slabs radiating from the main trunk, from which they stand out like the buttresses of a Gothic cathedral. . . . These buttresses are sometimes so large that the spaces between them if roofed over would form huts capable of containing several persons. (*Tropical Nature* 30–31)

As architectural forms crowd out natural ones in the reader's vision, and the distinction between architectural styles becomes the primary imagistic concern, the trees themselves are both perceived as and suddenly remade into human structures. Wallace has gone from seeing architectural forms in trees to fashioning trees into architectural forms. His deft progression from equatorial tree to pillar to Gothic column to crude hut enacts both the progression from imagined to manufactured artifact and from raw material to constructed object; Wallace's glance performs both the creative mental process of the architectural designer and the reshaping and manipulation of trees by the house builder. Wallace's Jamesian landscape thus involves both the perception of the foreign landscape as a familiar one as well as the transformation of that landscape into a familiar one.

The synchronic mental motion from Malaysian visual stimulus to remembered European form is thus naturalized as the diachronic motion from primitive to civilized and from raw material to manufactured product. Wallace's stated strategy of biological analogy masks an unstated strategy of historical analogy that becomes apparent in the primitive hut standing at the foot of the cathedral. The tropical landscape is visually analogous to a civilized landscape (the great civilizations of Egypt, Greece, and Europe) except that it has not been built up yet. Wallace's narrative eye, like Darwin's, allows him to transcend time through visual analogy, but it is the European model of cultural progress rather than biological history that flashes before the reader. The narrative motion of the European mind searching backward through its own memory is obscured, and the narrative motion of the tropical landscape advancing into the European landscape is foregrounded. Wallace's representation suggests that in looking at the trees he is not simply experiencing perceptual confusion; he is perceiving future forms in present ones. The link between trees and pillars, between tropical and European, is thus seen as a historical inevitability rather than an optical illusion or perceptual accident.

Where Darwin's illusions increase formal variety, however, Wallace's limit it. Rather than a single form blossoming into multiple analogous forms, Wallace's eye perceives several different species in terms of a single European form. The distinction between Darwin's and Wallace's representational strategies roughly correlates to the differences in their evolutionary theories. Darwin believed in random competitive evolution while Wallace believed in adaptive, environmental evolution. Malcolm Jay Kottler explains that in Wallace's model,

> The conditions in the external environment establish an absolute standard that must be met if an individual is to survive and reproduce. . . . All those individuals that fail to meet the absolute standard are automatically eliminated, while all of those (if any) meeting the standard survive.   (Kottler 371–72)

Wallace's evolution thus progresses through the elimination of unfit forms. Darwin emphasizes competitive selection, in which each organism "is struggling primarily against the other individuals of the species" rather than against the hardships of the environment. The driving engine of the evolutionary process is, for Darwin, the spontaneous appearance of many variations and modifications in individuals, not the leveling scythe of environmental hardship. While Wallace's nature is continually at work paring off the numbers of the unfit, Darwin's is increasing the numbers of the unusual and various.

Moreover, Wallace's evolution is adaptive, selecting only useful variations, while Darwinian selection involves other factors, such as habit, sexual selection, and correlation (inherited traits that are coincidentally linked). Wallace offers the example of the long necks of giraffes, which, he claims, probably became dominant when a climatic change made vegetation scarce, and all those giraffes that were unable to feed from the tops of trees were killed off. Darwin did not rule out this kind of selection, but would have suggested that long necks may have been selected because they allowed the giraffes to win mating battles, because female giraffes preferred long necks, or because long necks were coincidentally linked with some other desirable trait, like speed or strength. Darwin's feverishly mutating nature produces variations without reason, and allows certain variations to be selected without reason. In Wallace's nature all selection is purposeful and relatively precise; nature tends toward utility, and clears away all forms that are not useful.

James's theory of vision can be seen as the perceptual corollary to Wallace's evolutionary theory. The Jamesian mind, like Wallace's evolutionary nature, establishes a formal standard that must be met, and all those forms that fail to meet that standard are eliminated; in Wallace's nature they die off, in James's vision they go unperceived. It is therefore appropriate that Wallace should use a Jamesian representational model. Where Darwin portrays visual forms mutating and multiplying as they compete for space in the reader's perceptual field, Wallace portrays the selection of forms according to an imageable standard of reference. Moreover, because this formal standard is European, the forms of nature are selected according to the standard of reference of European experience—the viewer perceives trees as pillars, and those trees that look less like pillars are ignored. Wallace's representation of evolution thus involves the reader in a more and more familiar world.

Furthermore, Wallace's evolutionary vision, like his evolutionary theory, is adaptive, so that all evolutionary transformations lead to the creation of more useful forms. When the formal standards of the landscape are European, the standards for the utility of variations will also be European. In Wallace's jungle an organism's inherited traits frequently seem to have more survival value for humans than for the organism itself. His description of the bamboo plant in *The Malay Archipelago* (1869), for example, offers no discussion of the biological structure of the plant, or of the adaptations of those structures for the environment; however, it does include a lengthy description of the characteristics that make the bamboo "one of nature's most valuable gifts" (*Malay Archipelago* 59).

> Their strength, lightness, smoothness, straightness, roundness, and hollowness, the facility and regularity with which they can be split, their many different sizes, the varying length of their joints, the ease with which they can be cut and with which holes can be made through them, their hardness outside, their freedom from any pronounced taste or smell, their great abundance, and the rapidity of their growth and increase, are all qualities which render them useful for a hundred different purposes. . . . (59)

Any reader unfamiliar with the appearance of bamboo images a smooth, straight, round, hollow tool—an easily manipulated organic cylinder rather than a plant. The subsequent portrayals of the bamboo's usefulness for flooring, ladder making, and bridge building only intensify this image. The plant seems to have evolved specifically according to visibly obvious standards of human utility. Wallace's reimagination of natural forms as products represents the logical extension of an evolutionary vision that is at once adaptive and anthropomorphic.

Wallace's transformative vision is thus more complete than is Hardy's. It is not overwhelmed by the pressures of population; rather, it offers an orderly and distinct portrayal of forms that the reader has already seen. Presented with a less familiar landscape than are authors describing the British countryside, the jungle author asserts the familiarity of natural forms more aggressively and, in the process, diminishes nature visually. Jamesian perceptual theory can be considered a more cerebral and subjective version of the nativistic perception of form; not only do we see standardized forms, we see our own memories. Similarly, jungle vision is a more humanizing and distorting version of Hardyan simplification that involves not only the clearing of the land of nonhuman nature but its repopulation with human forms. If Hardyan perception can be seen as a sort of agrarian perceptual labor, Wallace's can be described as the perceptual colonization and industrialization of the new world.

II

In his travelogue, *The Sea and the Jungle,* H. M. Tomlinson carries the perceptual colonization of the landscape even farther by reimagining the jungle as a nearly urban landscape, crowded with human architectural forms.

> Individual sprays and fronds, projecting from the mass in parabolas with flamboyant abandon and poise, were as rigid as metallic and enamelled shapes. The diversity of forms, and especially the number and variety of the palms, so overloaded an unseen standing that the parapets of the woods occasionally leaned outwards to form an arcade above our masts. . . . Often the heavy parapets of the woods were upheld on long colonnades of grey palm boles; or the whole upper structure appeared based on low green arches, the pennate fronds of smaller palms flung direct from the earth. . . . Occasionally we brushed a projecting spray, or a vine pendent from a cornice. (127)

Tomlinson's representational strategy differs from Wallace's in one important particular, however. Where Wallace shows natural forms being imaginatively transformed into human artifacts, Tomlinson offers the reader a landscape in which this transformation has already taken place. Like the British travel writers described by Pratt, Tomlinson attempts "to make those [European] informational orders natural, to find them there uncommanded, rather than assert them as the products/producers of European knowledges or disciplines" (Pratt 144). Tomlinson portrays the jungle landscape as a skyline of architectural forms rather than as an individual tree reimagined as a set of artifacts. Terms such as *parapets, arcade, cornice, colonade,* and *arches,* seem to be the normal vocabulary for describing the jungle; tropical vegetation is composed of metal, enamel, and emerald. Tomlinson's reader perceives the jungle as a utopian city the architectural structures of which are roughly analogous to jungle forms, but more familiar and more brilliantly visual than the jungle itself.

The rhetorical power of Tomlinson's method lies in his use of unannounced visual analogy. The first image of the jungle simply gives a detailed account of the play of light across its architectural forms: "Suddenly sunrise ran a long band of glowing saffron over the shadow to port, and the vague summit became remarkable with a parapet of black filigree, crowns and fronds of palms and strange trees showing in rigid patterns of ebony" (111). Urban architecture is not a standard to which the natural world is openly compared and translated; rather, it is a material structure already present in the landscape. The extreme geometrical regularity of the jungle edge is indicated by the action of light against it; the jungle wall is envisioned as a "cliff" of mineral deposits:

> The morning light brimmed at the forest top, and spilled into the river. The channel filled with sunshine. There it was then. In the northern cliff I could see even the boughs and trunks; they were veins of silver in a mass of solid chrysolite. (112)

Tomlinson seems to see in brilliant hallucinations. He does not observe a form and then create a visual comparison that overtakes that form, as does Wallace; rather, he looks at the jungle and immediately sees a city.

One of Tomlinson's most rhetorically powerful descriptions is that of the urban jungle, in which the bleakness of the urban landscape is invoked to demonstrate the desolation of nature. Here, the darkness itself seems to inspire Tomlinson's narrative eye to more intense perception.

> The forest was nothing like the paradise a tropical wild is supposed to be. It was as uniformly dingy as the old stones of a London street on a November

> evening. . . . This central forest was really the vault of the long forgotten,
> dank, mouldering, dark, abandoned to the accumulations of eld and decay.
> The tall pillars rose, upholding night, and they might have been bastions of
> weathered limestone and basalt, for they were as grim as ancient and ruinous
> masonry. There was no undergrowth. The ground was hidden in a ruin of
> perished stuff, uprooted trees, parchments of leaves, broken boughs, and
> mummied husks, the iron globes of nuts, and pods. . . . The crowded
> columns mounted straight and far, almost branchless, fading into indistinc-
> tion. Out of that overhead obscurity hung a wreckage of distorted ca-
> bles. . . . We would crawl round such an occupying structure, diminished
> groundlings, as one would move about the base of a foreboding plutonic
> building whose limits and meaning were ominous but baffling. (294–95)

The urbanized and industrialized jungle is vividly and sinisterly complete
down to the "iron globes of nuts" and the "wreckage of distorted cables"
hanging from the roof. Tomlinson is able to make the unnaturalness of
dingy London seem part of the jungle landscape itself, just as he earlier
adopted the gardenlike abundance of the jungle as a characteristic of an
imaginary urban paradise. In both cases the reader does not notice the
absence of the jungle landscape he or she is supposed to be seeing because
of the visual complexity of the European landscape presented.

The absolute separateness of these perceived and natural landscapes is
continually emphasized by Tomlinson. Where Wallace's civilized jungle is
manufactured from the raw material of nature, Tomlinson's is created in
reaction to nature's emptiness.

> The equatorial forest is popularly pictured as a place of bright and varied
> colours, with extravagant flowers, an abundance of fruits, and huge trees
> hung with creepers where lurk many venomous but beautiful snakes with
> gem-like eyes, and a multitude of birds as bright as the flowers. . . . Those
> details are right, but the picture is wrong. . . . [T]he virgin forest itself
> soon becomes but a green monotony which, through extent and mystery,
> dominates and compels to awe and dread. You will see it daily, but will not
> often approach it. It has no splendid blossoms; none, that is, which you will
> see, except by chance . . . they are lost in the ocean of leaves as are the
> pearls and wonders in the deep. You will remember the equatorial forest but
> as a gloom of foliage in which all else that showed was rare and momentary,
> was foundered and lost to sight instantly. (291–92)

The world "popularly pictured" is full of vivid, intricate life, but nature
itself is a monotony, nearly a void. The beauty and intricacy of the jungle
can only exist in the imagination of the traveller, for his eye will never
catch it. Tomlinson promotes the human ability to perceive an apparently
empty landscape as dynamic and full of life; we are reminded of Lyell's

injunction to the scientist to "picture" the invisible processes of nature. Where Lyell's vision is fundamentally scientific, however, Tomlinson's is fundamentally aesthetic. The task of the travel writer is more to give a luminous portrayal of the landscape than an accurate one.

> Where are the Spanish Main, the Guianas, and the Brazils? At last I had discovered them. I found their true bearings. They are in Raleigh's "Golden City of Manoa," in Burney's "Buccaneers of America," with Drake, Humboldt, Bates and Wallace; and I had left them all at home. We borrow the light of an observant and imaginative traveller, and see the foreign land bright with his aura; and we think it is the country which shines. (107)

For Tomlinson, the country itself has no hope of shining. His jungle, like Conrad's, consists of an undifferentiated darkness that is frequently portrayed as a thick, opaque liquid. Where the snakes, birds, and flowers that the traveller expects are brilliantly distinct, the actual jungle forms blend together into an ocean of dark organic fluid.

> The few openings I have seen in the forest do not derange my clear consciousness of a limitless ocean of leaves, its deep billows of foliage rolling down to the only paths there are in this country, the rivers, and there overhanging arrested in collapse. There is no land. One must travel by boat from one settlement to another. The settlements are but islands, narrow footholds, widely sundered by vast gulfs of jungle. (178–79)

Tomlinson writes with the visual models of a sailor, and he makes use of the many dynamic representations of the sea from the first third of the book to reimagine the jungle as ocean. But this fluidity is not Darwin's formal fluidity; the oceanic jungle is uniformly dark. Such liquid vision allows for a material inversion through which the jungle landscape becomes liquid and the river connecting settlements becomes solid land. The less easy the access from a landscape region to the civilized world, the less material that region becomes.

The jungle is thus portrayed as an unseen and unseeable flux of darkness against which the familiar forms of human artifact and architecture stand vividly forth. When Tomlinson looks at the dark flood with imaginative eyes the landscape looms up with "quasi-hallucinatory strength." Tomlinson must overcome the visual monotonousness of the jungle by engaging in intense, familiarizing perception, and he chooses familiar architectural forms as the perceptual triggers that will bring about the most vivid imaging process. James states that "no object not probable, no object which we are not incessantly practiced in reproducing, can acquire this vividness in imagination" (James 893). Nature itself is disillusioning and nonvisual; the human mind, specifically the European mind, is that which makes vision possible.

The extreme contrast between Tomlinson's perceptual and imaginative portrayals of the jungle results in a form of representation that William James would have described as hallucinatory. James outlines a steady progression from illusion to hallucination; "hallucinations are often only *extremes* of the perception process, in which the secondary cerebral reaction is out of all normal proportion to the peripheral stimulus which occasions the activity" (758). An illusion occurs when the viewer looks at an unfamiliar form and perceives it as a familiar one; a hallucination occurs when the viewer looks at a very small or insignificant form and perceives it as an intensely, expansively, or vividly familiar one. James describes a hallucination incited by hypnotism in which the hypnotist will

> point to a dot on a sheet of paper, and call it "General Grant's photograph," and your subject will see a photograph of the General there instead of the dot. The dot gives objectivity to the appearance, and the suggested notion of the General gives it form.   (770)

Hallucination thus represents an extension of illusion in which the perceptual sign is so insignificant as to be almost nonexistent, and the accessed memory so vivid and dynamic as to offer an alternative world. Tomlinson continually points to the absence of perceptual signs in the jungle.

> Still the forest glides by. It is a shadow on the mind. . . . It should have convinced me now that it is something material. But why should I suppose it is that? We have had no chance to examine it. It does not look real. It does not remind me of anything I know of vegetation.   (138)

For the reader the jungle is, in effect, less "real" than the Jamesian "real" forms that appear in Tomlinson's hallucinatory vision. As in Hardy, the perceptual clearing of the landscape allows familiar emotion and experience to be infused into it. Hallucination is not so much a result of an empty landscape, as the emptying of the landscape is a prerequisite for intense hallucination.

The hallucinatory imaging of familiar forms culminates in the imagined world becoming so intense that it ceases to parallel the natural one, and launches into utter fantasy.

> The sooty limbs of the cacao trees grew low, and filled the view ahead with a perplexity of leafless and tortured boughs. They were hung about with fruit, pendent lamps lit with a pale greenish light. We saw nothing move there but two delicate butterflies, which had transparent wings with opaque crimson spots, such as might have been served Titania herself; yet the gloom and

> black ooze, and the eerie globes, with their illusion of light hung upon
> distorted shapes, was more the home of the fabulous sucuruju, the serpent
> which is forty feet long.   (144)

At this point, Tomlinson's travel writing has ceased to be informative and
has become entirely fantastic. The reader is plunged into a world of gothic
structures and nightmarish forms, but he or she is learning nothing about
the forest itself. Do the butterflies really have crimson-spotted wings or is
this just another fabulous image, like Titania, or the forty-foot long suc-
uruju? It does not really matter, for Tomlinson's jungle is largely an imaginary entity. The foreign land is not only illuminated but created by the
imaginative travel writer. Where Wallace reimagines the perceived landscape, Tomlinson perceives an imaginary one, and the imperialism of his
discourse is thus at once less substantial and more inclusive. At the end of
his discussion on hallucinations James indicates that it is possible for hallucinations to be "centrally initiated"—to occur when the perceptual trigger
has grown so small as to disappear. James states

> When an hallucination is complete, it is much more than a mental image. *An
> hallucination is a strictly sensational form of consciousness, as good and
> true a sensation as if there were a real object there.* The object happens not to
> be there, that is all.   (James 759)

The jungle is one such centrally initiated hallucination; rather than its own
land, the Amazon is the dreamworld of Western culture.

This dream is not always a good one. The strain of constantly asserting
the perception of a familiar landscape in the place of an unfamiliar one, of
living in a world of shadows, sometimes bears heavily on Tomlinson.

> Yet it was not easy to be sure that we saw anything at all, for these were not
> trees, but shapes in a region below the day, a world sunk abysmally from the
> land of living things, to which light but thinly percolated down to two
> travellers moving on its floor, trying to get out to their own place.   (295)

Tomlinson's familiar forms dominate the unfamiliar forms of the jungle
because, in the Jamesian sense, they are "real," while the jungle is "a
shadow on the mind" (138). It is ultimately necessary to return to the
source of such reality, as Tomlinson does at the end of *The Sea and The
Jungle* when he returns to England:

> The colours were faint enough to be but tinted mists. . . . The orderly
> hedges, the clean roads, the geometrical patterns of the fields, gave him
> assurance once more of order and security. Here was law again, and the
> permanence of affairs long decided upon. . . . Here again was the centre of
> the world.   (332)

Tomlinson sees the familiar English countryside as composed of luminously "real" forms; perceived and exterior nature are the same. What Gillian Beer calls the "green control" of the orderly, geometrical English countryside embodies the ideal, humanized landscape that Tomlinson has been struggling to create from the unfamiliar jungle landscape. The close of the book thus offers both an imaginative and an emotional fulfillment; the landscape that the narrator, and the reader, have been straining to perceive in the tropical darkness is found in its actuality at "the centre" of the British empire.

For Tomlinson the act of perception mimics the straightforward perception of one's own land, not the colonization of a foreign land; foreignness is only a passing mental shadow, a vision, sometimes a nightmare from which the reader ultimately awakens into an orderly and familiar visual world. Familiar forms are the only visible ones because they are the only real ones; the rest is "a phantom and indeterminate country." Implicit in Tomlinson's portrayal is the impossibility of Western eyes perceiving the landscape in anything but Western terms; Tomlinson's representational stance is thus directly opposed to Darwin's, who wished to offer readers an experience of nature's chaotic unfamiliarity. For Tomlinson, the ability to perceive a foreign landscape in one's own forms represents the peak of civilized human endeavor; seeing nature's evolutionary variety is not only anti-aesthetic, but in certain senses it is antihuman. The presentation of the jungle through a hallucinatory mode thus diminishes the psychic impact of its otherness, allowing the reader to perceive the world in comfortably familiar terms, while the jungle itself remains unseen.

III

In "Books" Joseph Conrad offers the following definition of the novelist's task:

> In truth every novelist must begin by creating for himself a world, great or little, in which he can honestly believe. This world cannot be made otherwise than in his own image: it is fated to remain individual and a little mysterious, and yet it must resemble something already familiar to the experience, the thoughts and the sensations of his readers. (*Conrad on Fiction* 79)

Like Hardy, Conrad emphasizes the necessity of an idiosyncratic artistic vision, but he urges universality through a steadfast appeal to the familiar "thoughts and sensations" of the reader's experience. Conrad's major concern is the accurate and insightful recreation of familiar worlds, not the representation of new ones; the artistic power of an imagined world can be judged, at least to some extent, by the reader's recognition of familiar thoughts and sensations. When representing a foreign landscape, therefore, Conrad must find a way of making that landscape resemble something already familiar to the experience of the reader, and all that cannot be made familiar must go unseen. It is not altogether surprising, then, that in *Heart of Darkness* Conrad, like Wallace and Tomlinson, offers the reader a blank, monotonous landscape; the jungle is

> an empty stream, a great silence, an impenetrable forest. . . . The long stretches of waterway ran on, deserted, into the gloom of the over-shadowed distances . . . along empty reaches, round the still bends, between the high walls of our winding way. (48–52)

Unlike Wallace and Tomlinson, however, Conrad offers no imagined landscape as an alternative to the monotonous perceived one. Ian Watt describes Conrad's technique of "delayed decoding" in which the reader is made to share in a character's confusion by the "protagonist's immediate sensations" being offered well before the "slower reflexive process of making out their meaning" (Watt 175) can take place. A technique similarly used in *Heart of Darkness* involves the protagonist's lack of immediate sensations preceding an almost endless process of speculation on what that absence might mean. Conrad frustrates the reader—telling him or her to look when there is nothing to look at—and establishes the jungle landscape as an abstract vista that, while it cannot be perceived, could be comprehended or defined if one could only remember the key. The representational strategy of *Heart of Darkness* centers largely on this mechanism of imagistic frustration, a sensory understimulation that is allowed no outlet within the text and which redefines the material world as an intellectual property.

Marlow's first perception of the jungle identifies it immediately as an intellectual landscape. "I watched the coast. Watching a coast as it slips by the ship is like thinking about an enigma" (19). Watching the jungle is not like watching a collection of raw materials, or an architectural pile; watching is like thinking. Appropriately, the jungle itself is not like a Cathedral or a city, but is "something great and invincible, like evil or truth" (37–38); it is "an implacable force brooding over an inscrutable intention," a "black and incomprehensible frenzy" (50), a "mysterious stillness" (56). Like Tomlinson, Conrad denies the possibility of seeing the jungle clearly or precisely; however, rather than replacing this absence with a lively imaginary world, Conrad meditates on it:

> Nowhere did we stop long enough to get a particularized impression, but the
> general sense of vague and oppressive wonder grew upon me. It was like a
> weary pilgrimage amongst hints for nightmares.

Gazing on the "inextricable, impenetrable forest" (*Selected Letters* 21) of
the Amazon launches William James into a speculative career; looking at
the darkened jungles of the Congo launches Marlow, and the reader, into an
extended process of narrative speculation.

In his writings on art Conrad suggests that while the scientist concerns
himself with aspect, the artist looks past the surface to interior essence. The
scientist is "impressed by the aspect of the world" and "plunges into
facts," while the artist "descends within himself" (*Conrad on Fiction*
161).

> To snatch in a moment of courage, from the remorseless rush of time, a
> passing phase of life, is only the beginning of the task. The task approached
> in tenderness and faith is to hold up unquestioningly, without choice and
> without fear, the rescued fragment before all eyes in the light of a sincere
> mood. It is to show its vibration, its coloring, its form; and through its
> movement, its form, and its colour, reveal the substance of its truth—
> disclose its inspiring secret: the stress and passion within the core of each
> convincing moment.   (*Conrad on Fiction* 163)

Conrad's description of the artist reminds us of Marlow's descriptions of
Kurtz; the artist "rescues" experience and, through a heroic act of articulation, makes the "substance of its truth" visible "before all eyes" of the
artistic community. This "substance," however, is "within the core," it is
"secret" and needs to be "disclosed." The role of the artist is to disclose—
to ferret out the truth underlying appearances, not to represent the appearances themselves. Ian Watt argues that Conrad conceives of sense perception in conceptual terms.

> For Conrad, the world of the senses is not a picture but a presence, a presence
> so intense, unconditional, and unanswerable that it loses the fugitive, hypo-
> thetical, subjective, and primarily aesthetic qualities which it usually has in
> the impressionist tradition.   (Watt 179)

If Conrad's visual sensations are registered as "presences" rather than
"pictures" they can hardly be considered to be responses to exterior nature
at all.[2] Moreover, this nonvisual vision is "unconditional" and "un-
answerable" rather than "fugitive" and "hypothetical"; these terms suggest an innate perception of substantial truths underlying the visible exterior. Conrad's much repeated embracing of sensory experience must be
read in the light of this disavowal of surface appearance.

> All art, therefore, appeals primarily to the senses, and the artistic aim when expressing itself in written words must also make its appeal through the senses, if its high desire is to reach the secret spring of responsive emotions. . . . My task which I am trying to achieve is, by the power of the written word to make you hear, to make you feel—it is, before all, to make you see. That—and no more, and it is everything.   (*Conrad on Fiction* 162)

As Bette London notes, Marlow fulfills Conrad's edict not by engaging in the reproduction of exterior nature but in the "manipulation of reality, the restructuring of experience: to *make* his audience hear what *he* hears, feel what *he* feels, see what *he* sees" (London 242). Artists must rescue or remove their experiences from one context and manipulate them to the point that they can be presented, as abstract "secrets" or "truths" to the members of their own cultural group by reaching the "secret spring of [their] responsive emotions," not their senses. The substitution of the abstract property for the original concrete property is thus heroic. The artist, like the Roman conquerer, is "[man] enough to face the darkness" of language and return to the community with a prize wrested from a foreign meaning and made part of his own. In doing so the visual aspects of experience become means to an end; the coloring, vibration, and movement all body forth the essential "secret" of the experience; what the artist makes an audience "see" is "truth" rather than objects. The European artist must describe the African landscape in such a way that its "inspiring secret" can be disclosed to the European audience; the visible substance of African flora and fauna must be transformed into a visible "substance of . . . truth."

Conrad portrays visual perception itself as an essentializing process. His perception is primarily cerebral; substances are rendered as essences and these essences, in the form of provocative words, become the most "visible" objects in the novel. We are not brought to an understanding of the jungle as an enigma through a series of intellectual steps; the narrative eye perceives it immediately as an essence. Conrad's narrative eye is thus as essentializing as the reasoning mind, while at the same time locked into the habitual mechanism of Jamesian visual perception. By combining the essentializing qualities of reason with the habitual structure of visual perception, however, Conrad's model of the mind diverges from James's. James asserts that a "thing inferred by reasoning need neither have been an habitual associate of the datum from which we infer it, nor need it be similar to it" (956). A reasoner in a strange landscape can, through association and the recognition of similarity, attempt to understand the initially unrecognizable surroundings. By adopting both familiarity and abstraction as aesthetic criteria, however, Conrad presents a form of perception that avoids association and similarity for the continual reiteration of the familiar.

Through this essentializing perception Conrad, like the other jungle writers, engages in the imposition of the familiar mental act over the unfamiliar one. Where Wallace and Tomlinson replace unfamiliar visual forms with familiar visual ones, Conrad replaces them with familiar intellectual abstractions. The fact that these abstractions—darkness, horror, primitiveness—tend to be associated with visual confusion and obscurity does not diminish their relative familiarity to the reader. Watching the jungle is like thinking about an enigma. The *Nellie* audience, and the European reader, is more used to thinking about enigmas than watching jungles. Moreover, as Patrick Brantlinger, Sandhya Shetty, and others have made clear, European audiences were especially used to thinking about Africa in terms of enigma, horror, and darkness. Shetty offers a particularly Jamesian formulation of this point:

> [I]n his depiction of a fictionalized landscape, Conrad not only pushed facts, but he seems to have pushed them along certain well-trodden paths, choosing the most powerful of the stereotypical images of Africa, recognizable images that would certainly have had the desired effect on the "minds and bosoms" of his contemporary readers.   (Shetty 471)

Because the familiar partakes of the invincible freshness of reality, as James suggests, the jungle as enigma seems more real to the European reader than does the jungle as populations of African plants and animals. Conrad thus applies the Jamesian process of perception to conceptual as well as perceptual activity by first replacing visual forms with thoughts, and then allowing familiar thoughts to take perceptual precedence over unfamiliar images. Like Wallace and Tomlinson, however, Conrad masks and naturalizes the process by which perception is manipulated, so that Marlow seems to actually perceive the jungle in abstract terms.

For Conrad, experience is "only the beginning." The artist must retell a tale, presenting its essential truth to a home audience; the true effort lies in holding it up "before all eyes." In *Heart of Darkness* the refinement of Africa from material to intellectual landscape coincides with the retelling of the tale on the *Nellie,* and its subsequent retelling by the frame narrator. The greater the narrator's distance from the original experience, and the more firmly located he is within a European literary context, the more abstract the African landscape becomes. Jakob Lothe has noted that in "An Outpost of Progress," a short story that prefigures *Heart of Darkness,* the narrator "is not only removed from the characters in time and space; he is also capable of entering their minds and explaining what they themselves do not comprehend'' (Lothe 48). He also enters their eyes and explains what they are unable to see.

> They lived like blind men in a large room, aware only of what came in contact with them (and of that only imperfectly), but unable to see the general aspect of things. The river, the forest, all the great land throbbing with life, were like a great emptiness. Even the brilliant sunshine disclosed nothing intelligible. Things appeared and disappeared before their eyes in an unconnected and aimless kind of way. The river seemed to come from nowhere and flow nowhither. It flowed through a void. Out of that void, at times, came canoes, and men with spears in their hands would suddenly crowd the yard of the station. (*Tales of Unrest* 92)

The narrator's condescending tone suggests that he can, from his omniscient perspective, perceive the "great land throbbing with life" in detail. As Lothe goes on to note, however, narrative distance does not bring about clearer perception of the object world. It creates instead a "tendency to generalize" through "philosophical reflection on, and evaluation of, the conditions of human existence" (Lothe 49). Consequently, the narrator's representations of the jungle offer philosophical, rather than material, entanglements; the jungle is filled with hopelessness and greatness rather than trees and animals.

> And stretching away in all directions surrounding the insignificant cleared spot of the trading post, immense forests, hiding fateful complications of fantastic life, lay in the eloquent silence of mute greatness. (*Tales of Unrest* 94)

> And out of the great silence of the surrounding wilderness its very hopelessness and savagery seemed to approach them nearer, to draw them gently, to look upon them, to envelop them with a solicitude irresistible, familiar, and disgusting. (*Tales of Unrest* 108)

The characters, like Wallace and Tomlinson, perceive familiar forms. The narrator perceives an embodied idea. Only as an idea, only as "hopelessness and savagery," does the jungle seem "familiar."

In *Heart of Darkness* Marlow occupies both positions of narrator and character for his own tale. Marlow the character steering his boat upriver concentrates, like Kayerts and Carlier in "An Outpost of Progress," on the familiar forms that occupy his daily life. When Marlow calls attention to his persona as the Buddhalike storyteller sitting aboard the *Nellie* ruminating on the jungle, however, the landscape becomes provocatively abstract. Marlow's perception of the station, and subsequent pronouncements on the spirit of the place, is highly reminiscent of the passages quoted earlier from "An Outpost of Progress." Marlow perceives his surroundings in much the

same way as Kayerts and Carlier; he sees the men working there, notices
the operation of trade, and little else.

> I saw this station, these men strolling aimlessly about in the sunshine of the
> yard. I asked myself sometimes what it all meant. They wandered here and
> there with their absurd long staves in their hands, like a lot of faithless
> pilgrims bewitched inside a rotten fence.   (37)

The narrative eye perceives the men, the yard, the fence, and the bright
sunshine of the clearing as visible forms, and is thus located in the African
visual context. Portrayals of the jungle as a primitive void, on the other
hand, are invariably accompanied by reminders of Marlow's presence on
the *Nellie* in a European context. Immediately after the preceding passage
the following rumination is offered.

> The word "ivory" rang in the air, was whispered, was sighed. You would
> think they were praying to it. A taint of imbecile rapacity blew through it all,
> like a whiff from some corpse. By Jove! I've never seen anything so unreal in
> my life. And outside, the silent wilderness surrounding this cleared speck on
> the earth struck me as something great and invincible, like evil or truth,
> waiting patiently for the passing away of this fantastic invasion.   (37–38)

The narrative seems to pull gradually back from visual perception as it
progresses, offering fewer visible details and more reminders of the story-
telling situation. The use of the second person pronoun, the shift from past
tense ("I asked myself") to present perfect ("I've never seen") and the
interjection ("By Jove!") all call attention to Marlow the old salt telling his
friends a story at the mouth of the Thames and clear the way for the
narratorial intrusion to follow. As we are reminded of this circle of European auditors the jungle suddenly becomes a place of darkness; it is "great
and invincible"—an abstract primordial essence "like evil or truth."
While the Marlow describing the station clearly dislikes the rapacity of the
imperialists, the one meditating on the jungle invokes the rhetoric of romantic imperialism.

   This disjunction between Marlow on the *Nellie* and Marlow in the
jungle remains consistent throughout the novel. Marlow describes the jungle as most mysteriously savage, most incomprehensibly primitive, when
the reader is most aware of his European audience. Bette London has
investigated the text's "hybridity," suggesting that "to read Marlow's
narrative persona against his narrated self" is to read "his displaced perfor-
mance of colonial power against his powerful topical critique" (London
242). While London effectively argues that the apparent resistance of these
two modes of discourse allows Conrad to reassert a dominant ideology, the

abstracting perceptual narrative of Marlow on the *Nellie* can also be read as an extension of the familiarizing perceptual narrative of Marlow in Africa. The major breaks in the narrative occur when the familiarizing perceptions of the European eye in the jungle escalate into abstractions, transferring the reader completely from an African perceptual context into a European intellectual one. This escalation is apparent in Marlow's perceptions of and meditations on the jungle just before his denial of the possibility of conveying the essence of experience and his assertion that "we live, as we dream—alone." He initially perceives the landscape vividly, if simplistically.

> [T]he high stillness of primeval forest was before my eyes; there were shiny patches on the black creek. The moon had spread over everything a thin layer of silver—over the rank grass, over the mud, upon the wall of matted vegetation standing higher than the wall of a temple, over the great river I could see through a sombre gap glittering, glittering, as it flowed broadly by without a murmur. (42)

Like Wallace and Tomlinson, Conrad uses artificial and architectural metaphor and perceives only a few simplified forms. In the subsequent passage, however, Conrad denies even this familiarized vision as he clears these landscape images away and allows the word *see* to take on a variety of more cognitive and less visual overtones.

> What was in there? I could see a little ivory coming out from there, and I had heard Mr. Kurtz was in there. . . . Yet somehow it didn't bring any image with it—no more than if I had been told an angel or a fiend was in there. I believed it in the same way one of you might believe there are inhabitants in the planet Mars. . . . I became in an instant as much of a pretence as the rest of the bewitched pilgrims. This simply because I had a notion it somehow would be of help to that Kurtz whom at the time I did not see—you understand. He was just a word for me. I did not see the man in the name any more than you do. Do you see him? Do you see the story? Do you see anything? (42)

Marlow's relinquishment of vision occurs through a transference of meaning across the word *see*. Seeing the jungle, seeing ivory, seeing Kurtz, seeing angels and fiends, Martians, and finally seeing the story itself become elided as Marlow progresses through his discourse. Dream states, systems of belief, and imagined possibilities are all conflated with visual perception until ultimately language rather than landscape becomes the object of vision; he asks his listeners to "see the story," transforming perception into a purely intellectual act and the landscape forms into conceptual absence.

Later in the text a relatively detailed description of the jungle gives way to a minute awareness of the steamboat, then finally to a discussion of the nature of reality just before the narrative breaks.

> The long stretches of waterway ran on, deserted, in the gloom of the over-shadowed distances. On silvery sand-banks hippos and alligators sunned themselves side by side. The broadening waters flowed through a mob of wooded islands; you lost your way on that river as you would in a desert . . .   (48)

For all its featurelessness this is perhaps the most detailed description of natural forms the reader ever receives. Like other jungle authors Marlow asserts the blankness of the landscape, reiterating the comparison between forest and desert, but we do see animals, banks, and wooded islands. As Marlow turns to ruminate on these perceptions, however, and starts to discuss the "truth" hidden behind appearance, these concrete forms disappear in a "mysterious stillness" and the narrative breaks into a direct address to the *Nellie* audience.

> When you have to attend to things of that sort, to the mere incidents of the surface, the reality—the reality, I tell you—fades. The inner truth is hidden—luckily, luckily. But I felt it all the same; I felt often its mysterious stillness watching me at my monkey tricks, just as it watches you fellows performing on your respective tight-ropes for—what is it? half-a-crown a tumble—   (49)

As Marlow describes "the truth" fading away behind "surface" reality, what actually fades from the reader's mind is the surface of the jungle. This "inner truth" seems to be associated with the inner forest, but it also lies beneath the surface of European life. Marlow attempts, apparently with some anxiety, to show the *Nellie* audience that the "mysterious stillness" is as present in England as it is in Africa; African darkness lurks just below the surface in the European historical subconscious. As he distills the landscape into an essential "truth" about history and culture the actual African forms fade from view and Marlow in Europe appears before the reader discussing an invisible and essential Africa.

The interruptions of Marlow's monologue, either by Marlow himself or by his audience, fail to surprise the reader, as any true interruption would, because they are actually culminations of the process of abstraction whereby the reader is moved from an African to a European context. Marlow's description of an African dance, for example, progresses into a meditation on his sense of "kinship" with African savagery and culminates in his demand "Who's grunting? You wonder I didn't go ashore for a howl and a dance?'' (51). The grunt (if it is not actually a snore from the sleepy listeners) does not stop Marlow in the midst of a narrative event or a landscape description so as to suddenly displace the reader; it caps his rhetorical dialogue with the *Nellie* audience that the reader has been following up to this point. Similarly, the question "Do you see anything?" (42) comes only after a long meditation on lying, belief, and vision when the listener has had nothing to "see" for quite a while. Marlow's tendency to pose questions for his audience—"Absurd?", "An appeal to me?" "You wonder I didn't go ashore?"—thereby assuming their level of knowledge and engagement is, as Bette London notes, one of his most powerful rhetorical devices. It is also a means by which he abstracts descriptive discourse into meditative discourse without admitting that he is doing so. By ascribing questions to the audience he seems to be responding to conceptual problems inevitably raised by the perception of the African landscape rather than actively conceptualizing his visual experience of that landscape into European intellectual categories.

Darkness emerges as the subject of Marlow's tale on the *Nellie* in the heart of European civilization because there it is at once the most politically crucial and the most conceptually problematic. He reveals this in his first spoken words when he decribes Britain as "one of the dark places of the earth" with reference to the Roman conquest. A landscape can only be perceived as a darkness when it is part of a tale told by an imperial foreigner "afterwards, to brag of what he had gone through in his time." Marlow thus establishes the operation of retelling, by which the visible details of a landscape are eliminated and replaced by politically useful conceptual qualities, as the proper mode for describing a foreign world. Because he openly discusses the perception of a landscape as a darkness Conrad's perceptual colonization of the jungle is subtler than Wallace's or Tomlinson's. Both Wallace and Tomlinson perceive familiar forms against emptiness, but they do not call attention to this emptiness. Conrad, on the other hand, emphasizes that the imperial eye fails to perceive foreignness. The Roman looking at Britain, like the Englishman looking at Africa, sees only a darkness. Rather than recognizing that this results from the foreigner's unfamiliarity with the landscape, however, Marlow suggests that the very failure of the imperial eye to perceive demonstrates its advanced, civilized condition.

> We were wanderers on a prehistoric earth, on an earth that wore the aspect of an unknown planet. . . . We could not understand because we were too far and could not remember because we were travelling in the night of the first ages, of those ages that are gone, leaving hardly a sign—and no memories.
>   The earth seemed unearthly.   (50–51)

Implicit in this mnemonic model is a monolithic imperialist history beginning in the jungle and ending in twentieth-century Europe. African culture
is primitive, not different, just as the African landscape is undeveloped
rather than unfamiliar.

Shetty and Brantlinger have discussed how this evolutionary model
operates within the Africanist conventions. By using darkness as a token
for the primitive spirit that underlies European consciousness Conrad once
again asserts the imperial narrative over the perceptual one. Wallace and
Tomlinson deemphasized the perceptual clearing of the landscape in order
to show African forms in European terms; Conrad goes one step farther by
claiming this very perceptually cleared area as proof of the imperialist
evolutionary model. The imperial eye first clears the landscape, then adopts
that emptiness as a token of primitiveness. According to Marlow the earth
seems "unearthly" and like "an unknown planet" because it is a "prehis-
toric" landscape seen through a modern eye, not because it is an African
landscape seen through a European one. The visible parts of the jungle—
the crumbling huts and languishing slaves—are perceived as examples of
the pretechnological stage of civilization. The invisible parts suggest an
even more ancient period of the evolutionary past: the primordial "night of
the first ages." The mind searches for a familiar form that corresponds to
the foreign ones, and not finding any, adopts that absence, that darkness, as
a sign for the forgotten memories of an evolutionary past. At the base of
cultural and personal memory lies the absence of memory; *darknesss* as a
visual term suggesting the inability to perceive is translated into *darkness* as
a conceptual term suggesting African savagery. Darkness is thus both a
"cue" for a whole set of specific African abominations, as Shetty and
Brantlinger have shown, and the evidentiary absence of European memories of abomination. The word evokes a range of stereotypical—that is,
habitually imaged—"African" behavior including cannibalism, violence,
lust, and cruelty; however, it also suggests, through its definition of visual
absence as lost memory, the developmental distance of "civilized" Europe
from darkest Africa. The great subtlety of Conrad's use of the word lies in
its ability to link such racist associations to Africa and to deny that any
European could have consciously created that linkage, thus naturalizing the
evolutionary model in an invisible prehistory.

The importance of the cleared landscape, of darkness as visual absence, to Conrad's portrayal of African primitiveness becomes clear in a
comparison between Conrad's actual travel diary from the Congo and his
use of that diary in Marlow's tale. Sandhya Shetty has shown that, in
comparison to the *Diary*, Conrad's portrayal of landscape in *Heart of
Darkness* "has the effect of under-emphasizing the extent to which colonial

development had proceeded'' (Shetty 472). Conrad, however, under-emphasizes more than just progress; the whole landscape is under-emphasized into invisibility. Conrad's observations of foreign forms become Marlow's meditations on absence. The *Diary* is filled with brief but vivid portrayals of both African cultures and African landscapes.

> General tone of landscape gray-yellowish (dry grass), with reddish patches (soil) and clumps of dark-green vegetation scattered sparsely about, mostly in steep gorges between the high mountains or in ravines cutting the plain. Noticed Palma Christi—Oil palm. Very straight, tall and thick trees in some places. Name not known to me. Villages quite invisible. Infer their existence from cal[a]bashes suspended to palm trees for the ''malafu.'' Good many caravans and travellers. (*Congo Diary* 8)

The passage portrays both perception and the curiosity resulting from perception; the narrative eye notices more and more detail as landscape features initially seen as patches of color are defined as natural forms. Conrad recognizes the species with most manufacturing value, as does Wallace. Rather than allowing the African forms to disappear beside the few familiar ones, however, he points out the strangeness and newness of the unfamiliar trees. Even the villages, which are invisible to the eye, are brought to the reader's attention by Conrad's description of the calabashes, and of the curiosity that causes him to infer the villages' presence. Conrad thus demonstrates a mind engaged to grasp perceptual clues or signals about the landscape and draw what conclusions he can based on his own culturally determined perceptions.

By contrast, in Marlow's trek to the Central Station, generally considered a fictional version of the *Diary* trek, Marlow emphasizes the absence of new or unusual forms, and makes no attempt to infer any presences but his own.

> No use telling you much about that. Paths, paths, everywhere; a stamped-in network of paths spreading over the empty land, through the long grass, through the burnt grass, through thicket, down and up chilly ravines, up and down stony hills ablaze with heat; and a solitude, a solitude, nobody, not a hut. (*Heart of Darkness* 34)

Marlow's passage seems to be specifically crafted to emphasize disorder and absence. He begins by denying the importance of the landscape, then proceeds to a description of paths that show an orderly culture unravelling. The landscape appears only in prepositional phrases so that the subject of the sentence, and of the narrative eye, is the ruinous, inextricable network of paths that move through an ''empty'' ''solitude'' without any apparent purpose. Conrad's perception of the landscape in terms of color that re-

solves into form, or of calabashes hinting at hidden villages, emphasizes
the perceptual progression from strangeness to conditional recognition.
Marlow's perception of the landscape as a ruined European form surrounded by emptiness offers the African landscape as a natural blankness
anterior to European culture. In the fictional version of the trek, Conrad
denies Marlow the more complicated perceptual act of recognizing only
partly visible or partly familiar forms, and rushes him directly from initial
perception into visual failure. Conrad's eye sees "nobody, not a hut," as
does Marlow's, but where Conrad goes to the trouble to search for signs of
huts Marlow denies the presence of any significant visual forms with the
sweeping disclaimer "a solitude." Consequently, the trek becomes a cir-
cuitous and meaningless trip through emptiness.

Moreover, in *Heart of Darkness* Conrad frequently generalizes the
specific observations of the *Diary* so that they become meditations on
absence.

> Camp, cook, sleep, strike, camp, march. Now and then a carrier dead in
> harness, at rest in the long grass near the path, with an empty water-gourd
> and his long staff lying by his side. A great silence around and above.
> Perhaps on some quiet night the tremor of far-off drums, sinking, swelling, a
> tremor vast, faint; a sound weird, appealing, suggestive, and wild—and
> perhaps with as profound a meaning as the sound of bells in a Christian
> country. (*Heart of Darkness* 34)

"Camp, cook, sleep, strike" extends the action of the trip into a timeless
present that seems to signify the loss of temporal awareness Marlow mentions earlier as typical of civilized humanity in a primitive context. The
specific visual details of walking, cooking, and camping, as well as the
landscapes in which they take place, all dissipate into nonspecific verbs. In
the *Diary*, these same incidents are portrayed very specifically.

> Marching across a chain of hills and then in a maze of hills. At 8:15 opened
> out into an andulating plain. Took bearings of a break in the chain of moun-
> tains on the other side. Bearing NNE. Road passes through that. Sharp
> ascents up very steep hills not very high. . . .
> Saw another dead body lying by the path in an attitude of meditative
> repose.
> In the evening three women of whom one albino passed our camp.
> Horrid chalky white with pink blotches. Red eyes. Red hair. Features very
> Negroid and ugly. Mosquitos. At night when the moon rose heard shouts and
> drumming in distant villages. Passed a bad night. (*Congo Diary* 9)

Rather than actions described without reference to landscape features or
situation, Conrad offers specific descriptions of directed motion through

time and space. The dead body is one of many strange and rather grotesque sights Conrad runs across. He views it with some irony, but does not locate it as a single emblematical perception surrounded by "a great silence." The albino women seem to interest him a good deal more. Conrad's *Diary* demonstrates a variety of emotional responses to a variety of scenes and situations, but in *Heart of Darkness* only a few emblematic images, stripped of visual detail and made to resonate with symbolic qualities, remain. While Marlow ascribes a "profound . . . meaning" to the drums that suggests a developmental relationship between primitive and civilized religion, Conrad complains about the drums disturbing his sleep. For Conrad the drums are just another incident in the trek, but for Marlow the drums, like the paths, the silence, the emptiness, and the dead body, demonstrate the malevolent primitive essence that he has come to confront. The investigation of African conceptual "darkness" is made possible by the perceptual abstraction of the landscape into a visual darkness. Conrad's observations become Marlow's narrative of conquest when the random visual details that demonstrate cultural difference are generalized and simplified into nonvisual expressions of numinous absence.

Conrad asks us to believe that the book's major concern is the way the African landscape affects the mind of the European traveller. The utter solitude and darkness of Africa sets off long-dormant sensations and memory patterns in both Kurtz and Marlow.

> He had taken a high seat amongst the devils of the land—I mean literally, You can't understand. How could you? . . . how can you imagine what particular region of the first ages a man's untrammelled feet may take him into by the way of solitude—utter solitude without a policeman—by way of silence—utter silence, where no warning voice of a kind neighbour can be heard whispering of public opinion? (64)

Kurtz is the test case for Marlow's evolutionary model, for Kurtz seems to be able to interpret the primordial urgings—to remember his ancient past— and thus demonstrate the African primitivism inherent in European consciousness. Kurtz cannot be said to be taking on native customs, for, as both Marlow's statements and Conrad's representations emphasize, he is surrounded by emptiness, "solitude," and "silence" (i.e., visual darkness) rather than a foreign culture. Rather than going native, he goes mnemonic; the primitive psychic "darkness" is recalled once visual forms are eliminated:

> I tried to break the spell . . . of the wilderness—that seemed to draw him to its pitiless breast by the awakening of forgotten and brutal instincts, by the memory of gratified and monstrous passions. (81)

Marlow may receive dim suggestions of primordial memory, but Kurtz has actually found evidence of African primitivism within his own European mind; he has remembered "forgotten brutal instincts" and "monstrous passions."

This shift from personal memory to cultural history is crucial to the work's imagistic logic. Conrad predicates evidence for the evolutionary model on the individual psyche; we know that Europeans are more evolved, not just more powerful, than Africans because Marlow can almost remember and Kurtz can fully remember a form of savagery that, as Brantlinger shows, must inevitably be interpreted as distinctly African. Just as the other jungle narratives we have seen mask the perceptual narrative of visual familiarization with colonial narratives of improvement, however, Conrad masks the perceptual narrative of visual abstraction with a psychological narrative of evolutionary reversion. The real story here is what the mind does to the landscape, not what the landscape does to the mind. The characters seem to be moving inward, toward their own long-lost, deep-seated memories of African savagery; in fact, they are actively defining and characterizing the landscape around them based on their lack of memories. Conrad's technique is so effective because he is masking a psychophysical process with a psychological one; memory-based perception is rewritten as cultural memory. The mind moving through its well-worn grooves is portrayed as the mind moving back through evolutionary residues. Familiar European ideas of African savagery and primitiveness are disguised as remembered sensations and come to replace actual perceptions of the landscape and culture. Conrad pushes the limitations of the European eye in the jungle to a kind of blindness that is counteracted by the mind's ability to abstract and control the landscape psychologically. The mind, rather than being a passive entity whose reactions demonstrate cultural memory, is actively defining the landscape in familiar abstractions.

This masking of the psychophysical with the psychological helps explain why critics are so quick to adopt the evolutionary model. It is apparent at any reading of the text that the narrative is organized around mental processes involving memory and unfamiliarity. The imperialist eye, checking through its own frame of reference, finds no corresponding forms and so abstracts and familiarizes the landscape. Critics emphasize this process of reaching backward or downward into some basic, infantile realm of memory, but they fail to recognize the leap involved in transposing cultural history onto personal perception, and thus take the leap along with Conrad. Ian Watt claims that *Heart of Darkness* "is not essentially a political work" because "Conrad mainly followed his own direct imaginative perceptions," portraying the jungle and its inhabitants from an "inward and subjective point of view" (Watt 160). The reason Africa can so easily be confused with the interior of Marlow's mind, Watt suggests, is that Marlow fails to relate his direct visual perceptions, replacing them with familiar European "imaginative perceptions" of Africa. A subjective description, however, is by no means necessarily an apolitical one, for it is through the concentration on subjectively familiar forms that Conrad, Wallace, and Tomlinson clear and appropriate foreign landscapes. Peter Brooks states that "Marlow's individual journey repeats, ontogenetically, a kind of reverse phylogeny, an unraveling of the threads of civilization. His quest, we might say, is also an inquest, an investigation leading toward beginnings and origins" (Brooks 243). The ontogeny of personal memory, however, does not necessarily recapitulate the phylogeny of racial and economic conflict. Brooks's image of unravelling cloth, and his later suggestion that the jungle "is beyond the system of human social structures which makes language possible and is itself made possible by language" (Brooks 252) echoes Conrad's insistence that the landscape is empty rather than foreign and that African language is silent because it is incomprehensible to European ears. In returning to its basic ground—"to the earth and its names"— Brooks claims that the mind reverts to a "realm beyond interlocution" (251). As we have seen, the European mind in the jungle does return to its basic ground, but this is not some transcultural savage "earth," it is the individual's culturally determined memory.

By using Marlow's metaphors to analyze Marlow's repetition critics end up repeating the story in the same terms and offering the same political message. Brooks closes by suggesting that "there are no primary narratives," but rather that Marlow is retelling "an ancient historical story" of "the Roman commander navigating up the Thames, into a land of savagery" (Brooks 261). This essential repetition—of words, images, and stories—suggests how the importance of perceptual memory and habit is registered in Conrad's novel. James's nativistic way of seeing is ordered around habits that leave repeatable patterns in the brain.

> The retention of an experience is, in short, but another name for the *possibility* of thinking it again, or the *tendency* to think it again, with its past surroundings. Whatever accidental cue may turn this tendency into an actuality, the permanent *ground* of the tendency itself lies in the organized neural paths by which the cue calls up the experience on the proper occasion . . . (616)

For both James and Conrad, seeing and describing the world involves a mental process of return and repetition; sensations move through well-worn neural grooves. These neural grooves, however, are culturally determined, as Brantlinger and Shetty have shown, and by allowing ourselves to fall into them we also engage in imperialist vision. The "primary narrative" of

Heart of Darkness is that of the European mind returning to its primary
sensations, not that of the civilized conquerer moving into a primitive
landscape. For Europeans the image of the conquerer moving through an
empty landscape is a habitual image, so that when it is alluded to it appears
with all the vividness of a disclosed substantial truth. By encouraging us to
reimage the emptiness, rather than the foreign landscape, Conrad participates in rather than critiques this form of cultural discourse.

At the beginning of the novel Marlow states that imperialism is re-
deemed by an "idea at the back of it"; by the end of it, Conrad has created
such an idea in the reader's mind—the idea of darkness itself. Pratt shows
how early nineteenth-century travel writers create the land for the European
reader by delineating its conquerable boundaries, but in the late nineteenth
century it is necessary to uncreate the jungle, to portray it as an insubstantial blankness anterior to European civilization. In Wallace's landscape the
unseen is the perceptual equivalent of the unfit; forms that have no significance to his culture are eliminated from the visual field, just as forms
without survival value are eliminated from nature. In Tomlinson's world,
darkness is a failure of aesthetic imagination against which European cultural artifacts shine brilliantly. In Conrad's jungle, darkness ceases to be a
visual phenomenon; instead, it becomes the idea through which imperialism operates. Kurtz's humanitarianism and his brutality both rely on the
idea of darkness: to bring light one must see a darkness; to create civilized
people one must clear the landscape of uncivilized ones, or "Exterminate
all the brutes!" (66). Implicit in an imperialist vision is the annexing of all
foreign forms into the culture's perceptual memory; jungle authors base
their representational strategies on processes of visual translation in which
the familiar world is made brilliantly visible by the intense invisibility of
the unfamiliar. The imperialist eye perceives only familiar forms, clearing the landscape of unfamiliar objects much as an army clears the landscape of indigenous peoples, and appropriating the resulting emptiness as
the open ground upon which it can build its own culture. The narrative of
civilization, of the evolution from primitive darkness to the shining city, is
always foregrounded in such portrayals, while the narrative action of the
eye and mind as it clears the visual field goes unrecorded. In order to
imagine a new world, as Darwin does, one must relinquish a normative
representational strategy and, as a result, one's norms must change. Darwin's jungle is able to overwhelm the European eye through an influx of
alien forms. A book, writes Conrad, "is a deed . . . the writing of it is an
enterprise as much as the conquest of a colony" (*Last Essays,* 132). By
adopting an aesthetic of familiarity, Conrad claims the colonial landscape
as an imaginative territory of the European mind.

4

Blossoms of Mutation: Field Theory in the Works of Richard Jefferies, W. H. Hudson, and D. H. Lawrence

Critics of D. H. Lawrence tend to be divided between those who believe Lawrence wishes to portray a literal, materially present landscape and those who consider his landscape a metaphor for human psychic states. The difference between these two positions can often be reduced to the juggling of tenors and vehicles. John Alcorn, echoing the long-standing critical appraisal of Lawrence as a "psychoanalytical" novelist, describes him as "internalizing landscape" and "developing an idiom through which the subtle ebb and flow of the unconscious life of his characters might be charted through the device of nature description" (Alcorn 90). Roger Ebbatson takes the opposite view, seeing the rhythms of nature charted on humanity; rather than nature serving as an expression of the characters' unconscious desires, human sexuality is "Lawrence's 'objective correlative' for the deep flow of Nature" (Ebbatson 52). Rather than the landscape being internalized, "the characters are dwarfed by the intensity of the realisation of the life of Nature . . . they are swamped by their environment. . . . The characters remain figures in a landscape, a small part of an overwhelming totality" (Ebbatson 52).

Yet, elsewhere in their arguments these critics seem to switch perspectives. Alcorn, while emphasizing psychological "interiority," also stresses how such interiority implies tangibility and exterior material presence; Lawrence "turned from the visual to the tactile and aural senses, from the static quality of graphic representation to the immediate and dynamic qualities of rhythm and touch" (Alcorn 92). While asserting that nature sets the pattern for human consciousness, Ebbatson proceeds to describe it as an "image" of human passion and of Lawrence's own feelings.

> Nature images in its wider totality that flow and recoil which characterises
> Lawrence's dramatisation of human relations—a dialectic of passion which,
> in his analysis, has been stifled in the modern world. It is this very flow and
> recoil of Lawrence's own feelings and ideas, charted in the novels and
> poems, which renders definitions of his position in terms such as "pantheist"
> and "vitalist" inappropriate.   (Ebbatson 29)

Such apparent contradictions emerge continually in critical discussions of
Lawrence's nature. Daniel R. Schwarz, who, like Alcorn, describes the
landscape of the modern novel as an expression of the author's psyche
suggests that Lawrence's metaphors bypass conceptualization to become

> sensuous, physical, instinctive and biological. . . . Such metaphors, rather
> than creating objective correlatives, are lyrical explosions whose rhythms
> and images are supposed to engage immediately the reader's libidinous self
> without the intervening cognitive process.   (Schwarz 72)

J. R. Watson, like Ebbatson, asserts that Lawrence's nature is

> always there in the novel, outside and beyond the characters . . . It is the
> force of the landscape accumulated over centuries that pulses in the blood of
> Tom, Anna and Ursula, making them what they are; they are shaped and
> possessed by a greater power than themselves.   (Watson 28, 30)

At another point in the same essay, however, Watson states that "a total
apprehension" of that exterior nature must include "a creative interaction
between the internal and external world which is a total experience, involving mind, body and accumulated understanding" (Watson 17). Critics who
describe Lawrence's nature as a manifestation of the human psyche also
emphasize its material presence, while those who describe it as a powerful,
shaping exterior reality seem drawn inexorably back to defining it in human
psychological terms.

   That Lawrence's conception of nature should include paradoxes, that
it should be, in Ebbatson's words, "dialectical," is not so surprising.
Lawrence's own love of paradox is apparent in his critical writings as well
as in critical writings about him. In order to investigate Lawrence's contribution to the nativistic diminishment of landscape, however, it is important
to find a structure that will help explain this paradox without simply restat-
ing it. How is it possible to portray a nature at once psychic and tangible, at
once materially and sensually exterior and psychologically interior? Is this
a uniquely and characteristically Lawrencian paradox, or is it a manifestation of a specific way of understanding matter and the perception of matter,
shared by other nature writers and thinkers? This chapter will demonstrate
that Lawrence's paradoxical conception of the relationship between psy-

chology and nature is based on a field conception of matter and that such a field model is apparent not only in his writing but in the work of other nature writers such as Richard Jefferies and W. H. Hudson.

Albert Einstein explains the emergence of field theory as follows.

> The old mechanical view attempted to reduce all events in nature to forces acting between material particles. . . . The field did not exist for the physicist of the early years of the nineteenth century. For him only substance and its changes were real. . . . In the new field language it is the description of the field between the two charges, and not the charges themselves, which is essential for an understanding of their action. The recognition of the new concepts grew steadily, until substance was overshadowed by field. . . . A new reality was created, a new concept for which there was no place in the mechanical description. (Einstein 151)

Einstein points out the radical change in conceptions of the material world brought about by the "new" physics of the late nineteenth and early twentieth centuries. Darwin's evolutionary theory, for all its questioning of the stability of organic form, portrayed the animal body as a material object. The material forms of nature, in wholes or in parts, overflow from Darwin's works; the reader experiences the natural world as a cornucopia of entangled organic matter. Einstein, however, suggests that in nineteenth-century physics material bodies were ceasing to be the primary units of representation. Nature writers of the late-nineteenth and early-twentieth centuries do not portray nature's forms as much as they do the forces between and around those forms. In the works of authors such as Richard Jefferies, W. H. Hudson and D. H. Lawrence, the representation of nature becomes a portrayal of fields of energy in which bodies are defined by forces and make forces visible. Einstein describes the concept of the field as an "interpreter" (134), an abstraction created to explain the unusual actions that bodies perform in certain electrical and gravitational contexts. As field theory grew, however, the objects came to be seen as the indicators of field forces, and "substance was overshadowed by the field."

Gestalt psychology was conceived around the principle that "the basic functional concepts of physics are applicable to brain dynamics" (Köhler 345). Gestalt psychologists believed visual forms were determined by the interaction of electrochemical forces in the brain and were by-products or manifestations of dynamic interactions. In the works of these authors, the forms of the English countryside are significant only insofar as they demonstrate underlying fields of force. For Richard Jefferies, the living world is a "stream of atmosphere," not an entangled bank; animals and landscape forms appear in dynamic patterns of motion, like so many iron filings arranging themselves around a magnet. W. H. Hudson's nature is a "living garment" of vividly contrasting color regions that interact according to field forces of chromatic contrast rather than biological laws. The world of D. H. Lawrence is populated by bodies that are at once sensual and dynamic, defined by their color and motion in a whirl of centrifugal and centripetal forces. Gestalt theory was nativistic in that it assumed the mind's electrochemical forces to operate by uniform measurable laws that also applied in exterior nature. Uniform forces will produce whole, regular forms and there will be a reliable correspondence between the exterior stimulus and the mental event. Lawrence's paradox, in which exterior presence and psychological interiority intensify rather than contradict one another, results from his definition of matter as energy operating by the same dynamic laws both in the mind and in nature. Like Darwin, these authors attempt to portray the invisible forces of nature as visually present; however, where Darwin portrays the biological interaction of bodies, these authors portray the field interaction of perceptual forces.

I

In Richard Jefferies's novel *Amaryllis at the Fair* (1887), an artist describes the difficulty involved in representing the motion of a bird's wings.

> Alere showed how impossible it was to show a bird in flight by the starling's wings. . . . [Y]ou see the wings in innumerable . . . positions . . . like the leaves of a book opened with your thumb quickly—as they do in legerdemain—almost as you see the spokes of a wheel run together as they revolve—a sort of burr.
>
> To produce an image of a starling flying, you must draw all this.
>
> The swift feathers are almost liquid; they leave a streak behind in the air like a meteor. (169)

Jefferies begins with a description of an illusion that results from residual imagery, much like Darwin's hand/paddle/wing passage. The individual images of the starling's wing are presented so swiftly to the eye that they blur together into a single form. Where Darwin uses the residual images of several forms to demonstrate their analogous physiology, however, Jefferies concentrates on the residual "streak" left by one form in motion, in order to demonstrate its swiftness. Consequently, where Darwin's reader sees several bodies coalesce into one, Jefferies's reader sees only a line.

> A black line has rushed up from the espalier apple yonder to the housetop thirty times at least. The starlings fly so swiftly and so straight that they seem to leave a black line along the air. (Looker 135)

The flapping of a bird's wings is perceived as a circle:

> A magpie flew up from the short green corn to a branch low down on an elm, his back towards me, and as he rose his tail seemed to project from a white circle. The white tips of his wings met—or apparently so—as he fluttered, both above and beneath his body, so that he appeared encircled with a white ring. (Looker 27)

Jefferies portrays the dynamism of natural matter by allowing natural motion to become more visually important than the bodies that are in motion. In effect, he offers us a record of the motion itself; the black line tells us nothing about the starling's form. In Darwin's work, the residual images of the hand/paddle/wing pile up in the reader's mind, allowing Darwin to multiply and complicate the animal body until one form appears to contain many others; Jefferies presents the residual image of a single moving body in such a way that not even that one form is imaged. Jefferies's visual nature is thus composed not of objects but of the perceptual traces left by dynamic forces.

Form is so insignificant in Jefferies's landscape that he pays little attention to whether a dynamic streak is made by one or by several forms in motion.

> The wet furrows reflect the [sun's] rays so that the dark earth gleams, and in the slight mist that stays farther away the light pauses and fills the vapour with radiance. Through the luminous mist the larks race after each other twittering, and as they turn aside, swerving in their swift flight, their white breasts appear for a moment. . . . The lark and the light are as one, and wherever he glides over the wet furrows the glint of the sun goes with him. Anon alighting he runs between the lines of the green corn. In hot summer, when the open hillside is burned with bright lights, the larks are singing and soaring. (Tickner 3–4)

It is not entirely clear whether the rising, swooping, and wheeling is that of the larks or of the sunbeams. Color, form, and motion create a dynamic field of paralleling activity in which the lark and the light become interchangeable units of natural energy. Both are white lines through the fog, both are bright semicircles at dawn, and both race through the corn rows and frolic across the summer landscape. The lark and the light seem to draw the same line through the air, and it is this line, rather than the objects that created it, that the reader images as the fundamental visual unit of nature.

This unification of streaks of motion is not a formal coalescence in the Darwinian sense, for the reader never sees the two forms of lark and sunbeam to be in any way similar—they simply leave the same dynamic trace. In another passage Jefferies portrays a typically Darwinian illusion— the transformation of one animal into another—in a distinctly non-

Darwinian fashion: "[Y]ou may see a covey [of partridges] there now and then, creeping slowly with humped backs, and at a distance not unlike hedgehogs in their motions" (Tickner 9–10). Under normal conditions, partridges look nothing like hedgehogs; only "in their motions" do the two animals become indistinguishable. While Darwin's coalescent perception of bear and whale concentrates on specific parts of the animals' bodies and results in a greater awareness of their physiology, Jefferies's concentrates on the line left by the bodies, and results in a comprehension of them simply as moving forms. The moving forms could be partridges, hedgehogs, spider monkies, or black dots, as long as they move in the same way. Had Darwin been making this comparison the reader would have come away with the impression of a large mouth, a rounded rib cage, or a sloping skull that could be matched between the two bodies. In Jefferies's portrayal the reader images a pattern of movement from one point to another; the fact that the points beginning and ending the motion are animals with distinct bodily forms remains unnoticed. The pheasants and the hedgehogs, like the lark and the light, become one being by ceasing to be visually significant as material forms and becoming the traces of dynamic motion.

Jefferies's portrayal of visual motion demonstrates a visual principle that Max Wertheimer was to investigate in a groundbreaking experiment on illusory motion two decades later. Wertheimer created a device that projected the image of a vertical line first on the left side, and then on the right side of a screen. If the images were flashed on and off successively, and for the correct duration, the viewer would perceive only one line moving back and forth from left to right. Moreover, given the correct conditions the viewer was able to describe either form, and was simply aware of having seen "something in motion" (Wertheimer in Hartmann 6). Furthermore, the illusion of motion was not affected when the two images were different. Thus, if one of the straight vertical lines was replaced by a wiggly one, the viewer would still perceive "something in motion." In a sense the viewer was perceiving motion itself. This is precisely what seems to occur in Jefferies's landscape.

> Westward the sun was going down over the sea, and a wild west wind, which the glow of the sun as it touched the waves seemed to heat into a fury, brought up the distant sound of the billows from the beach. A line of dark Spanish oaks from which the sharp-pointed acorns were dropping, darkest green oaks, shut out the shore. A thousand starlings were flung up into the air out of these oaks, as if an impatient hand had cast them into the sky; then down they fell again, with a ceaseless whistling and clucking; up they went and down they came, lost in the deep green foliage as if they had dropped in the sea. (Williamson 331)

The dynamism of this passage results from the narrative accumulation of natural processes of rising and falling. The sun going down, the waves and wind rising, the acorns falling, the trees rising against the sky, and the birds flying up then coming down are all objects flashed before the reader in separate positions and at such duration that they seem to create an overall pattern of rising and falling. If someone were shown a picture of a wave, then above it a picture of the sun, then below it a picture of acorns, that viewer would be given the impression of up and down motion even though the sequence of images made no logical sense. Even so, a series of successively positioned moving forms that bear no necessary relationship to one another but which are perceived in a continuous pattern of motion give the reader a sense of nature's intense, dynamic, unified undulation. Nature is composed of rising and falling rather than sun, acorns, ocean, and trees; the landscape is a seething medium of physical movements rather than of physiological objects.

Jefferies's concept of nature is based on the dynamic forces that shape it rather than the material units of which it is composed. Kurt Koffka, Wertheimer's subject in the motion experiment and one of the founders of Gestalt psychology, makes a similar claim for the Gestalt conception of the universe.

> Man the builder assembles his bricks and erects his house. . . . He forgets that he has piled these bricks in a gravitational field and that without this gravitational field he can build a house as little as without bricks. But the bricks are so much more palpable than gravitation that he thinks of them alone, and thus he models his concept of reality. Substance assumes for human thought the role of being the embodiment for the real. . . . But this difficulty arises for the philosopher only, and not for the architect or the physicist. The physicist is far from such crude realism. As a matter of fact he finds it harder and harder to lay his hands on "substances." Organized fields of force assume for him the chief reality. (Koffka 57–58)

Wertheimer, Koffka, and their associate Wolfgang Köhler suggested that, while previous theorists had explained perception in terms of the accumulation of points of light on the retina, it was better explained as the interaction of electrochemically charged fields in the brain cortex. According to Wertheimer the illusion of motion created in his experiment was caused by a "short circuit" in the brain. Rather than a set of specific neural receptors, like telephone lines, Gestalt theorists saw the brain as a netlike cortex; visual stimulations are "not restricted to small areas of the cortex but form a pattern pervading the whole area of the cortex with areas of highest activity varying with the kind of stimulation" (Koffka 61). The two forms perceived in the Wertheimer experiment create two separate electrochemical responses in the brain, each response creating an "excitation ring" (Hartmann 6) of electrochemical charge. When the excitation rings are close enough and of the correct frequency a current flows between them, causing an electrochemical "motion" in the brain; the motion of the current through the brain from one cortical region to another is the *physiological correlate* (Köhler 281) of object motion. The basic units of perception, therefore, are not minimum visibles adding up to forms, or even complete forms, but the currents that create an impression of visible form through their dynamic interactions.

Koffka and Jefferies, like Einstein, portray a world composed of dynamic fields of force that ebb and flow around one another. Darwin, like empirical perception theorists and what Einstein calls "mechanical" physicists, thinks of nature as a collection of minimum units, or particles (Koffka's "bricks"), that are rearranged when different forms are perceived. For field theorists, form is simply the result of two fields interacting. In Gestalt perceptual theory, for example, a black circle on a white background is perceived because the black area and the white create two different field responses in the brain. As someone looks at the circle, two different electrochemical responses will be generated in the netlike brain cortex, causing an *inhomogeneous field*. In order to balance this inhomogeneity the currents corresponding to the black area will flow together, as will those corresponding to the white area, and the field will be divided into two field parts. As Koffka states:

> [I]f the proximal stimulation is such that it consists of several areas of different homogeneous stimulation, then the areas which receive the same stimulation will organize unitary field parts segregated from the others by the difference between the stimulations. In other words the equality of stimulation produces forces of cohesion, inequality of stimulation forces of segregation . . .   (Koffka 126)

The point of distinction between the field parts, or *leap of stimulation* (135) as Koffka puts it, will be perceived as the edge of a form.

> [E]xactly the same proposition holds in physics. Thus . . . if oil is poured into a liquid with which it does not mix, the surface of the oil will remain sharply determined in the violent interaction of molecules, and if the liquid has the same density, then the oil will form a sphere swimming in the other liquid.   (Koffka 126)

A Gestalt form is thus not an actual object, but the product of the balancing of perceptual forces. Consequently, a form has no material shape or dimension, but rather it consists of the currents that determine it. Perceived forms, like oil in water, will often be regularized or "smoothed" by the currents surrounding them. A slightly irregular form, such as the one in Fig. 7 (Koffka 140), will be perceived as a circle. Jefferies's narrative eye regularizes natural forms in a similar fashion. "At a distance," he writes, "the enclosed fields seem surrounded with hedges, not merely cropped, but smoothed and polished, so rounded and regular do they appear" (Tickner 31). Animals are similarly smoothed and polished by visual effects.

Fig. 7. From Kurt Koffka, *Principles of Gestalt Psychology* (1935).

> Rude and uncouth as swine are in themselves, somehow they look different under trees. The brown leaves amid which they root, and the brown-tinted fern behind lend something of their colour and smooth away their ungainliness. Snorting as they work with very eagerness of appetite, they are almost wild, approaching in measure to their ancestors, the savage bears.   (Looker 200)

The rudeness of the hog's form is "smoothed" by the mind; the reader's impression of the hog is reduced to that of a malleable colored region that is being molded by the forces of the visual field. Like the passage in which the pheasants become hedgehogs, Jefferies offers us no comparison of animal parts between hog and bear, but reduces the hog and bear bodies to a formally malleable visual region. The Darwinian represention of the body as an object composed of variable parts becomes impossible in a Gestalt world because the visual form is only malleable as a whole. Darwin's visual representation of nature relies upon the fragmentation and shuffling of body parts. He makes the pigeon bodies "fluid" only in the sense that a brick wall being continually made and unmade is fluid; the reader must see the tumbler's beak, the pouter's crop, and the carrier's carunculated skin to understand nature's dynamism. Jefferies is able to show the animal body transforming without parts; we do not see an evolutionary force at work in this change, only a perceptual one.

The Jefferian naturalist is a physicist at heart, looking past matter to the forces that impel it. Where the variety of natural forms dazzled Darwin's eye, Jefferies's is overwhelmed by the speed and dynamism of natural motion. The eye perceives matter, but the essence of life is an immaterial flash that only an extraordinarily swift eye, like the swallow's, can catch.

> Swift and mobile as is the swallow's wing, how much swifter and much more mobile must be his eye. . . . [H]is eyes are to our eyes as his wings are to our limbs. If still further we were to consider the flow of the nerve force between the eye, the mind, and the wing, we should be face to face with problems which quite upset the ordinary ideas of matter as a solid thing. (Tickner 28)

Jefferies's speculations on matter grow out of his aesthetic awareness of nature's dynamic motion. A natural world that is composed of so many dynamic, meteoric forms can only be perceived by a mind that is itself dynamic and thus immaterial. For both Jefferies and the Gestalt psychologists the dynamic laws of neural activity also apply to matter in general; the fluid dynamism of the mind mirrors and is mirrored by the fluid dynamism of the universe. The speed and power of the imagination thus calls into question the solidity of matter. Gestalt theorists saw their theory calling into question a part-based model of perception, just as Einstein's work called into question the fundamental units of matter.

> Wherein does the similarity of the two views [Gestalt theory and relativity] lie? Primarily in the opposition of both systems to the summative and additive treatment of data. Each strikes at the discreteness of the cosmos . . . sensations are not independent, velocities and spaces and times are not absolute.   (Humphrey in Hartmann 51)

Form is not like a building, composed of so many different pieces, but like oil in water, adapting its shape to the dynamic conditions surrounding it.

Despite what appears to be a disorderly conception of matter Koffka claimed that Gestalt theory reasserted an order that was lost by nineteenth-century materialism.

> Materialism accomplished the integration [of life and nature] by robbing life of its order and thereby making us look down on life as just a curious combination of orderless events; if life is as blind as inorganic nature we must have as little respect for the one as for the other. But if inanimate nature shares with life the aspect of order, then the respect which we feel directly and unreflectively for life will spread over to inanimate nature also. (Koffka 17)

Darwinian theory undercut the possibility of a formal order in nature, but Koffka hopes to establish a dynamic one by demonstrating the similarity of exterior material forces to interior mental forces, what he refers to here as the order of "life"; the nativistic similarity of exterior and perceived forms and the perceptual reliability associated with those forms would thus be assured by the regularity of the physical forces determining them. Jefferies's vision of nature is ordered in just this way; the dynamic patterns that affect very different forms are consistent and stable. The lark and the light, the birds and the acorns, and the pheasants and the hedgehogs are all moved by the same underlying forces. Forms only serve to demonstrate this order. The chaos of form created by Darwin is thus subsumed into energy structures that, although powerful and dynamic, operate according to consistent and predictable patterns.

Koffka, however, stresses that his theory is not "vitalist." By demonstrating the "order" of the human mind "as a characteristic of *natural* events and therefore within the domain of physics," Gestalt theory is able to "accept it in the science of life without introducing a special vital force responsible for the creation of order" (Koffka 17). Similarly, Jefferies is not simply transposing a psychological order onto nature. W. J. Keith claims that Jefferies, "realizing that it is the human mind which, in a sense, creates order out of the prolific chaos of nature . . . penetrates the surface to discover the generalized but no less vivid reality" (Keith 160). For Jefferies, however, there is no surface to penetrate; matter is not significant as an exterior crust surrounding an interior spirit—both exterior and interior life manifest the same fundamental motion.

> Summer shows us Matter changing into life, sap rising from the earth through a million tubes, the alchemic power of light entering the solid oak; and see! it bursts forth in countless leaves. Living things leap in the grass, living things drift upon the air, living things are coming forth to breathe in every hawthorn bush. No longer does the immense weight of Matter—the dead, the crystalized—press ponderously on the thinking mind. The whole office of Matter is to feed life—to feed the green rushes, and the roses that are about to be; to feed the swallows above, and us that wander beneath them.   (Tickner 65)

It is not only the sap rising from within, but also the sun pulsing from without that makes the leaves burst forth. Action overwhelms form as verbs overwhelm nouns; Jefferies's narrative eye perceives leaping, drifting, and breathing, not the visually nonspecific "living things." The human mind participates in this order rather than creates it. Like all other matter, the Jefferian mind feeds the dynamic motion of life, and the Jefferian narrative eye perceives the dynamic patterns of natural energy that unify the mind with nature.

II

Like Jefferies, W. H. Hudson portrays a landscape in which form is less significant than the forces that create it; however, for Hudson these forces are manifested in color rather than motion.[1]

> Looking round upon the living garment of many colours, especially where the glowing orange-yellow patches of ragwort are most conspicuous, one can fancy that the strayed pack-horses of a silk merchant of the olden time have passed this way, and that the sharp claws of the bramble have caught and pulled the packages to pieces, scattering far and wide the shining fabrics of all the hues in the rainbow. (*Nature in Downland* 41)

Hudson's landscape consists of so many differently colored fabrics—each one pure in its own hue and standing out vividly against its ground, like forms segregated by the Gestalt mind. The multiple shades of the forest that dazzle the Darwinian eye and demonstrate the multiple possibilities of the empirical visual field are here replaced by segregated groupings. The reader gets a strong sense of the visual purity and intensity of organisms seen in a natural setting, not of evolutionary flux, or even, as in Hardy, of powerful formal interaction. Each form portrayed by Hudson seems to be vividly and uniformly colored, and set against a contrasting background.

> That was a beautiful picture I had to look at, with the doorway for frame; a round yellow hill and the blue sky beyond, and between the hill and the church a green meadow, low outhouse and fences, and a small paddock or enclosure with rooks and daws and small birds coming and going. And by-and-by, into that green enclosure came a white calf, and remained there for some time, standing motionless in the centre of the picture. The brilliant sunlight made it luminous, and it was like a calf hewn out of a block of purest white chalk. (*Nature in Downland* 10)

Hudson's forms do not combine or interact like Darwin's, but neither are they tangibly distinct like Hardy's. The yellow hill and the blue sky are separate because their colors are vividly distinct, allowing no blending. The calf seems to rise away from the ground—one gets no sense of the calf's hooves pushing through the grass or leaving dents in the soil. While Jefferies's nature displays motion, Hudson's displays color; nature is worth seeing because of the brilliance of its colors, and the task of the nature writer is to capture that brilliance. Consequently, Hudson attempts to emphasize coloring by homogenizing and intensifying natural hues.

John Alcorn states that "Hudson's landscape is itself a source of light, rather than a reflection of it. His plants and animals seem to burn with an intrinsic fire of vitality which is invariably portrayed in vivid primary

hues'' (Alcorn 56). The energy that seems to radiate from Hudson's landscape results from his use of contrast to homogenize and intensify color in
ways that are consistent with Gestalt color theory. Gestalt theorists claimed
that the current fields of the brain both regularize forms and tend to make
them more vividly and homogeneously colored. Koffka notes that there is a
''connection between high degree of articulation and coloring'' (Koffka
186); the cohesion and segregation of form also involves a cohesion and
segregation of color. A gray figure on a white ground looks darker than one
on a black ground because ''a white process induces a black process in its
whole surrounding'' (Koffka 133), and vice versa. Furthermore, a mottled
or varicolored white figure will appear more homogeneously colored on a
dark ground because ''a strongly unified part of the field will look as
uniform as possible'' (135). If a piece of paper is layed across the center of
the circle in Fig. 8 (Koffka 134), for example, the viewer will perceive it as
red against the green background and green against the red. When the
divider is removed and the circle becomes a complete form, it is perceived
as grey so as to be as uniform as possible. Color is therefore not a ''summative and absolute affair'' (Koffka 134), but a dynamic process, defined by
the chromatic context in which any one color is perceived.

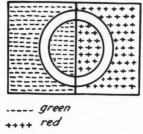

----- *green*
++++ *red*

Fig. 8. From Kurt Koffka, *Principles of Gestalt Psychology* (1935).

Hudson's brightly colored ''living garment'' (*Nature in Downland* 25)
displays the homogenization and intensification of contrast typical of Gestalt color vision. In the following passage, for example, a chaos of color is
transformed into a static collection of segregated color regions.

> There was nowhere a mass or patch of bright colour, but over the whole
> surface a sprinkling of yellow, red, white, purple, and blue colour, the
> flowers everywhere mixed with golden brown and silvery brown grasses,
> while under this thin herbage appeared the red ground flecked with white
> flints. It was a curiously beautiful and fascinating picture. . . . [W]e get an
> effect of this kind in a few stained-glass windows. The one I have in my mind

> at this moment has given me more pleasure than any other window in any church or cathedral in England; and it is without design, for it was destroyed some three or four centuries ago, but the fragments were gathered up by pious hands, and after many years restored to their place pieced anyhow together. (*Nature in Downland* 34)[2]

Because the Gestalt landscape is composed of physical forces rather than of biological forms, it is no more "entangled" than are oil and water. Hudson reimagines an entangled bank as a collection of distinct, colored pieces of glass. While he begins the passage by asserting the absence of bright homogeneous color regions, the effect of the stained-glass metaphor is to homogenize and intensify the irregular entanglements of a Darwinian nature into monochromatic regions. The "extraordinary variety of plants" become "yellow, red, white, purple, and blue colour" set rigidly into a window frame. It is this transformation of "plants" into "colour," of biology into physics, that makes Hudson's world as relativistic and dynamic as the Gestalt mind. As plants, the flowers have organically significant forms that, although they may only represent a moment of evolutionary flux, are biologically functional. As colors they are formless, demonstrating only the field forces that determine them. In the following passage, for example, the transformation of organic forms into colors becomes explicit, and the formal variety of nature is replaced by a variety of color.

> Crane's-bill and musky stork's-bill—merely specks of red; little round-leaved mint, a faint misty purple; and the scented plaintain, its leaves like leaves cut out of green cloth, pressed flat and sewn upon the green fabric. . . . Woodruff, round and among the furze bushes, like powdery snow newly fallen on the green earth: and curiously named squinancy-wort, exceeding small and fragrant, blooming all over the turfy downs, here white, there rose-red, or deep red, or purple. (*Nature in Downland* 43)

The distinction between the Darwinian observer, who is ravished by nature's biological complexity, and the Hudsonian observer, who is moved by "colour effects not often seen" is, roughly, that between the natural scientist and the travelling aesthete. For Darwin, to be ravished by nature is to perceive its formal variety; the more intensely the Darwinian observer sees, the more forms are apparent in nature. Hudson's reader, on the other hand, is encouraged to observe the landscape at its most intensely colored, and therefore its most formless.

> The South Downs, in their cultivated parts, are seen at their best in July and August, when the unreaped corn turns from green to red gold: whether the tint be yellow or red, it strikes one as more intense than on the lower levels. (*Nature in Downland* 25)

Hudson invariably directs the reader's eye to the most vivid color combinations and to the most homogeneously colored vistas. In large part, Hudson's works are structured around such visual direction; his representations of nature are records of visually intense experiences. The way nature "strikes one" is of primary importance.

Kim Herzinger notes that

> The Georgians, like so many others in England, were well aware that the center of English life had moved away from the rural, and toward the city. Much of their worst poetry come from a kind of fragile nostalgia derived from their recognition that a whole, authentic way of life had been lost. (Herzinger 73)

Hudson manifests a similar nostalgia. Many of his works, published in the first two decades of the twentieth century, chronicle the disappearance of the landscape that they celebrate. He says of *Nature in Downland*, published in 1900, that it is an attempt to paint "vividly on our minds" the Sussex landscape so that it may become part of the "spiritual geography" of England. Herzinger's description of this nostalgia as "fragile" is particularly appropriate because Hudson is attempting to produce a literary monument, to counteract the historical fragility of the downs by giving them an imagistic presence that is larger and more vivid than life. Mervin Nicholson argues that Hudson "thinks of art chiefly as an effort at preservation. The element of art or form in a 'living picture' is what enables memory to preserve the experience, as though art were an aid to memory" (Nicholson 316). Hudson's frequent comparison between landscape forms and art forms, such as the calf statue or the stained glass window, serve as memory aids. An adder "is like a richly-coloured or brightly-embroidered garter, or ribbon, dropped by chance on the pale colourless ground" (*Nature in Downland* 77). Perceiving nature as artificial always involves the intensification of its colors. In the following passage he records a vivid visual effect in which the cattle of the downs take on monumental proportions due to the simplicity of their coloring.

> The arrangement of the group as well as the form of the creatures composing it—men and great rough-hewn cattle—was wonderfully fine; but I also think that colour was a principal element in the fascinating effect the spectacle produced—the contrast of those large living black masses with the shining red and gold of the wheat. (*Nature in Downland* 29–30)

Seeing this effect leads Hudson to imagine the oxen as actual statues.

> If unlimited wealth were mine I should be tempted to become the owner of one of these great hills, to place upon it, as a gift to posterity, a representation

> in some imperishable material of these black cattle engaged with their human
> fellow-creatures in getting in the harvest. . . . To begin with, a sculptor of
> genius would be required, a giant among artists; and the materials would be
> gigantic blocks of granite and marble—red, black, grey, and yellow. From
> these would be wrought, twice or thrice the size of life, a group—a partly-
> loaded waggon, drawn by three couples of great bullocks, attended by four or
> five labourers in their rough grey garments. . . . [It] would remain un-
> ruined by time and weather for at least a thousand years.   (29)

The fineness of the bullocks' "effect" is created by the contrast between
the black figures and their red and gold background, and the overall grand-
ness of the figures themselves is caused by their chromatic uniformity.
Hudson emphasizes the size of the sculptures in part by emphasizing the
purity of the colors that make them up. The narrative eye perceives them as
more monumental, more like the statues Hudson hopes to erect, because of
their intense color contrast. Thus, paradoxically, visual intensity comes to
suggest material weight and endurance. Nicholson characterizes the statues
as "inadequate and impermanent" (Nicholson 316), but Hudson constructs
the image so that the perceptually intensified oxen are more substantial, and
more enduring, than their actual counterparts.

Similarly, Hudson describes an "immense basin-shaped combe" with
yews growing on the sides and beeches on the bottom that, on a particular
winter evening, gives the effect of being a natural temple.

> For the tall beeches on which I looked down appeared as innumerable white
> or pale columns standing on a floor of red or russet gold, and white columns
> and golden floor were all the more beautiful for being seen through the almost
> cloud-like tracery of innumerable purple and purplish-red or 'murrey'-
> colored branchlets. The rich colour of that temple and palace of nature—the
> golden floor and purple roof—made the wide band of the yew wood seem
> black by contrast; and above the black yews the smooth turf of the hill-top
> looked a pale green.   (*Nature in Downland* 228)

Again, it is the particular effect of contrast between the beeches and the
yews—the white trunks, the golden leaves, and the purple branches—that
cause the natural landscape to be intensified and homogenized into an
artificial and monumental structure. Hudson's monumental transformation
of nature is somewhat reminiscent of the architectural transformations used
by the jungle writers, and both can be considered examples of nativistic
simplification of landscape. Hudson, however, while homogenizing formal
detail into color, does not darken sections of nature; he wishes to intensify
the landscape rather than to familiarize it.[3] The transformation of the landscape into an artifact does not leave the reader's vision empty, but full of

forms that seem brighter and more massive than ever. He turns the combe into a monumental structure so that it will remain vividly in the reader's mind after the real trees are gone.

Form becomes so malleable in Hudson's world, so dependent upon color, that it ceases to be useful as a biological concept. Darwin's redefinition of static species allowed for a more plastic conception of the body, but Hudson has gone beyond bodies entirely into a world of colored expanses. His plants and animals are made up of interacting blue, red, and yellow fields rather than fur, petals, and stems, and this chromatic intensity comes to suggest material weight and longevity. Again, the Lawrencean paradox of greater physical presence linked to intense mental dynamism allows a perceptually formless nature to be materially present.

III

Where Jefferies and Hudson perceive color and motion as indicators of natural dynamism, D. H. Lawrence addresses the relationship between matter and energy directly. In doing so he calls into question the artistic portrayal of material form.

> [W]e realize finally that matter is only a form of energy, whatever that may be, in the same instant matter rises up and hits us over the head and makes us realize that it exists absolutely, since it is compact energy itself. (*Phoenix* 568)

Paradoxically, matter seems most obviously material when we "realize" its immateriality. Lawrence is not positing a physically lawless universe; if matter is "compact" there must be some set of forces that serve to keep it compacted. These forces are themselves unpredictable, however, making surprise an essential attribute of matter. If we conceive of matter as solid we will see it spark and flow into energy; if we conceive of it as energy it will hit us over the head. Lawrence thus asserts the dangerous physicality of objects that are themselves composed of energy, striking at the core of the issue that Hudson and Jefferies allude to. In Lawrence's work the body is at risk from the physical presence of immaterial forms: for every stimulus there is a response; for every dissipation of matter into energy there is an inverse impulse that causes matter to "rise up" and reassert its substantiality. Thus Lawrence's material world continually fluxes between energy and matter, form and formlessness.

The portrayal of form as a momentary balancing of forces is entirely consistent with field theory. Koffka describes the operation of perception as a continual struggle between "interior forces" (those that regularize shapes by balancing the field) and "exterior forces" (those that destabilize the field and make shapes irregular).

> In our psychophysical case, then, we have two kinds of forces, those which exist within the process in distribution itself and which will tend to impress on this distribution the simplest possible shape, and those between this distribution and the stimulus pattern, which constrain this stress towards simplification. (Koffka 138)

In "A Study of Thomas Hardy," Lawrence offers a very similar description of the male "Will to Motion" and the female "Will to Inertia" that, through their struggle, make and unmake material forms.

> The goal of the male impulse is the announcement of motion, endless motion, endless diversity, endless change. The goal of the female impulse is the announcement of infinite oneness, of infinite stability. When the two are working in combination, as they must in life, there is, as it were, a dual motion, centrifugal for the male, fleeing abroad, away from the center, outward to infinite vibration, and centripetal for the female, fleeing in to the eternal centre of rest. (*Phoenix* 457)

Although Lawrence describes these forces in terms of motion and rest, rather than of regularization and dissolution, the stability of perceived material forms is at stake in both schemes. The Lawrencian struggle between motion and inertia can be understood in terms of the Gestalt struggle to establish figure and ground. In the following passage from *The Plumed Serpent* Kate perceives the initially still, round papayas flowing through their own formal boundaries and moving outward into motion.

> Kate read this long leaflet again, and again, and a swift darkness like a whirlwind seemed to envelop the morning. She drank her coffee on the verandah, and the heavy papayas in their grouping seemed to be oozing like great drops from the invisible spouting of the fountain of non-human life. She seemed to see the great spouting and urging of the cosmos, moving into weird life. . . . So monstrous the rolling and unfolding of the life of the cosmos, as if even iron could grow like lichen deep in the earth, and cease growing, and prepare to perish. (*Plumed Serpent* 266–67)

The papayas on the table are segregated into distinct groupings, yet, paradoxically, are in motion. They are, as Lawrence describes Cézanne's apples, "mobile but come to rest," ready to ooze apart even as they are being perceived. Even the deepest geological strata can spout and run like liquid. On Lou Witt's ranch the flowers are both liquid and flaming.

[The] herb honeysuckle: a tangle of long drops of pure fire-red, hanging from slim invisible stalks of smoke-colour. The purest, most perfect vermillion scarlet, cleanest fire-colour, hanging in long drops like a shower of fire rain that is just going to strike the earth.   (*Saint Mawr* 150)

Like Jefferies and Hudson, Lawrence makes motion and color more visually determining than form. Where Hudson's color patches and Jefferies's dynamic motions follow predictable patterns, however, Lawrence's landscape is most notable for its unpredictability. Lawrence delights most in the moments of dissipation from matter to energy or of combination of energy into matter. "Life, the ever-present, knows no finality, no finished crystalization," he states, adding "the perfect rose is only a running flame . . ." (*Phoenix* 219). This emphasis on combative rather than parallel or uniform forces sets Lawrence's representations apart from Jefferies's and Hudson's, and, in an odd way, makes form more significant to his landscape than to theirs. Where Hudson's and Jefferies's narrative eyes simply lose form in motion or color, Lawrence's eye is always hovering around the points where it is being made or unmade. Like Darwin, Lawrence makes form fluid, thus calling into question the stability of the material world, but where Darwin's fluidity expresses the variety of actual biological forms Lawrence's reflects the precariousness of any form. Paul Morrel states that the artist must paint the "shimmering protoplasm in the leaves and everywhere, and not the stiffness of the shape" because "the shape is a dead crust" (*Sons and Lovers* 152). Throughout his portrayals of nature Lawrence, like Paul, attempts to reveal the "shimmeriness" or "quickness" of real living, rather than the dead crust. The artist, he states, must describe "that which was enacted, where the two wills met and intersected and left their result, complete for the moment . . . the portraying of the moment of union between the two wills . . ." (*Phoenix* 447). The artwork is a record of a point at which life forces are momentarily balanced, just as a Gestalt form is the perceptual manifestation of the balancing of dynamic forces in the mind.

One of Lawrence's most extended portrayals of matter dissipating into energy and recombining again is the horses' pursuit of Ursula at the end of *The Rainbow*. Here, rather than appearing as individual objects, the bodies of the horses become a dynamic force that ebbs and flows, recombining into solid forms to block Ursula, or flashing and crackling electrically as they pursue her. Ursula's body is itself on the verge of melting or dissolving under the emotional pressure of the pursuit.

She knew they had gathered on a log bridge over the sedgy dike, a dark, heavy, powerfully heavy knot. . . . And tense, and more tense, became her nerves and her veins, they ran hot, they ran white hot, they must fuse and she must die.

But the horses had burst before her. In a sort of lightning knowledge their movement travelled through her, the quiver and strain and thrust of their powerful flanks. . . .

She was aware of the great flash of hoofs, a bluish irridescent flash surrounding a hollow of darkness. Large, large seemed the bluish, incandescent flash of the hoof-iron, large a halo of lightning round the knotted darkness of the flanks. . . .

They slowed down, and cantered together into a knot once more, in the corner by the gate and the trees ahead of her. They stirred, they moved uneasily, they settled their uneasy flanks into one group, one purpose. . . .

Her heart was gone, her limbs dissolved, she was dissolved like water. All the hardness and looming power was in the massive body of the horse-group.   (*Rainbow* 451–53)

The physical and emotional tension of Ursula's situation is manifested both in the resolution and dissipation of the horse group as well as in the conflict between her body and the body of the group; their resolution signals her dissipation and vice versa. The horses embody Lawrence's paradox of matter; they are at once physical forms with muscles that "quiver and strain" under the flesh of their "powerful flanks" and a mass of kinetic and electrical energy that crackles in a "halo of lightning." Lawrence makes no attempt to portray the horses as individuals; they are a mass of matter flashing into energy then combining again. Nor are they simply an expression of nature's joyous dynamism, for this fluid, electrical mass is clearly capable of doing Ursula great harm, of rising up and hitting her over the head with its materiality. The Lawrencian paradox offers us the dynamism of Darwin's material world and the threat of Hardy's, along with an uncertainty more ominous than that of either. The struggle of Ursula and the horses parallels the underlying struggle of opposing forces in nature that results in matter only when there is a momentary and precarious balance, and that makes Lawrence's world at once sensual and mercurial.

In the paintings Lawrence analyses throughout the "Study of Thomas Hardy" it is the record of this struggle for balance that he most admires. In Botticelli's *Mystic Nativity* (Fig. 9) Lawrence sees the struggle between masculine and feminine forces in the figures' motion inward to form regular circles and in their straining outward to fly apart.

> Still there is the architectural composition, but what an outburst of movement from the source of motion. The Infant Christ is a centre, a radiating spark of movement, the Virgin is bowed in Absolute Movement . . . whilst the Angels fly round in ecstacy, embracing and linking hands. . . . They two

Fig. 9. Botticelli, *Mystic Nativity.* Courtesy of the National Gallery, London.

are the ecstatic centre, the complete origin, the force which is both centrifugal and centripetal. (*Phoenix* 455)

The madonna and child, as well as the angels above and below the stable,
are being pulled into circular forms, like dollops of oil combining into a
single sphere under water, even as the intensity of their desire makes them
radiate outward in a dance. The viewer of Botticelli's painting is caught in
the midst of a process of visual resolution in which the internal forces of

cohesion, which impel the viewer to perceive the two forms as one circle, are battling against the exterior forces that impel the viewer to perceive them as two separate irregular forms, and the bodies seem to be whirling around charged poles. The opposition between embrace and dance parallels the opposition between internal and external forces. What Lawrence sees when he looks at Botticelli's painting is the interaction of mental forces generated by the perception of objects rather than the objects themselves; his primary perception is of the forces that, at that moment of perception, interact to create those forms rather than of angels, mother, and child. The same can be said of Correggio's *La Notte,* or *Madonna with the Basket,* in which Lawrence sees the woman as "part of a stream of movement," and in which he sees "everything as motion" (456). Here, rather than three separate poles, the vortex of the painting is single and central; but again, the bodies warp or move along patterns of force. The bodies of the angels just discussed, of Joseph, and even of the Virgin herself are either partially obscured or transgress the edge of the canvas, emphasizing the insignificance of individual forms relative to the total pattern of motion.

Lawrence's own paintings, with their highly colored, oversimplified forms, almost seem more like portrayals of interactive fields than of bodies in space. The struggle between interior and exterior forces, between the resolution and dissipation of regular form, is one of the most notable features of paintings such as *Fight with an Amazon* and *Leda and Her Swan.* The bodies of the man and woman in *Fight with an Amazon* (Fig. 10), one of whom is physically straining inward and the other outward, are perceived by the viewer as two closely associated figures on a ground, whose general outline, when combined, is that of a circle. The internal forces thus impel combination of the forms, but the external forces, the stimuli of the differences in coloring and outline, strain outward, away from this simplification. Lawrence's sense of centrifugal and centripetal motion is demonstrated in this same struggle. The figures are moving toward one another, yet there seems to be the danger that their motion will burst out, past one another, and break the circle. All the elements of the landscape—trees, hills, animals—follow the lines of the bodies' motion, and the bodies spread beyond the canvas, emphasizing both the inward pull of centripetal motion and the outward thrust of centrifugal force. The paintings seem to be enactments of Lawrence's gendered description of dynamic forces.

> For it is as if life were a double cycle, of men and women, facing opposite ways, travelling opposite ways, revolving upon each other, man reaching forward with outstretched hand, woman reaching forward with outstretched

Fig. 10. Lawrence, *Fight with an Amazon.* Collection of Mr. Saki Karavas.

hand . . . till the two are abreast, and side by side, until even they pass on again, away from each other, travelling their opposite ways to the same infinite goal. (*Phoenix* 448)

Roger Ebbatson has shown that Lawrence's primary debt to Darwin was a sense of nature's checks and balances, and that this influence extends through Spencer, Huxley, and Ernst Haeckel. Haeckel's *The Riddle of the Universe,* which Lawrence read in 1908, was a particularly strong influence, Ebbatson suggests, because it helped Lawrence move from a rational to a "pantheist" conception of matter by claiming that "every living cell possesses psychic properties, and the psychological life of multicellular

organisms is simply the sum total of the psychic functions of their cells''
(Ebbatson 35). These psychic properties are manifested in attraction and
repulsion, and evolution results from the endless alternation between motion and stillness. Lawrence read this, Ebbatson suggests, as a "reintegra-
tion of matter and spirit" that allowed him to make "the great Lawrencean
assertion against a world of dead matter" (Ebbatson 38–39). Haeckel's
conception that "all mental phenomena are dependent on a definite material
substratum" (Ebbatson 36) can also be read as a restatement of the psychophysical postulate. In his chapter entitled "The Law of Substance" Haeckel offers a description of J. C. Vogt's "pyknotic theory of substance" that
makes the operation of field dynamics vividly imageable.

> By means of certain "constellations, centres of perturbation, or systems of
> deformation," great masses of centres of condensation quickly unite in im-
> mense proportions, and so obtain a preponderance over the surrounding
> masses. By that process the primitive substance, which in its original state of
> quiescence had the same mean consistency throughout, divides or differenti-
> ates into two kinds. The centres of disturbance, which positively exceed the
> mean consistency in virtue of the pyknosis or condensation, form the ponder-
> able matter of bodies; the finer, intermediate substance, which occupies the
> space between them, and negatively falls below the mean consistency, forms
> the ether or imponderable matter. As a consequence of this division into mass
> and ether there ensues a ceaseless struggle between the two antagonistic
> elements, and this struggle is the source of all physical processes. The
> positive ponderable matter, the element with the feeling of like or desire, is
> continually striving to complete the process of condensation . . . the nega-
> tive, imponderable matter, on the other hand, offers a perpetual and equal
> resistance to the further increase of its strain and to the feeling of dislike
> connected therewith.   (Haeckel 218–19)

If all psychological dynamics are fundamentally material, as Haeckel suggests, then this field system would also apply to brain dynamics; not sur-
prisingly, Haeckel's description is quite similar to Gestalt portrayals of
brain activity. Haeckel certainly revitalizes the natural world in a way
Lawrence would find attractive, but he also suggests that the mental world
is configured in a way identical to the material world. His "pantheist
vision" reintegrates spirit and matter, but it also reintegrates mind and
matter in a way that is more scientific than pantheistic.

Lawrence's conception of "mutation in blossom" (219), the momentary vision of form in a seething passage of formlessness, is central to his
artistic vision. Because the role of the artist is not to portray the forms of
nature, the dead crusts, but rather the forces that underlie and determine

form, Lawrence's landscape forms are subject to the precarious change of interactive fields. The reader does not see flowers or papayas as much as the strident interaction of forces that momentarily determine flowers and papayas. "The 'object,'" says Lawrence, "was always slightly repulsive to me . . ." (Phoenix II 604). Like Hardy, Lawrence focuses on the points that define the edges of the material world, but here the edge is not one between form and form, but between form and formlessness. His flowers, rather than the sticky buds that rub against Tess with substantial roots and petals, are more the ephemeral and "forever-unfolding" blossoms of mutation.

IV

Lawrence's material forms, continually fluxing between matter and energy, seem to be so precarious as to be barely embodied. Oddly enough, however, Lawrence frequently states that his goal is to "confront" the reader with the "living procreative body" (*Phoenix* 561). He wrote that "the intuitional faculty, which alone relates us in direct awareness to physical things and substantial presences, is atrophied and dead, and we don't know what to feel" (*Phoenix* 558). Through "intuition," Lawrence suggests, we can return to the physical. While the eye is incapable of perceiving nature's palpable weight, the "intuitive" perception can do so. In his critique of Cézanne's work Lawrence suggests that it is this "intuitive" organ, rather than the physical eye, that recognizes substance.

> For the intuitive apperception of the apple is so tangibly aware of the apple that it is aware of it all round, not only just the front. The eyes see only fronts, and the mind, on the whole, is satisfied with fronts. But intuition needs all-aroundness, and instinct needs insideness. The true imagination is forever curving round to the other side, to the back of presented appearance. (*Phoenix* 579)

There is no tangible element to looking; the eye, used to its two-dimensional world, is "satisfied" with two dimensions, and even the mind deals in "fronts." In order to represent a palpable nature, Lawrence must portray the world through the "true imagination"; "intuition" and "instinct" must be his guides, rather than optical vision. Cézanne managed to "shove the apple away from him" and express "what he suddenly, convulsedly knew! the existence of matter," because "his intuitive consciousness triumphed, and broke into utterance."

But what does Lawrence mean by "intuition"? Later in the essay the qualities of "intuitive perception" are described to be much like Gestalt forces. Intuitive perception regularizes and simplifies visual form.

> [W]hile he was painting the appleyness he was also deliberately painting out the so-called humanness, the personality, the "likeness," the physical *cliché*. He had deliberately to paint it out, deliberately to make the hands and face rudimentary, and so on, because if he had painted them in fully they would have been *cliché*. (579)

Cézanne's figures are accurately "appley" because of their "rudimentary" rendering. Lawrence thus links "rudimentary" perception, the diminishment of unique characteristics that define "personality" and "likeness," with an impression of physical externality and wholeness. An "artistically palpable" world will be one in which forms are segregated and simplified; regularization becomes the perceptual equivalent of palpability. Consequently, when Lawrence wishes to portray tangibly distinct objects, he does not portray one form touching another, but forms being intensified and resolved from their contrasting ground, impelled by invisible forces to become brighter and more vivid. In the following passage, the tangible presence of the lemons is portrayed through their visual distinctness from their ground.

> Between the lemon trees, beside the path, were little orange trees, and dozens of oranges hanging like hot coals in the twilight. When I warm my hands at them the Signore breaks me off one twig after another, till I have a bunch of burning oranges among dark leaves, a heavy bouquet. (*Sea and Sardinia* 247)

The radiating heat of the oranges is rendered as a corollary to their intense color—a color that grows more brilliant as the reader ponders it. The oranges seem warmer because they are "among dark leaves," but it is color, rather than heat, to which the leaves serve as background. Heat, weight, and intensity of color are linked in the passage; physical realness, roundess, and externality are the corollaries of brilliantly visible segregation. The internal processes of the mind as they curve around and set apart the oranges seem to disentangle the form from its landscape, and, like the Signore gathering oranges, bring them to the reader as individual objects. As the orange grove fades into a twilit ground, the oranges grow brilliant, hot and heavy.

The physical weight of a form thus becomes a corollary of its resolution into an intense figure–ground contrast rather than of its tangible distinctness from the surrounding forms.

> I see curious slim oak-looking trees that are stripped quite naked below the boughs, standing brown-ruddy, curiously distinct among the bluey-grey pallor of the others. They remind me, again and again, of glowing, coffee-brown, naked aborigines of the South Seas. They have the naked suavity, skin-bare, and an intense coffee-red colour of unclothed savages. And these are the stripped cork trees. Some are much stripped, some little. Some have the whole trunk and part of the lower limbs ruddy naked, some only a small part of the trunk. (*Sea and Sardinia* 103)

As in Hudson's description of the cattle, vivid color contrast suggests material presence. Where Hudson's cattle are coldly statuesque, however, Lawrence's trees, like his lemons, grow tender, soft and humanly naked because the figure–ground contrast seems to intensify before the reader's eyes. They are first shown to stand out as different colored trees in a grey forest. Then, through anthropomorphic comparisons to human bodies, they appear rounder, softer, more flesh-colored than the other forms. Just as the color of the lemons is elided with heat, the color of the "stripped" trees is elided with the sensitivity of naked flesh. The longer the reader ponders them, the more "intense coffee-red" they become, and the more human they seem. Ultimately the imagery of stripping bark, stripping clothing, and stripping skin are combined in a painful combination of tangible sensations, all depending upon the distinct coloration of the trees. Lawrence's use of figural contrast to incite a tangible sensation is more impressive here than in the description of the oranges because the cork trees are merely seen from afar; the narrator never touches them and their texture is not described, yet the reader has a strong impression of them as physically present and sensually significant forms. The visual intensification of form, caused by the internal forces in the brain cortex, thus becomes the representational equivalent of the sense of touch; we experience the interaction of fields as heat or tenderness.

Interestingly, the same association between physicality and cerebral forms exists in Köhler's discussion of externality. Attempting to refute empirical assertions that the phenomenal world is a human mental creation, Köhler points out that, according to Gestalt theory, each observed form creates a separate response in the cortex. Because we can see our bodies, then our bodies must also create a separate response, and the other responses, which occur at other points in the cortex, cannot be contained within this single response.

> [T]he idea that things ought to be experienced as being inside ourselves can surely not be defended. There is no more reason for this expectation than for assuming that the pencil ought to be seen within the book, or a cloud, or the moon . . . the brain processes which underlie the visual book, the visual

pencil and all the other visual objects around me must be external to the
processes which underlie the visual arm, feet, chest and nose. (Köhler
209–12)

The dynamic forces that make perceived forms "rudimentary" are also
those that set them apart, thereby establishing a physiological correlate in
the brain for their physical externality in nature. If the world is within us,
then forms must be within other forms, as in a Darwinian empirical coalescence. If, however, forms cannot be within other forms, if all natural forms
can only be perceived through their segregation, then the world must not be
within us. Lawrence, through his praise of Cézanne's "appleyness,"
equates cerebral perception with an awareness of a physically exterior
world. Köhler makes an identical equation by making a case for a world of
forms that are exterior from the self by being perceptually segregated in the
mind. For, both mental segregation indicates material segregation.

    To see the body in all its nakedness, then, we must look to its moments
of resolution and dissipation. In his "Introduction to these Paintings"
Lawrence describes optical vision as "a sort of flashy coloured photography of the eye" that concentrates on clothes rather than on bodies, and sees
the world in visual "clichés."

> [M]odern people are nothing inside their garments, and a head sticks out at
> the top and hands stick out of the sleeves, and it is a bore . . . a mere
> cliché, with very little instinctive or intuitional perception to it. ("Ap-
> ropos" 25)

Only the "instinctive or intuitional perception," the perception that sees
the body at the moments when matter becomes energy, can see the "gleam
of the warm procreative body" through the clothes. Lawrence portrays
sexuality as a loss of form resulting from the flow of energy between
bodies. In "Pornography and Obscenity" Lawrence describes sex as having "a give and take. A new stimulus enters as the native stimulus departs.
Something quite new is added as the old surcharge is removed" (73).
Hardy, as we have seen, emphasizes the contiguity of forms by concentrating on the points of intersection between one form and the other, thus
pointing out at once their distinctness and proximity. Lawrence also concentrates on points of tangency, but, rather than showing them to be bar-
riers, he portrays them as points of exchange by which two segregated
bodies dissipate into a formless energy field. In *The Trespasser* a kiss
causes the bodies to melt and fuse. "[A]t the mouth," he wrote, "they
seemed to melt and fuse. . . . The fire, in heavy flames, had poured
through her to Siegmund, from Siegmund to her" (Trespasser 23). In

Women in Love, Ursula and Rupert's lovemaking creates an electrical circuit.

> She traced with her hands the line of his loins and thighs, at the back, and a living fire ran through her, from him, darkly. It was a dark flood of electric passion she released from him, drew into herself. She had established a rich new circuit, a new current of passional electric energy, between the two of them, released from the darkest poles of the body and established in perfect circuit. (*Women in Love* 305–6)

The description immediately reminds us of Hardy, with the close attention to the very points of tangency, and the shrinking of the bodies down to their points of intersection. Where Hardy continues to focus on these points repeatedly, however, by emphasizing the firmness of their edges, Lawrence immediately replaces the specific body parts with an image of flowing current.

Moreover, taken chronologically Lawrence's representations of lovemaking reaveal his growing ability to conceive of and represent matter as a field entity. Lawrence did not read Einstein or study the human nervous system until rather late in his literary career, and the majority of his pronouncements on the nature of matter and energy are found in the "Introduction to these Paintings," written in 1929. His early attempts to express sexual formlessness involve heat; bodies either melt or burst into flame. Although these show the precariousness of matter, they still treat the body as fundamentally material. Later, electricity and radiation become his primary metaphors for the exchange of sexual energy, as Alcorn has noted (Alcorn 100); the body thus becomes an element in a dynamic interaction of forces. When Gudrun and Gerald embrace beneath the railway arch she feels "as if he were soft iron becoming surcharged with her electric life" (*Women in Love* 323). Afterward she touches him in order to "gather" his energy into her body.

> There seemed a faint, white light emitted from him, a white aura, as if he were a visitor from the unseen. She reached up, like Eve reaching to the apples on the tree of knowledge . . . touching his face with her infinitely delicate, encroaching, wondering fingers. Her fingers went over the mold of his face, over his features. . . . He was such an unutterable enemy, yet glistening with uncanny white fire. She wanted to touch him, and touch him and touch him, till she had him all in her hands, till she had strained him into her knowledge. . . . For the time, her soul was destroyed with the exquisite shock of his invisible fluid lightning. . . . How much more of him was there to know? Ah, much, much, many days harvesting for her large, yet

perfectly subtle and intelligent hands upon the field of his living, radio-active
body. (*Women in Love* 325)

Einstein points out that while earlier physics had conceived of a universe of
"forces acting between material particles," field physics concentrated on
"the field between the two charges, and not the charges themselves"
(Einstein 151). Rather than defining their material presence Gudrun's touch
leads the reader to an awareness of the current dynamics between the
bodies. By creating a current between herself and Gerald, by introducing a
new stimulus into the "field of his living, radio-active body," Gudrun has
made his single balanced energy field into an imbalanced one in which
energy must flow and shift to create a new balance. The fingers and arm
become a bridge of interchange, expanding and complicating the field of
body energy, so that her "electric life" flows to him while his "invisible
fluid lightning" flows to her. Gudrun's hands are significant as pathways
rather than as edges; both the agricultural and the electrical "harvesting" of
Gerald involve the opening up of his body beneath her hand. Thus Gudrun
and Gerald's touch does not have the tragic implications of Tess touching
Angel, for rather than emphasizing material distinctness it releases radioac-
tive dynamism.

In *Lady Chatterly's Lover* Lawrence portrays the sexual interaction of
bodies as a single field in which two influences are at work. Constance fears
that Mellors body will have a sharp, tangible edge like "the thrust of a
sword in her" but instead, when he enters her, she is "gone in the flood"
(*Lady Chatterly* 187).

> And it seemed she was like the sea, nothing but dark waves rising and
> heaving, heaving with a great swell, so that slowly her whole darkness was in
> motion, and she was ocean rolling its dark, dumb mass. Oh, and far down
> inside her the deeps parted and rolled asunder, in long, far-travelling billows,
> and ever, at the quick of her, the depths parted and rolled asunder. (187)

The reader images undulations in fluid, the action of a field of erotic energy
created by Constance and Mellors, rather than the two bodies themselves.
Although the "flood" can be generally interpreted as Constance's body,
the undulating water suggests a pyschophysical energy field in which sensations and emotions are not tied to any specific body parts. The characters do
not appear as distinct visual forms, whether with solid or fluid edges; the
"flood" contains and expresses both bodies, as a field does charges.

Gestalt theorists posited a molar conception of the nervous system in
which sensual stimulations create "a pattern pervading the whole area"
(Koffka 61) of the brain's cortex, rather than smaller, "molecular" areas.
Lawrence's portrayals of sexuality move toward such a molar conception of

physical experience. Mellors attempts to express this to Constance in his definition of "cunt": "An' doesn't ter know? Cunt! It's thee down theer; an' what I get when I'm i'side thee, and what tha gets when I'm i'side thee; it's a' as it is, all on't" (*Lady Chatterly* 191). Mellors suggests that the sexual body should not be conceived of in terms of individual parts, but as an element in a sensual interaction. Molar theory allowed Gestalt theorists to suggest that perception does not proceed by the responses of individual points on the retina, just as Mellors suggests that sexuality does not consist simply of the responses of the individual points on the body. "Cunt" is not just a body part; the definition must also include the psychic results of the interaction of one body with another—of the moment when bodies cease to be composed of parts. Mellors thus bends the definition away from objects toward the energy field created by them. In Lawrence's sexual language, as in Einstein's "new field language," an awareness of the field between the forms "is essential for an understanding of their actions" (Einstein 151). As Constance runs home from her lovemaking she is open not only to her own erotic identity, but to the field dynamics of the entire landscape: "the trees in the park seemed bulging and surging at anchor on a tide, and the heave of the slope to the house was alive" (*Lady Chatterly* 191).

In "Introduction to these Paintings" Lawrence criticizes English landscape painters for failing to portray a world of physically substantial objects, and makes several cryptic linkages between the "deep conflict" of the "intuitional consciousness" and the "living procreating body."

> But for me, personally, landscape is always waiting for something to occupy it. Landscape seems to be meant as a backdrop to an intenser vision of life, so to my feelings painted landscape is background with the real subject left out. . . . It doesn't call up the more powerful responses of the human imagination, the sensual, passional responses. . . . There is no deep conflict. The instinctive and intuitional consciousness is called into play, but lightly, superficially. It is not confronted with any living procreating body. (*Phoenix* 561)

Like Hardy, Lawrence wants a human figure to be the center of any landscape painting, but where Hardy's central figure brings about the visual simplification of the landscape, Lawrence's is itself simplified so as to become palpable. In the most powerful imaginative responses we find the most physical body, and these imaginative responses are incited by paintings that aggressively confront the eye with vivid figure and ground distinctions and thus create intensely combative perceptual fields in the viewer's mind. The homogeneous English landscape paintings lack the bright colors and intense figure and ground relationships that characterize Lawrence's own paintings and thus fail to create the deep conflicts between interior and exterior forces in the mind. The lack of visual confrontation and resulting mental conflict causes English landscape paintings to become both visibly and tangibly uninteresting.

For Lawrence, as for the Gestalt theorists, cerebral and cereal matter operate by the same laws. While empiricist theory rejected the essential link between interior and exterior states, the Gestalt use of the psychophysical postulate assures the continuity of mind and nature. Metaphorical readings of the relationship between nature and the human psyche in Lawrence's landscapes suppose a rift between interior and exterior perception that must be bridged by literary means. Ebbatson is one of many to define Lawrence's major "theme" as "the reunification of man, woman and nature" (Ebbatson 61). Keith Sagar explicitly points to literary metaphor as the means by which the reunification of mind and nature can take place.

> The grail Lawrence sought and found in his quest was wholeness. Wholeness means atonement. And atonement means imaginative vision. . . . The imaginative is simply a charge that links up again and makes operative those senses and powers of perception which our rationalistic culture has allowed to atrophy. . . . The metaphor is the linguistic equivalent of touch. It is the link, the bridge, the meeting, the marriage, the atonement, bit by bit reconstructing the world as a unity, blissfully skipping over the supposed chasms of dualism.   (Sagar 122–24)

Certainly Lawrence makes the same claims himself, and Sagar is simply reasserting their legitimacy, just as Ebbatson reasserts Lawrence's literary historical claims when he describes his "reconciliation of scientific and romantic apprehensions of Nature upon the anvil of his creative will" (Ebbatson 260). The heroic image of Lawrence pounding the two prongs of the scientific and romantic, or the human mind and the natural spirit, together, is common to all such metaphorical readings of Lawrence's landscape, regardless of which end of the metaphor nature occupies. As we have seen, however, Lawrence perceives nature through a narrative eye that is already attuned to natural rhythms. While the characters often betray anxiety over their distance from nature, Lawrence's style demonstrates underlying unities; the eyes through which both characters and narrator perceive demonstrate the reassuring nativistic congruity between perceived and exterior forms implicit in the psychophysical postulate. What most critics describe as Lawrence's great imaginative achievement is in fact a given of his representational style and is also apparent in the works of other nature writers. Lawrence's use of a psychophysical unity does seem revolutionary set against empirical models of mind, as it is in Sagar's description of the Lawrenceian imagination.

> Starting from the narrow world we all inhabit, with its hubristic human perspectives and habitual complacencies, the imagination reaches inward toward the roots of our being in the psyche and outward toward the powers of the nonhuman world. Its goal is atonement, the healing of the split between the mind and the rest of our faculties which has brought us to our present chronic, perhaps terminal, condition. The analytical reason, operating in a void, is absurd. It has no validating or vitalizing contact with either inner or outer realities. If thought were a matter of mind only, man would be a windowless monad, an ego-bound obscenity. (Sagar 123)

Sagar describes Lawrence's "imagination" as a force that generates a nativistic continuity between internal and external worlds from the interiorized isolation of the empirical mind. Lawrence, however, does not start in the narrow, windowless world of the empirical mind, but in the nativistic mind in which interior forms correspond to their exterior counterparts. While Lawrence's stated and apparent task is the reconciliation of humanity with nature, his representations of nature demonstrate a fundamental, underlying unity already extant between exterior and perceived form, between mind and matter, that assures the success of this reconciliation. Nature is an expression of the psyche in that perceived forms manifest the characteristics of cerebral field forces; the psyche is an expression of nature in that those cerebral forces are the same as material forces operating outside of the mind. It is thus equally accurate to say that Lawrence's nature expresses the "ebb and flow of the unconscious life of his characters" (Alcorn 90) and that the characters' minds are "shaped and possessed by a greater power than themselves" (Watson 28). Given this nativistic conception of mind, no metaphorical bridge is necessary; Lawrence's goal of "wholeness" is one of the primary characteristics of his style.

While Hudson and Jefferies emphasize the visual malleability and intensification of nature, Lawrence links that visual malleability to material malleability, so that, as in Darwin, the limitations of the narrative eye reveal essential truths about nature. Lawrence's portrayals come closest to Darwin's both in their dynamism and in their scope, which purports to be cosmic rather than simply idiosyncratic or politically useful, like Hardy's and Conrad's. While Darwin's is a nature so overrun with different forms that the eye cannot perceive them all, Lawrence's is one in which material and perceived forms operate by the same dynamic rules. Paul A. Kolers writes that

one of the important achievements of the Gestalt psychologists, we now
realize, was the demonstration that the study of illusions revealed not ephemeral or defective processes in the visual system, but fundamental aspects of
its normal functioning.   (Kolers 16)

Lawrence's world, too, is functioning normally when it flows, spills, and
heaves. The fluid forms perceived by Lawrence's characters are visual
"effects" brought about by color contrasts and figure and ground formations; however, they are also manifestations of the nature of matter. Where
Darwin portrayed a world of dynamic forms, Lawrence, Hudson, and
Jefferies portray a world of formless dynamism; their ultimate units of
representation are the arc of motion and the chromatic hue. As in Hardy and
Conrad, the failures of the physical eye allow for a kind of strength;
Lawrence's narrative vision allows us to see the essential mechanisms of
nature, but they are nonformal mechanisms. Darwin's theory was instru-
mental in loosening conceptions of organic form, thus allowing it to be
portrayed as less and less central to a cultural vision of nature. Lawrence
frees his narrative vision from nineteenth-century depictions of nature that
celebrate matter to participate in twentieth-century representations that celebrate energy.

Epilogue

In offering the reader a vision of nature's otherness, Darwin succeeds in doing what none of the post-Darwinian nature writers attempt; his natural world continually mutates into new and strange forms. Darwinian theory allowed for transgressions of the species boundary, and Darwinian vision was similarly transgressive. As Gillian Beer notes, Darwin's *Beagle* experience showed him that in strange, unfamiliar landscapes the "full range of sense experience fills out and disturbs the narrowly descriptive authority of the scientific collector" (34). As we have seen, Darwin himself was disturbed by the "entire newness, & therefore absence of all associations" (*Beagle Diary* 60) of the entangled tropical landscape, and only his delight in perceiving biological variety kept him from fleeing to the "rural quiet & retirement" of his native home. The nature writers in this study engage in a such a flight representationally by selecting, simplifying and regularizing Darwin's nature until it manifests the "green control" the English countryside had long expressed. In certain ways Darwin's portrayal of entangled nature came just at the wrong time. The English countryside in the mid- and late nineteenth century was already the focus of nostalgia; it had become the ideal image of a pristine and familiar landscape in an increasingly industrial society, representing to the English mind "chidhood & times past, where all that was unpleasant is forgotten" (*Beagle Diary* 60). Glen Cavaliero's study of *The Rural Tradition in the English Novel 1900–1939* demonstrates how rural novelists following Lawrence offered nostalgic portrayals of an English countryside that had become emblematic of traditional value and social order. That Darwin should entangle this precious landscape, precious in part because of its familiarity and orderliness, was perhaps too much for the English sensibility. Nature may cease to be a significant artistic concern so soon after Darwinian theory pushes it to the forefront of cultural debate because nature writers so effectively reinscribe it into orderly, familiar, and predictable representational modes. We can perhaps best understand the modernist transformation of biological nature "from an organic setting into a summoned or remembered *idea*" (Howe 30) as the attempt to perceive the familiar face of a remembered landscape in Darwin's entangled nature.

Notes

INTRODUCTION

1. Levine makes a similar point in his discussion of observation and narrative authority in *Darwin and the Novelists*. His chapter "The Perils of Observation" serves as a useful counterpart to my physiological discussion of narrative perception. By investigating "observation" in the nonphysiological sense, Levine demonstrates how the Darwinian "themes of abundance and entanglement" complicate social and political observation, undercutting the observer's authority and access to the truth. As such, Levine's discussion shows how metaphorical, as well as physical, conceptions of sight are transformed in the presence of an entangled Darwinian nature.

2. See *Imagery*. Ned Block, ed. In his introduction Block states that "recent experimentation has shown that imagey and perception share much of the same physiological machinery" (9). He describes one experiment by Stephen M. Kosslyn that demonstrates that the eye's ability to perceive vertical stripes at greater distances than horizontal stripes is also a characteristic of the mind; imaginary horizontal stripes blur sooner than imaginary vertical ones. Another experiment performed by C. F. Stromeyer and J. Psotka demonstrates that a two-dimensional figure appears to have stereoscopic depth when combined with a remembered image. Jerry Fodor states that "it seems hard to deny that imaging is like perceiving when it is possible to produce typical perceptual illusions whose objects are images rather than percepts" (Block, 84).

3. See R. L. Gregory. *Eye and Brain*, p. 106, for a more thorough discussion of this illusion. Gregory's descriptions of optical illusion are always eloquent and informative.

4. I follow the general outline of the nativist–empiricist conflict that Nicholas J. Pastore sets up in his superb *Selective History of Theories of Visual Perception*, particularly in his attention to arguments over wholes and parts and the psychophysical postulate. The great value of Pastore's work is its specific emphasis on visual perception theory rather than philosophy and psychology in general. While more attention could be given to optical and psychological experimentation, I adopt Pastore's approach of concentrating on major theoretical texts because it allows for a unity and clarity of argument that is useful for my purposes here.

5. This appeal to common sense and everyday experience was common among nativist theorists. Hamilton poses his examples in terms of familiar objects, such as the face of a friend or the appearance of a sheep to a shepherd. Empiricists,

on the other hand, tended to use metaphors drawn from mystical experience. Berkeley continually describes uneducated vision in terms of spiritual enlightenment or ecstacy. Herman von Helmholtz describes uneducated vision as "optical phantasmagoria" and John Stuart Mill compares construction of complex ideas from simple ones to the bedazzlement of the eye "when the seven prismatic colours are presented . . . in rapid succession" so that "the sensation produced is that of white" (Mill 558). As we shall see, this portrayal of vision in the quasi-mystical terms of fantasy and ecstasy also characterizes Darwinian perception.

6. Johannes Muller, in his *Elements of Physiology* (1840), describes how pressing on the eyeball will create perceived form: "If, however, it were possible to confine the pressure accurately to determinate portions of the retina we should doubtless be able to produce perfectly defined images by mechanical means" (1088). Such a precise, literalistic conception of the connection between retinal regions and brain regions was fairly common. The links between points on the retina and points in the brain were often described as being like telegraph lines.

7. While I link James to the nativists, elements of his theories of perception are also empiricist (Pastore 229). He believed that an infant's primary perception was chaotic, but throughout his theories he asserts the wholeness of perceived forms. Gestalt psychologists are nativistic in the sense that they asserted formal wholeness, but not nativistic in that they believed in no innate perceptual knowledge.

CHAPTER 1

1. Darwin's sense of visual uneasiness is demonstrated by his continual assertions of lack of confidence in his own vision. "I examined pretty accurately a Caryophyllia," he writes to Henslow, "and if my eyes were not bewitched, former descriptions have not the slightest resemblance to the animal" (*Collected Papers* 3). He finds the organization of some marine species "so marvelous that I can scarcely credit my eyesight" (*Collected Papers* 4), and belittles the strangeness of a new species of bird because it is seen through "my unornithological eyes" (*Collected Papers* 5). Some of this is no doubt hyperbole, meant to emphasize the uniqueness of his surroundings, but this cannot account for the great number of such statements. Darwin's lack of confidence in his vision also crops up in Frank J. Sulloway's content analyis of Darwin's early writing. "Perhaps the most noteworthy aspect of Darwin's early letters to Henslow," states Sulloway, "is Darwin's repeated use of expressions that indicate a lack of self confidence in his own observations and opinions" (Sulloway 128). Although here, in his private letters and journals, Darwin's expressions of self-doubt must be taken at face value, he later develops this humility into an effective rhetorical strategy and employs it in his major theoretical works.

2. Darwin's rhetorical humility involves the description of the extreme lengths to which he has gone to discover, organize, and process data, followed immediately

by the assertion that the data is insufficient, the reasoning flawed, and the conclusions therefore suspect. In Glen Roy, Darwin emphasizes the limits of his observation, while at the same time pointing out the great and unparalleled effort he has taken to garner these observations. He thus demonstrates the limitations of all human vision while asserting his authority as the most experienced observer. For an excellent discussion of the "cautious deviousness" of Darwin's "charming, self-deprecatory style" see Levine, pp. 86–90.

3. In his discussion of visual art and optical theory Crary argues that while the eigteenth-century observer "confronts a unified space of order, unmodified by his or her own sensory and physiological apparatus" (55), vision in the nineteenth century is "always an irreducible complex of elements belonging to the over-viewer's body and of data from an exterior world" (70). Nineteenth-century visual experience is thus "given an unprecedented mobility and exchangeability" (14). While Crary describes this transformation occurring in the 1820s, I believe such a "corporealization" of the visual occurs later in literary art because the eighteenth-century model of vision adheres so powerfully to modes of literary narration. Only when the limitation of vision becomes a rhetorical necessity, as in Darwin's work, is the omniscient perspective abandoned.

4. This does not suggest intellectual sloppiness on Darwin's part so much as the freedom of his scientific thought. In his "Owen and Darwin Reading a Fossil: Macrauchenia in a Boney Light," Stan P. Rachootin offers an interesting example of Darwin's intellectually impressionistic method. During his travels in South America, Darwin found the bones of an extinct quadruped that, he was inaccurately informed by Owen, belonged to an ancient form of camel. Later, Owen was to revise his analysis and pronounce the bone to be that of a pachyderm. Darwin's analysis of the bones as those of a camel, however, helped him to make significant headway in his evolutionary speculations. Rachootin describes Darwin's approach as displaying "a certain innocence about the home truths of comparative anatomy," but emphasizes that "what he did not see . . . allowed him to read stories in bone that were invisible to Owen" (Rachootin 156). This is not to say that innocence is intellectual bliss, but that Darwin's way of thinking always involves a blurring of firm intellectual distinctions and a transgression of proven scientific approaches. According to Rachootin, "one of the triumphs" of Darwin's method is "his ability to misprise in a strong and creative way what experts in other fields have done. . . . [Darwin] practices unrestricted science . . . and, in a case such as the taphonomy of guanaco bones, an unexpected science" (Rachootin 179).

CHAPTER 2

1. Bullen concentrates on Hardy's aesthetic statements in Chapter 1 of *The Return of the Native* as a straightforward claim for a modernist landscape aesthetic of "beauty in ugliness." Hardy does not mean to emphasize the actual ugliness of the landscapes described in the passage so much as their emptiness. Moors, seas,

and mountains are notable for their emptiness rather than for their ugliness, and Hardy would be hard put to suggest that they have never been considered beautiful before. These landscapes appear beautiful to the modern mind because they are empty and therefore more easily used as canvases for the modern mind's associative processes. Hardy is describing both historical change in moods as well as a change in the way of seeing nature. Rather than expressing themselves through the physical ordering of the landscape into "vineyards and myrtle gardens," humans now concentrate on the psychological ordering of open spaces around human figures. The eighteenth-century vision of an orderly, gardenlike nature is replaced by the twentieth-century vision of natural absence. The unacknowledged step between these two ways of seeing, and the one that makes the second desirable, is entangled Darwinian nature. Bullen writes that "the modern mind . . . will find an appropriate vehicle of expression in the sad and desolate landscape" (93), but these landscapes are not really sad and are only desolate in the physical sense. Moreover, rather than serving as "vehicles" for human emotion they serve as manifestations of the human perceptual ability to humanize a Darwinian landscape by emptying it.

2. J. Hillis Miller's contention in *Distance and Desire* that the narrator, because he is distanced, sees the "true pattern of existence" (10) also places too much emphasis on the authority of distance. Daniel R. Schwarz's study of Hardy's narrator as a character demonstrates the idiosyncratic character traits of this apparently objective viewer; through the narrative eye that narrator is tied to the equivalent of an idiosyncratic body. Miller claims that the narrator is "separate from the universe by the detached clarity of his mind," participating only in nature through his body (17); however, the perceptual properties of the narrative eye and mind are determined by the body—his nativistic narrative vision is physiologically grounded. The image of the single thread in the cloth that, to Miller, suggests the narrator's ability to perceive the whole fabric is strongly reminiscent of the the single pattern in the carpet which, to Hardy, demonstrates the impossibility of doing so. While Hardy's narrative position may mimic that of the Immanent Will, it is too self-consciously human to be omniscient.

CHAPTER 3

1. The comparison of nature to the middle class drawing-room was not limited to portrayals of foreign landscapes. A good many popular natural history books were written at the turn of the century to engage middle-class readers, particularly children and young women, with a nature that had become increasingly unfamiliar and inaccessible. Works such as Mrs. J. T. Gumersall's *Cameos from Nature,* Margaret Cameron's *By Common, Pinewood and Bog,* and Catherine Pullein's *How to Observe* portray the natural world through forms and operations more familiar to their readers. For example, Catherine Pullein writes

> The mosses are very fine this month. There is one that looks like a tiny dark-green bottle brush; anoher shaped like a small fern frond; and there is aso the grey cup-moss,

> the fairy wine glasses. . . . You older girls who do so much pretty crewel embroidery, if you would use observation, could find an endless variety of patterns from leaf designs. . . . You will seldom find two ivy leaves alike.   (11)

As in Wallace, the move from familiarized perception to manufacture is a rapid one. Ivy leaves are worth noticing because they can easily become leaf patterns for embroidery; nature is perceived in the ways we are used to imitating it. Pullein's stated desire to move middle-class girls out of their houses and into the landscape has just the opposite effect; the landscape becomes like a middle-class house.

2. Ian Watt describes Conrad's aesthetic as symbolist in its attention to the unveiling of "a spiritual order thought to exist beneath or beyond surface appearance." The symbolists believed that this order could be accessed through "those modes of perception which are the most opposed to rational observation of analysis—notably dreams, drug-induced hallucinations, and occult rituals" (Watt 185). Like Tomlinson, Conrad offers a jungle dreamscape that is meant to open a "Platonic" pathway to the "ultimate changeless ideas." In Jamesian terms, however, the spiritual order manifested in dream states consists of the individual's past experience. The changeless symbolist world underlying the jungle's aspect would, therefore, be composed of British forms.

CHAPTER 4

1. Jefferies's work also offers much attention to color and to the artificiality of vividly perceived landscapes. He describes summer fields as

> Large squares of green corn that was absorbing its yellow from the sunlight; chess squares irregularly placed, of brown furrows; others of rich blood-red trifolium; others of scarlet sainfoin and blue lucerne. . . . It was something like the broad folio of an ancient illuminated manuscript, in gold, gules, blue, green.   (Williamson 335).

His primary concern with the dynamism of nature prevents even color regions from remaining homogeneous for long, however; color seems to heave and shimmer with life, as in "on the ruddy golden coat of the warrantable deer the bright sunlight shone, so that the colour seemed unsteady, or as if it was visibly emanating and flowing forth in emanations" (Tickner 38).

2. Although the random recombination of glass fragments may seem chaotic, it is not a Darwinian entangled chaos that combines to create an ecological whole. A traditional stained glass window, like a Darwinian empirical landscape, is summative; smaller panes of glass combine, like minimum visibles, into a complete form. In Hudson's world, however, each pane is separately significant; the conception of the organic form as an entity composed of variable parts is abandoned. Instead, Hudson's natural forms are homogeneously colored wholes that have no significant relation to one another and which impress the reader primarily as a thrilling "effect" of coloration.

3. Hudson, of course, was a jungle novelist himself, with *Green Mansions* being his best-known novel. I have not included him in the previous chapter be-

cause, having grown up in Argentina, he could not accurately be described as a European viewing an unfamiliar jungle landscape. His portrayals of the jungle, like those of the other authors, tend to be structured around architectural metaphors. His emphasis, however, is more often on the interaction of light and color within such architectural spaces than on the forms themselves. He describes the forest "roof" as follows:

> Nature, we know, first taught the architect to produce by long colonnades the illusion of distance; but the light excluding roof prevents him from getting the same effect above. Here Nature is unapproachable with her green, airy, canopy, a sun-impregnated cloud—cloud above cloud; and though the highest may be unreachable by the eye, the beams yet filter through illuming the wide spaces beneath—chamber succeeded by chamber, each with its own special light and shadows. (32–33)

Hudson is somewhat more self-conscious about his use of architectural and artificial metaphor than are the other jungle authors because his vision is more aesthetic and less controlling than are theirs. Nevertheless, his vision in the jungle does familiarize foreign forms; while his portrayals of the English landscape always involve a close attention to species, his jungle vision is less specific and more metaphorical.

General Bibliography

Achebe, Chinua. "An Image of Africa." *The Massachusetts Review*. 18 (1977): 782–94.

Alcorn, John. *The Nature Novel from Hardy to Lawrence*. New York: Columbia University Press, 1977.

Beer, Gillian. *Darwin's Plots: Evolutionary Narrative in Darwin, George Eliot and Nineteenth-Century Fiction*. Boston: Routledge, 1983.

Berkeley, George. *Works on Vision*. Colin Murray Turbayn, ed. New York: Bobbs-Merrill, 1963.

Block, Ned, ed. *Imagery*. Cambridge: The MIT Press, 1981.

Brantlinger, Patrick. *"Heart of Darkness:* Anti-Imperialsim, Racism or Impressionism." *Criticism*. 27:4 (Fall 1985): 363–85.

———. *The Rule of Darkness: British Literature and Imperialism, 1830–1914*. Ithaca, NY: Cornell University Press, 1988.

———. "Victorians and Africans: The Genealogy of the Myth of the Dark Continent." *Critical Inquiry*. 12 (Autumn 1985): 166–203.

Brewster, Sir David. "On the Law of Visible Position in Single and Binocular Vision, and on the Representation of Solid Figures by the Union of Dissimilar Plane Pictures in the Retina." *Transactions of the Royal Society of Edinburgh* 15 (1844): 349–68.

———. "On the Same Subject." *Report of the British Association, Transactions of the Sections*. (1844): 10.

Bullen, J. B. *The Expressive Eye: Fiction and Perception in the Work of Thomas Hardy*. Oxford: Clarendon, 1986.

Cannon, Walter F. "Darwin's Vision in *On the Origin of Species*." *The Art of Victorian Prose*. George Levine and William Madden, eds. New York: Oxford University Press, 1968, 154–76.

Carlisle, Janice. *The Sense of an Audience: Dickens, Thackeray, and George Eliot at Mid-Century*. Athens, GA: University of Georgia Press, 1981.

Cassagrande, Peter J. *Hardy's Influence on the Modern Novel*. Totowa, NJ: Barnes & Noble, 1987.

Cavaliero, Glen. *The Rural Tradition in the English Novel 1900–1939*. New York: Macmillan,. 1977.

Cheselden, W. "An account of some observations made by a young gentleman, who was born blind &c." *Royal Society of London Philosophical Transaction.* 35 (1728): 447–50.

Conrad, Joseph. *Congo Diary and Other Uncollected Pieces.* Zdzislaw Najder, ed. New York: Doubleday, 1978.

———. *Heart of Darkness.* 1902. Ross C. Murfin, ed. New York: St. Martin, 1989.

———. *Joseph Conrad on Fiction.* Walter F. Wright, ed. Lincoln: University of Nebraska Press, 1967.

———. *Last Essays.* London: Dent, 1926.

———. *Tales of Unrest.* New York: Doubleday, 1925.

Crary, Jonathan. *Techniques of the Observer: On Vision and Modernity in the Nineteenth Century.* Cambridge: The MIT Press, 1990.

Culler, A. Dwight. "The Darwinian Revolution and Literary Form." *The Art of Victorian Prose.* George Levine and William Madden, eds. New York: Oxford University Press, 1968, 224–46.

Darwin, Charles. "An Autobiographical Fragment, Written in 1838." Gavin de Beer, ed. *Charles Darwin, Thomas Henry Huxley Autobiographies.* New York: Oxford University Press, 1983.

———. *The Collected Papers of Charles Darwin.* Paul H. Barrett, ed. Chicago: University of Chicago Press, 1977.

———. *The Descent of Man, and Selection in Relation to Sex.* Princeton: Princeton University Press, 1981.

———. *Diary of the Voyage of H.M.S. Beagle.* Nora Barlow, ed. *The Works of Charles Darwin,* Vol. I. Paul H. Barrett and R. B. Freeman, eds. New York: New York University Press, 1987.

———. *The Life and Letters of Charles Darwin.* Francis Darwin, ed. New York: Appleton, 1896.

———. "Observations on the Parallel Roads of Glen Roy." *Philosophical Transactions of the Royal Society of London,* pt. 1, 1839: 39–81. *The Collected Papers of Charles Darwin.* Paul H. Barrett. ed. Chicago: University of Chicago Press, 1977.

———. *On the Origin of Species, A Facsimile of the First Edition.* 1859. New York: Atheneum, 1967.

Dickens, Charles. *Bleak House.* 1853. London: Oxford University Press, 1971.

Ebbatson, Roger. *Lawrence and the Nature Tradition: A Theme in English Fiction 1859–1914.* Sussex: Harvester, 1980.

Einstein, Albert, and Leopold Infeld. *The Evolution of Physics.* New York: Simon and Schuster, 1961.

Eliot, George. *Adam Bede.* New York: Collier, 1962.

Enstice, Andrew. *Thomas Hardy: Landscapes of the Mind.* New York: St. Martin's, 1979.

Genette, Gérard. *Narrative Discourse: An Essay in Method.* Jane E. Lewin, trans. Ithaca, NY: Cornell University Press, 1980.

Gregory, R. L. *Eye and Brain: The Psychology of Seeing*. New York: McGraw-Hill, 1978.

Grundy, Joan. *Hardy and the Sister Arts*. London: Macmillan, 1979.

Guerard, Albert J. *Conrad the Novelist*. Cambridge: Harvard University Press, 1965.

Haeckel, Ernst. *The Riddle of the Universe*. Joseph McCabe, trans. London: Harper, 1901.

Hamilton, Sir William, Bart. *Lectures in Metaphysics*. H. L. Mansel and John Veitch, eds. London: Blackwood, 1859.

Hardy, Thomas. *A Changed Man, the Waiting Supper and Other Tales*. London: Macmillan, 1962.

———. *Life and Art*. New York: Haskell House, 1966.

———. *The Life and Works of Thomas Hardy*. Michael Millgate, ed. Athens, GA: University of Georgia Press, 1985.

———. *The Literary Notebooks of Thomas Hardy*. Lennart A. Bjork, ed. New York: New York University Press, 1985.

———. *The Mayor of Casterbridge*. Robert B. Heilman, ed. New York: Houghton Mifflin, 1962.

———. *The Return of the Native*. New York: New American Library, 1959.

———. *Selected Stories of Thomas Hardy*. John Wain, ed. London: Macmillan, 1966.

———. *Tess of the D'Urbervilles*. Ayelesbury: Penguin, 1978.

———. *The Woodlanders*. New York: Oxford University Press, 1985.

Hartman, Geoffrey H. *The Unmediated Vision: An Interpretation of Wordsworth, Hopkins, Rilke, and Valery*. New York: Harcourt Brace, 1966.

Hartmann, George W. *Gestalt Psychology*. New York: Ronald, 1935.

von Helmholtz, Hermann. *Helmholtz's Treatise on Physiological Optics*. James P. C. Southall, ed. Optical Society of America, 1924.

Herzinger, Kim. *D. H. Lawrence in His Time: 1908–1915*. Lewisburg, PA: Bucknell University Press, 1982.

Howe, Irving, ed. *Literary Modernism*. Greenwich, CT: Fawcett, 1967.

Hudson, W. H. *Green Mansions*. London: Duckworth, 1966.

———. *Hampshire Days*. Oxford: Oxford University Press, 1980.

———. *Nature in Downland*. London: Futura, 1981.

Hull, David L. *Darwin and His Critics: The Reception of Darwin's Theory of Evolution by the Scientific Community*. Cambridge: Harvard University Press, 1973.

Hunter, Allan. *Joseph Conrad and the Ethics of Darwinism*. London: Croom Helm, 1983.

James, William. *The Letters of William James*. Henry James, ed. Boston: Atlantic Monthly Press, 1920.

———. *Principles of Psychology*. Cambridge: Harvard University Press, 1981.

———. *The Selected Letters of William James*. Ed. Elizabeth Hardwick. New York: Farrar, Strauss & Cudahy, 1961.

Jefferies, Richard. *Amaryllis at the Fair*. London: Westaway, 1887.

―――. *Selections from Richard Jefferies*. F. W. Tickner, ed. London: Longmans, 1909.

―――. *Selections from His Works*. Henry Williamson, ed. London: Faber, 1937.

―――. *The Spring of the Year and Other Nature Essays*. Samuel J. Looker, ed. London: Lutterworth, 1946.

Keats, John. "Ode to a Nightingale." *The Norton Anthology of English Literature*. 4th ed. Vol. 2. M. H. Abrams, et al., eds. New York: Norton, 1979, 823–25.

Keith, W. J. *Richard Jefferies: A Critical Study*. London: Oxford, 1965.

King, Alec. *Wordsworth and the Artist's Vision: An Essay in Interpretation*. London: Athlone Press, 1966.

Koffka, Kurt. *Principles of Gestalt Psychology*. London: Kegan Paul, 1935.

Köhler, Wolfgang. *Gestalt Psychology*. New York: Liveright, 1947.

Kolers, Paul A. *Aspects of Motion Perception*. Oxford: Pergamon Press, 1972.

Kottler, Malcolm Jay. "Charles Darwin and Alfred Russel Wallace: Two Decades of Debate over Natural Selection." *The Darwinian Heritage*. David Kohn, ed. Princeton: Princeton University Press, 1985, 367–434.

Lawrence, D. H. *Apropos of Lady Chatterly's Lover and Other Essays*. Harmondsworth: Penguin, 1961.

―――. *Lady Chatterly's Lover*. New York: Bantam, 1983.

―――. *Phoenix*. Edward D. McDonald, ed. New York: Viking, 1936.

―――. *The Plumed Serpent*. 1926. New York: Vintage, 1959.

―――. *The Rainbow*. 1915. Harmondsworth: Penguin, 1979.

―――. *Sea and Sardinia and Selections from Twilight in Italy*. New York: Doubleday, 1954.

―――. *The White Peacock*. Cambridge: Cambridge University Press, 1983.

―――. *Women in Love*. New York: Viking, 1960.

Levine, George. *Darwin and the Novelists: Patterns of Science in Victorian Fiction*. Cambridge: Harvard University Press, 1988.

Lodge, David. "Tess, Nature and the Voices of Thomas Hardy." *Hardy: The Tragic Novels*. R. P. Draper, ed. New York: Macmillan, 1975.

―――. "Thomas Hardy and Cinematographic Form." *Novel*. 7 (1973–1974): 246–54.

London, Bette. "Reading Race and Gender in Conrad's Dark Continent." *Criticism*. 31, 3 (Summer 1989): 235–52.

Lothe, Jakob. *Conrad's Narrative Method*. Oxford: Clarendon, 1989.

Lyell, Charles. *Principles of Geology or The Modern Changes of the Earth and Its Inhabitants*. 2 vols. New York: Appleton, 1873.

Mill, John Stuart. *An Examination of Sir William Hamilton's Philosophy*. London, 1865.

Miller, J. Hillis. *Fiction and Repetition: Seven English Novels*. Cambridge: Harvard University Press, 1982.

―――. *Thomas Hardy: Distance and Desire*. Cambridge, MA: Belknap, 1970.

Müller, Johannes. *Elements of Physiology*. William Baly, trans. London: Taylor and Walton, 1840.

Nicholson, Mervin. "'What we see we feel': The Imaginative World of W. H. Hudson." *University of Toronto Quarterly* 47 (1977–1978): 304–22.

Paley, William. *Natural Theology or Evidences of the Existence and Attributes of Deity. Collected from the Appearances of Nature*. London: Longman, 1802.

Paradis, James. "Darwin and Landscape." *Victorian Science and Victorian Values: Literary Perspectives*. James Paradis and Thomas Postlewait, eds. New York: New York Academy of Sciences, 1981.

Pastore, Nicholas. *Selective History of Theories of Visual Perception: 1650–1950*. New York: Oxford University Press, 1971.

Pinion, F. B. *Thomas Hardy: Art and Thought*. New York: Macmillan, 1977.

Pratt, Mary Louise. "Scratches on the Face of the Country; or, What Mr. Barrow Saw in the Land of the Bushmen." *"Race," Writing and Difference*. Henry Louis Gates, Jr., ed. Chicago: University of Chicago Press, 1985. 138–62.

Pullein, Catherine. *How to Observe: Suggestions to Young Folk about Country Life*. London: Society for Promoting Christian Knowledge, 1901.

Rachootin, Stan P. "Owen and Darwin Reading a Fossil: Macrauchenia in a Boney Light." *The Darwinian Heritage*. David Kohn, ed. Princeton: Princeton University Press, 1985, 115–84.

Reid, Thomas. *An Inquiry into the Human Mind*. 1764. Timothy Duggan, ed. Chicago: University of Chicago Press, 1970.

Richards, Robert J. *Darwin and the Emergence of Evolutionary Theories of Mind and Behavior*. Chicago: University of Chicago Press, 1987.

Ruskin, John. *The Elements of Drawing*. New York: Dover, 1971.

Sagar, Keith. "D. H. Lawrence: The Man and the Artist." *The Modernists: Studies in a Literary Phenomenon*. Lawrence B. Gamache and Ian S. MacNiven, eds. London and Toronto: Associated University Press, 1987. 114–25.

Scarry, Elaine. "Work and the Body in Hardy and Other Nineteenth-Century Novelists." *Representations*. 3 (1983): 90–123.

Schwarz, Daniel R. *The Transformation of the English Novel, 1890–1930*. New York: St. Martin's, 1989.

Shetty, Sandya. *"Heart of Darkness:* Out of Africa Some New Thing Never Comes." *Journal of Modern Literature 15:4* (Spring 1989): 461–74.

Stelzig, Eugene L. *All Shades of Consciousness: Wordsworth's Poetry and the Self*. Paris: Mouton, 1975.

Stevenson, Lionel. *The English Novel: A Panorama*. Boston: Houghton Mifflin, 1960.

Stone, Donald David. *Novelists in a Changing World: Meredith, James, and the Transformation of English Fiction in the 1880s*. Cambridge: Harvard University Press, 1972.

Sulloway, Frank J. "Darwin's Early Intellectual Development: An Overview of the

Beagle Voyage (1831–1836)." *The Darwinian Heritage.* David Kohn, ed. Princeton: Princeton University Press, 1985, 121–54.

Swan, William. "On the Gradual Production of Luminous Impressions on the Eye, and Other Phenomena of Vision." *Transactions of the Royal Society of London* 16 (1849): 581–603.

Taylor, Dennis. *Hardy's Poetry 1860–1928.* New York: Columbia University Press, 1981.

Tomlinson, H. M. *The Sea and the Jungle.* New York: The Modern Library, 1928.

Vigar, Penelope. *The Novels of Thomas Hardy: Illusion and Reality.* London: Athlone, 1974.

Wallace, Alfred Russel. *The Malay Archipelago.* New York: Dover, 1962.

———. *Tropical Nature and Other Essays.* London: Macmillan, 1878.

Wardrop, James. "Case of a lady born blind, who received sight at an advanced age by the formation of an artificial pupil. *Philosophical Transactions of the Royal Society London* 116 (1826): 592–40.

Watson, J. R. "'The country of my heart': D. H. Lawrence and the East Midlands." *The Spirit of D. H. Lawrence.* Gamini Salgado and G. K. Das, eds. Totowa, NJ: Barnes & Noble, 1988.

Watt, Ian. *Conrad in the Nineteenth Century.* Berkeley: University of California Press, 1979.

Wheatstone, Sir Charles. "Contributions to the Physiology of Vision—Part the First. On Some Remarkable, and Hitherto Unobserved, Phenomena of Binocular Vision." *Philosophical Transactions of the Royal Society* 128 (1838): 371–94.

———. "On the Singular Effect of the Juxtaposition of Certain Colours under Particular Circumstances." *Report of the British Association, Transactions of Sections* (1844): 10.

Wordsworth, William. *The Prelude. The Norton Anthology of English Literature.* 4th ed. Vol. 2. M. H. Abrams et al., eds. New York: Norton, 1979, 255–313.

Young, Robert M. *Darwin's Metaphor: Nature's Place in Victorian Culture.* Cambridge: Cambridge University Press, 1985.

Index